HONEYVOICED

Also available from Bloomsbury

PINDAR AND THE SUBLIME: GREEK MYTH, RECEPTION, AND LYRIC EXPERIENCE
by Robert L. Fowler

PREPOSTEROUS VIRGIL: READING THROUGH STOPPARD, AUDEN, WORDSWORTH, HEANEY
by Juan Christian Pellicer

THE POEMS OF OPTATIAN: PUZZLING OUT THE PAST IN THE TIME OF CONSTANTINE THE GREAT
by Linda Jones Hall

HONEYVOICED

A TRANSLATION OF PINDAR'S SONGS
FOR ATHLETES

BLOOMSBURY ACADEMIC
LONDON · NEW YORK · OXFORD · NEW DELHI · SYDNEY

BLOOMSBURY ACADEMIC
Bloomsbury Publishing Plc, 50 Bedford Square, London, WC1B 3DP, UK
Bloomsbury Publishing Inc, 1359 Broadway, 12th Floor, New York, NY 10018, USA
Bloomsbury Publishing Ireland, 29 Earlsfort Terrace, Dublin 2, D02 AY28, Ireland

BLOOMSBURY, BLOOMSBURY ACADEMIC and the Diana logo
are trademarks of Bloomsbury Publishing Plc

First published in Great Britain 2024
This paperback edition published 2025

Copyright © James Bradley Wells, 2024

James Bradley Wells has asserted his right under the Copyright,
Designs and Patents Act, 1988, to be identified as Author of this work.

For legal purposes the Acknowledgments on p. vii constitute
an extension of this copyright page.

Cover design: Terry Woodley
Cover image © Vincent van Gogh, *The Olive Trees*, 1889
Wikimedia Commons

All rights reserved. No part of this publication may be: i) reproduced or transmitted in any form, electronic or mechanical, including photocopying, recording or by means of any information storage or retrieval system without prior permission in writing from the publishers; or ii) used or reproduced in any way for the training, development or operation of artificial intelligence (AI) technologies, including generative AI technologies. The rights holders expressly reserve this publication from the text and data mining exception as per Article 4(3) of the Digital Single Market Directive (EU) 2019/790.

Bloomsbury Publishing Inc does not have any control over, or responsibility for, any third-party websites referred to or in this book. All internet addresses given in this book were correct at the time of going to press. The author and publisher regret any inconvenience caused if addresses have changed or sites have ceased to exist, but can accept no responsibility for any such changes.

A catalogue record for this book is available from the British Library.

Library of Congress Cataloging-in-Publication Data
Names: Pindar, author. | Wells, James Bradley, translator.
Title: Honeyvoiced : a translation of Pindar's songs for athletes / James Bradley Wells.
Description: New York : Bloomsbury Publishing Plc, 2024. |
Includes bibliographical references and index.
Identifiers: LCCN 2023039088 (print) | LCCN 2023039089 (ebook) |
ISBN 9781350226401 (hardback) | ISBN 9781350226449 (paperback) |
ISBN 9781350226418 (pdf) | ISBN 9781350226425 (ebook)
Subjects: LCSH: Athletes–Poetry.
Classification: LCC PA4275.E5 W37 2024 (print) | LCC PA4275.E5 (ebook) |
DDC 884/.01—dc23/eng/20231115
LC record available at https://lccn.loc.gov/2023039088
LC ebook record available at https://lccn.loc.gov/2023039089

ISBN: HB: 978-1-3502-2640-1
PB: 978-1-3502-2644-9
ePDF: 978-1-3502-2641-8
eBook: 978-1-3502-2642-5

Typeset by RefineCatch Limited, Bungay, Suffolk

For product safety related questions contact productsafety@bloomsbury.com.

To find out more about our authors and books visit www.bloomsbury.com
and sign up for our newsletters.

CONTENTS

Preface	vi
Acknowledgments	vii
Note on Text and Translation	viii
Pronunciation Guide	xi
Chronology	xiii
Introduction	1
Olympians	32
Pythians	109
Nemeans	196
Isthmians	258
Glossary	291
Notes	319
Bibliography	325
Index	328

PREFACE

In addition to a general introduction to Píndaros, ancient Hellenic athletics, and the poetics of Píndaros' *epiníkia* (victory songs), a brief introduction precedes each poem. I provide a glossary, but do not include a commentary or notes, preferring to keep intrusions upon the experience of the poetry to a minimum, but expect that the general introduction, introductions to each poem, and the glossary will sufficiently enable readers to appreciate Píndaros' proverbially difficult poetry. As I explain further in my "Note on Text and Translation," I use original Hellenic language transliterations for all proper nouns and some common nouns that occur in Píndaros' songs. The "Pronunciation Guide" will facilitate the pronunciation of such ancient Hellenic words. I deviate from the practice of transliterating ancient Hellenic in the case of words that are very naturalized in English. Conventional abbreviations refer to Píndaros' victory songs, as follows: *O* refers to Olympian songs, *P* to Pythian songs, *N* to Nemean songs, and *I* to Isthmian songs. Thus O.1.1 refers abbreviatedly to "*Olympian 1*, line 1." All line numbers for the verses of Píndaros' poetry refer only to original Hellenic line numbers, which are noted in the translation. In the "Introduction" and bibliography of this volume, I do not ambition to represent the extensive scholarship on Píndaros and his *epiníkia*, but register debts where I have directly drawn upon the research of particular scholars and suggest points of departure for readers who would like to explore further. All translations from all languages are my own.

ACKNOWLEDGMENTS

It is a pleasure to express my gratitude to those who have supported me in the course of writing this book. Reginald Gibbons, William Levitan, Richard Martin, David Schenker and Jane Springer generously responded to my appeals for their advice about writing choices by reading drafts of the manuscript, providing thoughtful suggestions, and stemming the riot of second-guessing as the book neared completion. Jay Wright has been a staunch advocate for this translation, and I am indebted to him for his encouragement, to say nothing of the ways in which his honeyvoiced poetry beautifully amplifies music's possibilities. The task of anonymously reviewing a manuscript renders prodigious service, especially when that task is taken seriously and performed with care. I thank the anonymous reviewer of my manuscript for their insights about how to improve this book and their guidance about pitfalls to navigate. This book would not have been possible without the vision and expertise of my collaborators at Bloomsbury Publishing. In the beginning of what has been a much too-long writing process, Alice Wright saw the promise of a new translation of Píndaros' victory songs and trusted in my ability to produce it. Lily Mac Mahon and Zoë Osman have guided my writing process with patience and unfailingly good humor. Sophie Beardsworth has efficiently and expertly led the production process. Merv Honeywood has been quick, adept, and affable at each step of the way in rendering the manuscript ready for printing. Especially given the foreignizing features of my translation and the conventions for line breaks and punctuation that I adopt, I am indebted to Sandra Creaser for her keen copyediting skills. This book will find its way to readers thanks to the creativity and knowhow of Elizabeth Morris and Brenna Akerman. Mike Smith and the extended Smith family have made it possible for me to pursue my writing vocation in fundamental and unaccountable ways, and I thank Tom Shelton in particular. What matters most to me about my writing practice is that it is entangled in the day-to-day life Stacey Giroux and I share together with feline and floral kin at MorrowHaven Gardens

NOTE ON TEXT AND TRANSLATION

My translation follows the Hellenic text of Bruno Snell and Herwig Maehler.[1] I also consulted the editions of C. M. Bowra[2] and William H. Race[3] for their treatment of problematic passages, which are infrequent and so insignificantly affect translation that I do not document them. I rarely identify different dates for the composition or performance for Píndaros' victory songs than those that Snell and Maehler give.

I seek to represent a degree of cultural and linguistic difference in the target language, English, with a modestly foreignizing translation of Píndaros' poetry.[4] Lawrence Venuti's *The Translator's Invisibility* presents foreignizing translation as an act of resistance to cultural, political, linguistic, and aesthetic hegemonies entailed in domesticating translation, which is predicated upon ideological conceptions of "standard" or "fluent" English that erase cultural difference.[5] I attend to English here not to privilege this language over others, but simply because it is the target language of my translation. I limit my foreignizing strategies to presenting all proper nouns and some common nouns that occur in Píndaros' poetry in transliterated Hellenic forms. This orthographic move, further explained in the "Guide to Pronunciation," will enable animators of the poetry to register (to voice) a degree of cultural difference that domesticating translation occludes.

How does such a foreignizing translation play out? Consider the name of the hero Hercules. In the first place, *Hercules* is a domesticated English form. Like many domesticated English words that derive from Hellenic language, *Hercules* arrives in English via Latin, the word for the hero being represented orthographically in that language as *Hercules*. The most striking examples of domesticating language transiting via Latin into English may perhaps be the words *Greece* and *Greek*, which derive from the ancient Roman colonialist denominations of *Hellás* and *Hellēnikoí* as *Graecia* and *Graeci*. This colonialist language persists in contemporary standard English, where *Greece* is the name for the nation whose people live in Elláda. If Latin *Hercules* is a Roman domestication of the original Hellenic word *Hēraklés*, the English pronunciation of that Latin word domesticates a domesticating form: although Latin *Hercules* is pronounced /ˈhɛrkuleːs/, standard English *Hercules* is pronounced /ˈhərkjəˌliz/. By transliterating the Hellenic word Ἡρακλῆς as *Hēraklés*, I represent this name in a way that indexes cultural artifacts and practices that are indigenous to ancient Hellás. Whereas domesticating translation erases such indigeneity, a foreignizing translation aspires to foreground and honor it.

The name of the hero Hēraklés illustrates one of several compromises in my representation of ancient Hellenic forms in the target language. Píndaros threads features of Doric and Aiolic varieties of ancient Hellenic into his poetic idiom. Instead of rigorously representing this polyphony, I regularly render proper and common nouns in their Attic forms; I use *Hēraklés* (Attic) rather than *Hērakléēs* (Píndaros' form), *Persephónē* (Attic) rather than *Phersephóna* (Píndaros' form), *Dēmétēr* (Attic) rather than *Dāmátēr*

Note on Text and Translation

(Píndaros' form). I use Attic forms only in the case of proper and common nouns that occur widely in ancient Hellenic sources. I cast many proper nouns for which Píndaros is the only or principal source in transliterated forms of Píndaros' poetic Hellenic. When nouns occur widely in both Attic and Doric varieties of ancient Hellenic, for example *Spártē* (Attic) and *Spárta* (Doric), I choose Doric forms because Doric culture, history, and language is salient for athletes from communities that identified as Doric.

Among other compromises in foreignizing translation I make, I do not foreignize Hellenic words that are hyperdomesticated into English. *Aiolic, Attic, Doric*, and *Hellenic* and English adjectives that refer to games and to each of Píndaros' victory songs—*Olympian, Pythian, Nemean*, and *Isthmian*—are so conventional in standard English that it verges upon pedantic or obscurantist to use more properly indigenous forms of these words, even if this concession compromises the aims of foreignizing translation. In contrast with my practice concerning such naturalized English adjectives, I prefer Hellenic toponyms—*Olympía, Pythó* or *Delphoí, Neméa*, and *Isthmós*—in the case of which, the difference between Hellenic and English is often more a matter of pronunciation than orthography. Although to transliterate word-initial ρ *rō* as *r*, ξ *ksî* as *ks*, and ζ *zdéta* as *zd* would more closely approximate the orthography of certain Hellenic sounds known on the basis of historical linguistics, I follow deeply engrained conventions by representing *rō* as *rh* (e.g. *Rhódos* rather than *Ródos*), *ksî* as *x* (e.g. *Xenophón* rather than *Ksenophón*), and *zdéta* as *z* (e.g. *Zeus* rather than *Zdeus*).

Poetic constraints guide my translation practice. I shape each line into four-foot (the strophe and antistrophe of *Olympian 11* and every line of *Olympian 14, Pythian 7*, and *Nemean 11*) or five-foot lines of sprung rhythm verse, as conceived by Gerard Manley Hopkins.[6] I subdivide these four- or five-footed sprung rhythm lines, occasionally for emphasis or to highlight instances of *rimalmezzo*, most often in order to clarify syntax in the absence of punctuation. I use punctuation only where it mitigates particularly challenging ambiguities. The absence of punctuation destabilizes the scriptural authority of the page and brings poetry into proximity with the embodied experience of language, affording a more synesthetic encounter with the verse. Limited punctuation also has a foreignizing effect: in the song culture of ancient Hellás, the material text of a given work of verbal art would have trafficked much less widely than the performance and reperformance of it. Punctuation is a function—for convenience I perilously simplify the vast research on such questions—of silent reading. I intend limited punctuation to pry this silence open into the polyphonic voicedness of varied and multiple animations of the translation. Punctuationless poetry is in any case hardly novel, so my explanation of the practice here is probably superfluous. I also wanted to experiment: given the artistic constraints—limited punctuation, sprung rhythm, coordinating syntax and line-breaks, and, yes, rendering Píndaros' challenging Hellenic into English—what might happen?

I would prefer to produce a translation whose language inclusively represents gender and sexuality, but I allow Píndaros and the cultural practices and norms embedded in his poetry to be accountable to audiences of this translation for their systemic patriarchy and sexism. To erase these distressing aspects of Píndaros poetry would be dishonest and implicitly, problematically apologetic. I accordingly translate forms of the Hellenic word

Note on Text and Translation

ánēr as gender-specific "man" or "men" and forms of the Hellenic word *ánthrōpos* as gender-neutral "people," "mortals," "humans," or "humankind." Indefinite pronouns often afford gender-neutral translation, but when they occur in the context of representation of domains of exclusively male-centric cultural practices or points of view, my translation reflects this. Such gender-neutral English nouns as *people*, *mortals*, *humans*, and *person* are Latinate, but the decidedly binary words *man* and *woman*, and their plurals, are Germanic. My preference for Germanic, rootedly English diction over Latinate diction conflicts at times with making inclusive word choices when to do so is not dishonest or apologetic. A related creative challenge is that the gender-neutral pronoun *one* and the gender-neutral possessive *one's* have a prosaic register, although they are Germanic. I therefore generally avoid using *one* and *one's*, but often use gender-neutral Germanic *they*, *them*, and *their* for both singular and plural referents. This practice may remain novel for some readers. Others who endorse outmoded and prescriptive conceptions of grammar, or who adhere to non-inclusive language ideologies concerning identity, will find my translation choices simply incorrect. No data, no argument, no revelation will assuage the desperation of those who deny that the world is all that is the case, to paraphrase Ludwig Wittgenstein. To these considerations about the translation of Píndaros' language for gender and sexuality, I will add that the poet, more than regularly suppressing the violence entailed in sexual assault that occurs in mythological stories, disturbingly juxtaposes "language of pleasure and consent . . . with the vocabulary of abduction and rape."[7] Although some readers might argue that Píndaros sanitizes depictions of sexual violence simply in order to observe religious propriety and to strike the right tone for the celebratory occasions that motivate the composition and performance of his victory songs, the fact remains that the violence of rape "is both obscured and exposed in the text: the poet has attempted to erase it, but the erasure marks remain."[8] My translation transmits these marks.

PRONUNCIATION GUIDE

As I explain in the "Note on Text and Translation," rather than translating ancient Hellenic proper nouns and some common nouns into their standard English equivalents, I transliterate them using English (i.e. Latin) orthography in order to represent something approximating their original Hellenic pronunciation. My transliteration practice follows Geoffrey Horrocks, *Greek: A History of the Language and Its Speakers*, except when I resort to pronunciation conventions typically presented in introductory ancient Hellenic language textbooks.[1] There are discrepancies between traditions of pronunciation represented in such textbooks and the linguistic description of ancient Hellenic pronunciation. My "Note on Text and Translation" acknowledges compromises and contradictions in my transliteration practice.

Consonants

Ancient Hellenic consonants are generally pronounced like English consonants, with the qualification that the Hellenic *g*-sound is always pronounced like the English *g*-sound in *gather* (/g/), never like the English *g*-sound in the word *rouge* (/ʒ/). The letter *h* after a consonant indicates that the preceding consonant is aspirated; the consonant sound includes a slight exhalation. This means that:

Hellenic *kh* sounds like English *c* (and *k*) in *cook*

Hellenic *ph* sounds like English *p* in *pot* (not like English *ph* in *phial*)

Hellenic *th* sounds like English *t* in *tug* (not like English *th* in *thew*)

Vowels

Letter	Pronunciation
a	English *a*-sound in *drama* (/a/)
e	English *e*-sound in *spate* (/e/)
ē	English *e*-sound in *fret*, but longer (/ɛː/)
i	English *i*-sound in *chic* (/i/)
o	English *o*-sound in *boat* (/o/)
ō	English *o*-sound in *boat*, but longer (/oː/)
y	French *u*-sound in (French) *sûr* (/y/)

Pronunciation Guide

My transliteration practice does not distinguish between long and short alpha *a*, iota *i*, or upsilon *y*. A stress-mark ´ indicates the syllable of a given word to be stressed, the other syllables in the word remaining unstressed. If *ē* or *ō* are stressed, I represent them only with the stress mark—*é* and *ó*—because the stressed sound is generally equivalent the sound represented by *ē* and *ō*.

Diphthongs

"Diphthong" is an English word derived from a Hellenic word that means "double sound." Hellenic diphthongs are accordingly sounds represented by two vowels. Although they are formed with two letters, diphthongs are monosyllabic. The following table summarizes the pronunciation of diphthongs:

Diphthong	Pronunciation
ai	Like English sound represented by *y* in *why*
au	Like English sound represented by *ow* in *how*
ei	Like English sound represented by *ay* in *day*
eu	This diphthong compresses the vowel sounds represented by *e* (/e/) and *u* (/y/) into single syllable. The Hellenic sound of this diphthong approximates the English sound represented by *ew* in *brew*.
oi	Like English sound represented by *oy* in *enjoy*
yi	Like English sound represented by *wee* in *between*

CHRONOLOGY

776 BCE	Athletic competitions at Olympía begin.
750 BCE	Conventional date for the *Iliad* and *Odyssey* of Hómēros and for *Theogony* and *Works and Days* of Hēsíodos.
518 BCE	Birth of Píndaros.
498 BCE	*Pythia 10* for Hippokléas of Thessalía.
490 BCE	*Pythian 6* for Xenokrátēs of Akrágas. *Pythian 12* for Mídas of Akrágas. Battle of Marathón between Héllēnes and Persians.
488 BCE	*Olympian 14* for Asópikhos of Orkhomenós.
486 BCE	*Pythian 7* for Megaklés of Athénai.
485 (?) BCE	*Nemean 2* for Timódēmos of Akharnaí. *Nemean 7* for Sōgénēs of Aígina.
483 (?) BCE	*Nemean 5* for Pythéas of Aígina.
480 BCE	*Isthmian 6* for Phylakídas of Aígina. Battle of Salamís between Héllēnes and Persians. Gélōn of Syrákousai and Thérōn of Akrágas ally against and defeat the Catharginians at the Battle of Himéra.
479 BCE	Battle of Plátaia between Héllēnes and Persians.
478 BCE	*Isthmian 8* for Kléandros of Aígina.
478 (?) BCE	*Isthmian 5* for Phylakídas of Aígina.
476 BCE	*Olympian 1* for Hiérōn of Syrákousai. *Olympian 2* and *Olympian 3* for Thérōn of Akrágas. *Olympian 11* for Hagēsídamos of Epizephyrian Lokroí. Hiérōn of Syrákousai founds Aítna.
476 (?) BCE	*Nemean 1* for Khromíos of Syrákousai and Aítna.
475 (?) BCE	*Pythian 2* for Hiérōn of Syrákousai. *Nemean 3* for Aristokleídas of Aígina.
474 BCE	*Olympian 10* for Hagēsídamos of Epizephyrian Lokroí. *Pythian 9* for Telesikrátēs of Kyrénē. *Pythian 11* for Thrasydaíos of Thébai. Hiérōn of Syrákousai defeats an alliance of Carthaginian and Etruscan forces in a naval battle off the coast of Kýmē.
474 (?) BCE	*Pythian 3* for Hiérōn of Syrákousai. *Nemean 9* for Khromíos of Syrákousai and Aítna. *Isthmian 3* for Mélissos of Thébai. *Isthmian 4* for Mélissos of Thébai.
473 (?) BCE	*Nemean 4* for Timásarkhos of Aígina.
470 BCE	*Pythian 1* for Hiérōn of Aítna.
470 (?) BCE	*Isthmian 2* for Xenokrátēs of Akrágas.
470 (or 466 ?) BCE	*Olympian 12* for Ergotélēs of Himéra.
468 BCE	*Olympian 6* for Hagēsías of Syrákousai.

Chronology

466 BCE	*Olympian 9* for Ephármostos of Opoús.
465 (?) BCE	*Nemean 6* for Alkimídas of Aígina.
464 BCE	*Olympian 7* for Diagóras of Rhódos. *Olympian 13* for Xenophón of Kórinthos.
462 BCE	*Pythian 4* and *Pythian 5* for Arkesílas of Kyrḗnē.
460 (or 456?) BCE	*Olympian 4* and *Olympian 5* for Psaúmis of Kamárina. *Olympian 8* for Alkimédōn of Aígina.
459 (?) BCE	*Nemean 8* for Deínis of Aígina.
458 (?) BCE	*Isthmian 1* for Hēródotos of Thḗbai.
454 (?) BCE	*Isthmian 7* for Strepsiádas of Thḗbai.
446 BCE	*Pythia 8* for Aristoménēs of Aígina.
446 (?) BCE	*Nemean 11* for Aristagóras of Ténedos.
444 (?) BCE	*Nemean 10* for Theaíos of Árgos.
443 (?) BCE	Píndaros dies.
393 CE	Last athletic competitions at Olympía.
1896 CE	First modern Olympics at Athína, Elláda.

INTRODUCTION

Píndaros was born in Kynoskephalai, a town near Thébai in Boiōtía, in *c.* 518 BCE.¹ When he composed *Pythian 10*, his earliest *epiníkion* (victory song) in 498 BCE, Píndaros would have been twenty years old. The poet died after 446 BCE, the date of *Pythian 8*, his last *epiníkion*. Píndaros identified as a member of the Aigeídai, an aristocratic family with mythological origins associated with Thébai and Spárta (cf. P.5.72), and celebrated Théba, the eponymous nymph of Thébai, as his "mother" (O.6.85 and I.1.1). According to the ancient historian Arrian (*c.* 86–160 CE), when Alexander the Great (356–323 BCE) attacked Thébai in 335 BCE, levelling the city and enslaving those who survived the onslaught, he spared Píndaros' house from destruction "because of his reverence for the poet" (*Anab.* 1.9.10). The travel writer Pausanias (active *c.* 150 CE), a crucial ancient source about the sites of athletic games and the games themselves, recounts that inside the temple of Apóllōn at Delphoí he witnessed the iron chair in which, according to tradition, Píndaros composed songs in honor of the god (10.24.5).

Píndaros worked in a variety of media: *hýmnoi* (hymns, praisesongs), *paiánes* (paeans, choral songs in honor of Apóllōn), *dithýramboi* (dithyrambs, choral songs in honor of Diónysos), *prosódia* (a type of processional song), *parthéneia* (choral songs performed by unmarried girls), *hyporkhémata* (a type of performance in which dance figured prominently), *enkómia* (encomia, a type of praise song), *thrénoi* (funerary laments), and the poetry translated in this volume, *epiníkia*, songs that celebrate victories in athletic competitions. Ancient editors generally organized the *epiníkia* first according to the site where an athlete attained his victory, Olympía, Delphoí (=Pythó), Neméa, or Isthmós, then according to event, field events following equestrian events. Although only a portion of Píndaros' corpus remains, his extant poetry surpasses that of other ancient Hellenic poets such as Sapphó (born *c.* second half of seventh century BCE) and Simōnídēs (born *c.* 556 BCE). While we possess fragments, some of them substantial, of Píndaros' other poetry, only his *epiníkia* remain intact.

The proverbial difficulty of Píndaros' poetry is partly attributable to the density and relative obscurity of historical events, historical figures, and mythological content in his poetry. The introductions to each *epiníkion* and the Glossary explain historical and mythological details that readers encounter in the poems.² Píndaros' figurative uses of language, probable syntax, and the complex tapestry of linguistic registers that occur in each poem also contribute to the strangeness of his victory songs. This introduction maps the historical and cultural context in which Píndaros' *epiníkia* are embedded and outlines artistic features of his poetry.

The poet Hēsíodos (*c.* 750 BCE) offers an ancient Hellenic point of view on the adaptive and destructive potentials of competition in his characterization of the two kinds of *éris* (strife; plural: *érides*), which he represents as a divine personification:

> There was not a single clan of Érides,
> but upon the earth two kinds exist.
> If you recognize one Éris, you
> would praise it, but the other Éris
> must be blamed. They have a twoway
> temper. One mercilessly inflames
> war's wickedness and conflict. No mortal
> loves it, but under compulsion's power
> they honor this backbreaking Éris
> by the will of undying gods.
> Gloomy Nux gave birth to the other
> elder Éris and Kronídes seated
> above, who inhabits ether, he made her
> the better Éris—for earth's roots, for men.
> She drives even lazybones to work.
> Someone really lacking industry
> sees another person who thrives,
> who hurries to plow, to plant, to build
> a solid home, neighbor rivals neighbor
> at being bent on abundance. This Éris
> is good for mortals. Potter spites potter,
> carpenter spites carpenter, beggar envies
> beggar, singer envies singer.
>
> Op. 11–26

In this portrait of the dual nature of *éris*, praiseworthy *éris* motivates one to rival a neighbor or someone employed in the same pursuit as oneself, while blameworthy *éris* is the source of conflict and warfare. These lines from the *Works and Days* depict competition as a potential asset: life itself may be lived productively on the basis of a competitive ethos. Hēsíodos' poetry illustrates how nuanced social conventions distinguish appropriate and beneficial competition from divisive competition. In a similar way, *philotimía* (love of honor) in ancient Hellenic culture may be a positive attribute when voluntary and mutual rivalry with another brings to fruition the aspirations to achieve and to garner the esteem of others. Iron sharpens iron. But *philotimía* may also connote the self-interested ambition that gives rise to ostentatious displays of wealth or power and to political conflict. I offer Hēsíodos' distinction between praiseworthy *éris* and blameworthy *éris* to illustrate that competitiveness was a salient feature of ancient Hellenic society. The word *agón* (contest, public gathering, ordeal) both evokes this cultural salience and enables us to explore the connection between ancient athletics and ritual.[3]

The two connotations of *agón*, "contest" and "public gathering," converge. Legal disputes, military conflict, and dramatic competitions among playwrights during the City Dionysia at Athénai are examples of *agónes* (the plural form of *agón*) in the sense of

Introduction

"contests." The *agónes* (contests) held at each of the Panhellenic religious sites, Olympía, Delphoí, Neméa, and the Isthmós during their regularly occurring festivals were the venues for competition that figures centrally in Píndaros' *epiníkia*.[4] These sites were also venues for *agónes* in the sense of "public gatherings"—in that case, Panhellenic gatherings: people travelled from communities throughout Hellás to participate in the religious festivities, including games, held at each of them. Panhellenism was an ideological and cultural development that emerged in the Archaic period (750–480 BCE) as individual Hellenic *póleis* (cities) began to identify with a larger community that shared language, religious practices, traditions of governance and cultural production, including mythology and the performance of verbal art and music.[5] The development of Olympía, Delphoí, Neméa, and the Isthmós as Panhellenic religious sites that hosted athletic competitions is a definitive feature of Panhellenism. These sites provided arenas for individual athletes to compete and to represent their families, their social class, and their home *póleis* before a Panhellenic audience.

Píndaros' *epiníkia* roughly map the Panhellenic world. He composed fifteen *epiníkia* for elite figures from Sikelía: Hiérōn (O.1, P.1, P.2, P.3), Thérōn (O.2, O.3), Psaúmis (O.4, O.5), Hagēsías (O.6), Ergotélēs (O.12), Xenokrátēs (P.6, I.2), Thrasýboulos (P.6, I.2), Mídas (P.12), and Khromíos (N.1, N.9).[6] He also wrote eleven *epiníkia* for competitors from the island of Aígina: Alkimédōn (O.8), Aristoménēs (P.8), Aristokleídas (N.3), Timásarkhos (N.4), Pythéas (N.5), Alkimídas (N.6), Sōgénēs (N.7), Deínis (N.8), Phylakídas (I.5, I.6), and Kléandros (I.8).[7] Three *epiníkia*, including his longest, *Pythian 4*, commemorate the victories of athletes from Kyrénē in northern Africa: Arkesílas (P.4, P.5) and Telesikrátēs (P.9).[8] In addition to Italy and Sikelía in the west, Kyrénē in northern Africa, and the island of Aígina, other *epiníkia* celebrate the achievements of figures from Rhódos and Ténedos in the eastern Mediterranean basin and from Épeiros, Thessalía, and Thrákē in northern Hellás.

The traditional date for the establishment of *agónes* at Olympía is 776 BCE. The people of Élis oversaw the religious site of Olympía and the games held there. The Áltis, as the precinct sacred to Zeus is known, was the location for the sole original athletic event, the *stádion*, a footrace of approximately 200 meters. The four-year cycle for convening games at Olympía, known as an Olympiad, provided the basis for scheduling festivals and games at other sites. The prize for victory at Olympía was a crown of olive leaves. The Pythian Games at Delphoí developed from an older convention of holding a citharodic contest, that is, singing to the accompaniment of the seven-stringed instrument known as the *kithára* every eight years (cf. Paus. 10.7.2–3). Athletic competitions were introduced in 582 BCE. As Píndaros' *Pythian 12* attests, musical competitions remained among the *agónes* of the Pythian Games, which were second in importance to the Olympian Games and took place every four years, two years after the festival at Olympía. Victors in Pythian games received a crown of laurel leaves. Dating from their foundation in 581 BCE, the Panhellenic *agónes* at the Isthmós were held on the isthmus that connects Attiké with the Pelopónnēsos, near the important city of Kórinthos, which administered them. The Isthmian Games took place biennially, in the spring of the same years when the Olympian and Pythian Games occurred, and commemorated Poseidón. Victors received a crown made of wild celery. In the Nemean Games the prize was also a crown of wild celery. Neméa was a religious sanctuary of Zeus, and the *agónes* were held there in honor of him, beginning in 573 BCE. The city of Kleōnaí originally administered games at Neméa, but later Árgos assumed their oversight. As at the Isthmian Games, the Nemean Games occurred biennially, in the summer of the years between Olympian and Pythian Games. Because winners received a crown as their prize, the athletic competitions at the Panhellenic sites of Olympía, Delphoí, Neméa, and the Isthmós are known as "crown games."

In the following overview of athletic events, I highlight details most relevant to Píndaros' *epiníkia*, without accounting for how the program of athletic events changed with the introduction and elimination of events through time. When presenting the data for distances, I generalize and approximate without specifying differences in regional conventions for units of measurement—though it is a fascinating fact that units of measurement were not standardized throughout Hellás. That said, the program of athletic events that eventually developed at Olympía provided a template for games at Delphoí, Neméa, and the Isthmós. This program included running events, field events, and equestrian events.

The running events included the *stádion*, a sprint of one length of the running course (200 meters), the *díaulos*, a race of two lengths, out and back (400 meters), and the *dolikhós*, a distance race of seven lengths of the running course at Olympía (1,400 meters), but elsewhere twenty (4,000 meters) to twenty-four (4,800 meters) lengths. There was additionally a footrace in which the athlete wore combat armor, the hoplite race (400 meters). The field events comprised the *péntathlon* and combat sports. The *péntathlon* included five contests, in the order in which they took place: *stádion*, *dískos* (discus throw), *hálma* (long-jump), *ákōn* (javelin throw), and *pálē* (wrestling). The athlete who won three of these contests won the *péntathlon*. If one athlete was victorious in three of the first four events, he was declared winner of the *péntathlon* without contesting the wrestling event. There were three combat sports: wrestling, boxing, and the *pankrátion*, which combined wrestling and boxing. Competitors in the boxing event wrapped their hands with leather strips to protect their knuckles and stabilize their wrists. Equestrian events included the *apénē* (mule wagon race), *kélēs* (the single-horse race), and the *téthrippon* (four-horse chariot race). With two turning posts set at a distance of 300 meters, the *hippódromos* (horse-race course) was elliptical. The *téthrippon* consisted of twelve laps around this elliptical circuit, so that the total distance of the chariot race was about 7 kilometers. An elaborate procedure ensured a fair start for the forty or more chariot teams that competed (cf. P.5.49–51). This event must have been loud, dangerous, and thrilling. Victory required consummate skill and the luck to avoid a wreck. Because horses were costly to acquire and maintain, the wealthy elite exclusively competed in equestrian events. Although they typically hired specially skilled jockeys and chariot drivers, the owners of the horses received recognition as competitors—and as victors if their animals won a race. There were separate competitions for boys at Olympía in the *stádion*, wrestling, and boxing. In addition to this program for running events, field events, and combat sports, the Pythian and Isthmian Games included musical competitions (cf. P.12).

Athletic competition was by no means limited to the crown games. Olympía hosted games—one event, the *stádion*—for women as part of the *Hēraía*, a festival celebrated every four years in honor of Héra (Paus. 5.16.2–3). Throughout Hellás there were many local games during festivals in honor of a god or hero specially worshipped by a *pólis* (city). When an athlete or members of his family prevailed in those local contests, Píndaros' *epiníkia* often celebrate those achievements.

Additional historical details offer a sense of the atmosphere of ancient Hellenic athletic competition. For each quadrennial festival at Olympía, the people of Élis selected Hellanodíkai, the officials charged with overseeing the sanctuary of Zeus at Olympía, arranging competitions, and judging the contests. Prior to the commencement of the festival, the Hellanodíkai dispatched six ambassadors, whose mission was at once diplomatic and sacred. These ambassadors each journeyed to the *póleis* (cities) in a designated region of Hellás in order to announce that Olympía would soon welcome athletes for games scheduled to occur during the second full moon after the summer solstice. These ambassadors also declared that a truce should be observed during the month before the games, when athletes were obligated to be present at Élis in order to train and when the Hellanodíkai verified the citizenship of each athlete, assessed the athletes' readiness for competition, and determined the category of contests, boys' or men's, in which they would compete. Rather than suspending all conflicts, the Olympic truce of one month more pragmatically ensured the athletes' safe travel from their home *póleis* to Olympía. Once at Olympía, the athletes, along with their fathers, brothers, and trainers, were obligated to swear by Zeus that they had committed no crime against the *agónes* and that they had trained properly during the ten consecutive months prior to their competition (Paus. 5.24.9). Athletes competed nude. They coated their bodies with olive oil. Ancient sources, including Píndaros' *epiníkia*, remark the sexual appeal of athletic events. Women were not allowed to attend Panhellenic games. An exceptional athlete became known as a *periodoníkēs* for achieving *níkē* (victory) in the *períodos* (circuit) of all four crown games. The leisure and wealth required to train, to travel to venues for athletic games, and to compete, especially in the case of equestrian events, generally limited participation to the aristocracy.

We have already seen that the ancient Hellenic word *agón* names both a contest and a public gathering and that games at Panhellenic religious sites are *agónes* in both senses. Another word, *áethlos* (contest) is synonymous to *agón* in the sense of a "contest." This verbal alignment sheds light on the ritual dimensions of athletic competition because Píndaros explicitly characterizes *áethloi* (contests) as *hieroí* (sacred, holy).⁹

    Melēsías would   O.8.61–4; cf. O.13.15
outreach all others
        in telling those tests of strength
would tell what training propels
        a man who intends
to carry home

> from holy games [*hieroí áethloi*]
>> the glory

If *áethloi* (contests) are *hieroí* (sacred, holy), then athletic competition is a matter of ritual. In Píndaros' poetry the word *áethlos* (contest) "applies equally to the contests of athletes and to the life-and-death ordeals of heroes" in mythological narratives.[10] Taking this linguistic evidence as a point of departure, I next describe two interrelated spheres of cultural practice in which *epiníkion* is embedded: the ritual backdrop of athletics and the sociological poetics of athletic competition.

The evidence of mythology and historical ritual practices retains vestiges of primordial, obsolescent ritual practices. For example, in the case of ancient athletics, separation from the community (for games at Olympía), the funerary attire of judges of games, and the garlands awarded to athletes for victory are vestiges of two kinds of rituals: initiation into adulthood and compensation for death.[11] Although no longer historical practices, these primordial rituals motivated the mythology and religious symbolism associated with ancient athletics. Furthermore, the rituals of initiation and compensation for death converge in the ritual of initiation into adulthood, which "ritualizes or symbolizes death and rebirth from one given status to another: one must 'die' to one's old self in order to be 'reborn' to one's new self."[12]

Mythological stories that recount the origin of each of the Panhellenic crown games portray the foundation of each site's festival as compensation for the death of a hero.[13] According to one story, Pélops founded games at Olympía to compensate for Oinómaos' death (cf. O.1). According to other traditional stories, Hēraklés founded the Olympian festival to compensate either for his ancestor Pélops' death (cf. O.2.2–3) or for the deaths of Augeías, Ktéatos, and Eúrytos (cf. O.10). Apóllōn founded the games at Pythó to compensate for slaying the primordial serpentine creature the Pýthōn. Sísyphos founded the festival at the Isthmós to compensate for the death of Melikértēs, who became the god Palaímōn. The seven heroes who attacked Thébai (see "Seven Against Thébai" in the Glossary) founded games at Neméa to compensate for the death of the child Ophéltēs, also known as Arkhémoros.

We find a parallel to this pattern according to which compensation for death motivates the foundation of religious festivals that feature athletic competition in the case of the establishment of local games at Rhódos. Píndaros' *Olympian 7* recounts the story that Tlēpólemos, son of Hēraklés, founded the Tlēpolémeia, a recurring local festival that included animal sacrifice and games, as a *lútron* (compensation) for murdering Likýmnios (O.7.27–30), his grandmother Alkménē's half-brother:[14]

> founded there for Tlēpólemos   O.7.77–80
>> as if for a god
>
> pioneer for Tíryns' people
>> a sweet compensation [*lútron*]
>
> for mournful misfortune
>> a procession

>   sacrifice
> and fatsavor of sheepflocks
>   awarding prizes for games

Significantly Píndaros relates in his very next words how the Tlēpolémeia crowned Diagóras, the boxer whose athletic victories *Olympian 7* celebrates, with victory garlands, illustrating the connection between the mythological foundation of games as compensation for death and the athlete's historical participation in those games, where the athlete's ordeal of competition replicates the mythological ordeal of death. In other words, "the ordeals of heroes, as myths, are analogous to the ordeals of athletes, as rituals, in that the themes of living and dying in myth are analogous to the themes of winning and losing in the ritual of athletics."[15] In light of this analogy, it is resonant to note that during the time when Píndaros was active, the representation of athletes' bodies in victory statues, discussed below, was so similar to that of heroes that scholars today debate whether many extant statuary remains represent historical athletes or mythological heroes.[16] The ancient Hellenic word for the ordeals of heroes in mythology and of athletes in competition is *agón*. This third connotation of *agón* (ordeal) pertains to the competitor's experience of adversity both in a contest and, as Píndaros often notes, in the arduous preparation required to compete in a contest. In the context of primordial ritual, *agón* in the sense of "ordeal" characterizes both the process of initiation into adulthood and the trials that heroes undergo in mythology.[17]

As an illustration, the ritual pattern for initiation into adulthood includes three phases: a young female or male undergoes, first, a phase of segregation from the community, then a phase of experiencing some ordeal that qualifies the initiate for a new status as an adult member of the community, and, finally, a phase of the initiate's reintegration into the community with their newly attained status. Ancient sources describe the sanctioned practices for such an initiation ritual for young males in Krḗtē:[18] an older man abducts a boy, separating him from the community; the boy undergoes the ordeal of being sexually forced and then remaining for a period of time in the wilderness where men and boys hunt; the boy then returns to his community with the new status of adult male. Solemnifying this transition to adulthood, the initiate receives gifts required by ritual conventions, including military equipment. Several aspects of the mythology of *Olympian 1* correspond to this pattern: Poseidón, motivated by erotic desire, abducts Pélops, translating him to the realm of the gods and separating him from his earthly community; Pélops sexually gratifies the god; as a result of his father Tántalos' crime, the gods send Pélops back, but notably to a foreign land, thematically extending the hero's separation from his community; Pélops then prays (O.1.75–85) to Poseidón for assistance in his impending *áethlos* (contest), the life-and-death chariot race against Oinómaos, specifically as compensation for his sexual gratification of the god; Poseidón gifts Pélops with a golden chariot and winged horses, equipment that is at once athletic and martial.

Again, although the rituals of initiation and compensation for death were not explicitly an aspect of athletic competition at the time when Píndaros lived and wrote, vestiges of these obsolescent rituals nevertheless surface in mythology and the symbolism of the games. This ritual context is entangled with the sociological poetics of ancient athletics and the social functions of the performance of *epiníkion*.

Píndaros was one of three poets who composed *epiníkia*. Simōnídēs (born *c.* 556 BCE) is credited with originating the practice of writing songs to commemorate athletic victory. Simōnídēs' nephew Bakkhylídēs (*c.* 520–450 BCE) composed, in addition to songs in other poetic genres, fifteen *epiníkia*, including three *epiníkia* composed for Hiérōn (Bacchyl. 3, 4, 5) and one for Pythéas of Aígina (Bacchyl. 13), two competitors whom Píndaros' *epiníkia* also celebrate. All three poets worked from the late-sixth century to the mid-fifth century BCE. This period coincides with the emergent practice of commemorating athletic victories by dedicating statue portraits of athletes at the four Panhellenic sites.[19] It was also a time of widespread social instability: "Pindar's era was heir to the crisis of aristocracy, the last flowering of tyranny, the rise of the democratic polis, and the shift from a premonetary to a money economy."[20] The explosion of victory commemoration arose at an inflection point when the aristocracy approached Panhellenic games as venues for displaying their power and wealth, as well as for building networks with other elite figures who travelled from throughout the Panhellenic world to these sites. The commemoration of athletic victory in the form of the public displays such as the performance of *epiníkia* and victory statues located in a prestigious site with Panhellenic traffic conferred durability upon the achievement and broadcasted it to wider audiences.[21]

Victory statues evidence a "display culture"[22] in which the human form—the bodies—of historical individuals, of heroes, and of images of gods represent the qualities captured by two adjectives that appear ubiquitously in Píndaros' poetry: *kalós* (beautiful, noble, good) and *ágathos* (worthy). These modifiers encapsulate the qualities of the person, hero, or god endowed with *areté* (excellence, prowess). The reception histories of ancient Hellenic visual culture have problematically promoted an axiomatic alignment between "classical" sculpture and "fine" art. In order to appreciate both the ancient statue habit in its own right and how the performance of *epiníkion* participates in the display culture evidenced by this habit, it is necessary to recognize that in the eyes of ancient viewers statue portraits were realistic and that they represented indigenous ideologies, rather than an abstract, absolute, universal idealism that stems from the conjunction of "classical" and "fine." In the first place, ancient statues did not appear originally as they do in the modern imagination and, until recently, in art history textbooks. The clothing, eyes, hair, and flesh of marble statues were painted.[23] Technological and artistic innovations in bronze sculpture in the early-fifth century BCE resulted in works that "were big, real-looking figures, with bright polished tan surfaces, that imitate skin, tendons, veins, muscles, inlaid with realist colour for eyes, lips, teeth, nipples, and fine cold-worked engraving for eyebrows, beards, hair, toenails, fingernails."[24] The austerity of unadorned, white marble statues such as Roman replicas of the originally bronze *doryphóros* (spearbearer) of Polýkleitos (active *c.* 460–410 BCE) or the "classicizing" patina of works such as the Riace bronzes (*c.* 460–450 BCE), qualities celebrated, again problematically, as idealizing and universal, differ from the experience of original viewers' encounters with ancient Hellenic statuary, for whom victor statues were realistic representations of a human form, so much so that "a primary ancient response to statues was as real persons: they can speak, sweat, move, be tied up, flogged, prosecuted, and executed."[25] Even the nudity of victory statues, which we might associate with a kind of "classical" idealization of the human form, is more appropriately understood as an aspect of lifelikeness: athletes competed nude.[26]

Victory statues were erected at Delphoí, Neméa, and the Isthmós, but since Olympía hosted the most prestigious crown games, the evidence for the statue habit as a form of victory commemoration is thickest there.[27] The travel writer Pausanias concedes that he does not include in his account all of the statues that he observed in situ at Olympía (6.1.2). Archaeological evidence hints at just how selective Pausanias was: of the approximately 100 inscriptions on the bases of victory statues that have come to light, roughly forty correspond to the victory statues that Pausanias describes. The other sixty or so statues which the remaining inscriptions would have accompanied do not appear in his account. Of the eighty statues dating to 400 BCE that Pausanias describes, forty-three are for athletes who were victorious during Píndaros' lifetime. Even then, roughly five hundred years before Pausanias, victory statues, along with the votive statues of Zeus that the travel writer also observed, crowded the Áltis. Visitors moving through that space would have encountered a throng of lifelike, three-dimensional images of nude portraits and the occasional imposing bronze chariot with chariot team, all presenting to viewers a wonderous spectacle of art and engineering. Statues were secured in place atop bases which bore inscriptions that replicated the *angelía* (proclamation) of the athlete's victory. Because the manner of "reading" at the time entailed oral reperformance of a text, to this visual experience we must add the aural experience that emanated from the inscriptions accompanying victory statues, litanies of *angelíai* (victory announcements) declaring athletes' names, families, home *póleis*, and the contests in which they were victorious.

At the time when Píndaros practiced his art, elite and powerful figures sought to display their successes in athletic competition, as well as the beauty, nobility, worthiness, and excellence that these successes symbolized, by commissioning statues to be erected in Panhellenic sanctuaries where viewers of them came from throughout the Hellenic world. The proliferation of the statue habit was so adventitious that eventually the Hellanodíkai regulated their size, number, and appearance.[28] A sense of competition with victory statues seems to motivate Píndaros' occasional disparaging comments about the practice, as in the following lines:

I am no portrait sculptor	N.5.1–2
who chisels statues	
that stand motionless on pedestals	

With such sentiments, Píndaros advocates for victory commemoration in the form of *epiníkion*: "the poet provides a self-moving production, capable of circulating, therefore superior."[29]

The formal *angelía* (victory announcement) and its symbolic significance pertains to the sociological poetics in which the commemoration of athletic victory participated. After the athlete had undergone the *agón* (ordeal) of competition, where representatives from Hellenic cities throughout the Mediterranean came together to form a Panhellenic *agón* (public gathering), during which the *angelía* proclaimed the athlete's name, patronymic, and home *pólis* (city), in addition to the athletic event in which he was victor. The *angelía* thus invoked three interconnected fields of social life especially relevant to aristocratic athletes: their *oíkos* (household), their aristocratic status, and their home *póleis* (cities).[30] Corresponding to each of these fields, Píndaros portrays himself variously "as a servant of the house of the victor, an aristocratic guest-friend, and a craftsman fashioning a public dedication on behalf of the victor."[31]

The spatial and metaphorical loop of *nóstos* (return home) and the economy of *kléos* (renown) depend crucially upon the significance of the *oíkos* in the sociological poetics of *epiníkion*.[32] The word *oíkos* (household) refers not only to the built space of a home, but approximates a meaning more akin to "homestead," especially given that agricultural yields and surpluses, much more than money, were the measure of the *ploútos* (wealth, abundance) of an *oíkos*, both symbolically and in terms of commodities. Taken together the primary meanings of the English words *wealth* (the condition of being happy and prosperous; well-being) and *weal* (wealth, riches, possessions) suggestively evoke the meaning of *ploútos*.[33] The Hellenic roots of the English word *economy*, *oíkos* (household) and *nómos* (management, tending), offer further insight into the meaning of *oíkos*: because it comprised all of the familial property, including buildings, land, animals, and enslaved persons, the Hellenic *oíkos* was the fundamental locus of economic activity for members of the *oíkos* and the basic economic and political unit of a *pólis* (city). The *oíkos* was, of course, also a familial institution, but a family that included past, present, and future members. The *oíkos* was fittingly the site for such rituals as revering past family members by maintaining ancestral tombs, observing funerals, celebrating marriages.[34]

We have already seen that the athlete departs from his community, both *oíkos* and *pólis*, in order to undergo an *agón* (ordeal) that results in a change of status that his *nóstos* (return home) affirms. The *oíkos* spatially orients this loop of *nóstos*: the *oíkos* is the point from which the athlete sets forth and to which he returns. The *oíkos* is also central in the economy of *kléos* (renown). *Kléos* is a possession of the *oíkos* rather than exclusively of the individual athlete. On the one hand, the athlete's victory confers *kléos* upon his *oíkos*, but the *oíkos* possesses and maintains a familial tradition of *kléos*. Because *kléos* is not static, but waxes and wanes through time, the vitality and currency of *kléos* requires its reanimation. The athlete's victory serves as a reminder of his *oíkos*' ancestral *kléos*, and the commemoration of athletic victory reawakens the dormant *kléos* of his *oíkos*. Without renewal, the social capital of ancestral *kléos* diminishes over time. As Píndaros writes:

> splendor slumbers   I.7.16–19
>   mortal memories falter
> if anything fails to reach the flowering heights
> of poetry yoked to a triumphant flow of lyrics

Leslie Kurke expertly encapsulates how these lines of Píndaros' verse elucidate the economy of *kléos*:

> The entropy of *kléos* results in a continual pressure to achieve: the house's reputation wanes if it is not periodically renewed. By the same token, each new achievement, properly publicized, reactivates all the symbolic capital of the house. Thus it is the poet's task to celebrate the current victory and recall the family's past achievements in order to consolidate and renew its stock of glory.[35]

One social function of *epiníkion*, then, is to reintegrate the returning victorious athlete into his *oíkos* when he completes the loop of *nóstos* and to align the achievement and prestige that attends victory with the intergenerational symbolic capital of the *oíkos*.[36]

The conventions of *xenía* (ritualized guest-friendship, hospitality) structure the rhetoric of *epiníkion* and the transactions between poet and athlete entailed in commissioning the composition and performance of the victory song. When the poet portrays his praise of athletic achievement and of the athlete's *oíkos* as *xenía*, he locates his art in the practices of aristocratic gift exchange.[37] The word *khréos* (duty) expresses the praise-poet's obligation to honor the reciprocity entailed in such gift exchange.

>   the Moúsa must   O.3.4–9
>   have stood
>   beside me
>   when I minted
>   a bright new style
>   to harmonize with Dorian sandal
>   the voice
>   of this gorgeous parade
>   garlands crowning an athlete's
>   waves of hair
>   give me this godsent duty [*khréos*]:
>   the lyre's
>   chordrange
>   the shout of auloí
>   composing verses—
>   to blend them beautifully
>   for the son of Ainēsídamos

Such rhetoric translates the dynamics of patronage, or payment for poetic services rendered, into a reciprocal exchange of valuable gifts.

To represent victory and the praise of it in terms of gift exchange is also significant because athletic competition at Panhellenic sanctuaries "provided a forum for aristocrats to vie for preeminence within their own class."[38] Here it is useful to recall Hēsíodos' distinction between blameworthy *éris* and praiseworthy *éris*. In the rhetoric of gift exchange, the poet undertakes the obligation to requite the expenditure and toil of competition and the achievement of victory itself with praise. "The community the poet creates," as Kurke writes, "by his act of praise extends beyond the single link between poet and victor, however, for the poem, like the victory, is a public act that addresses an audience [here, the aristocracy] and implicates them in its obligation to praise."[39] In this way the poet both celebrates the athlete's effort and signals that these qualities of diligence and prowess characterize the aristocracy. Píndaros' *epiníkion* transforms the potentially divisive consequences of blameworthy *éris*—in this context, competition for prestige—into an affirmation of the distinction that members of the aristocracy share.

In addition to being a node in networks of relations with other members of the aristocracy through the rhetoric and practice of *xenía*, the *oîkos* was also a constituent element the *pólis*. Athletes needed to manage the threats that the magnitude of the symbolic power of victory posed to their homecities. The means of exchange available to avert these potential tensions was the civic "virtue known as *megaloprépeia*, the lavish public expenditure of wealth by those who can afford it" on behalf of the *pólis*.[40] *Megaloprépeia* (munificence) taps into the principles of gift exchange: wealth and status obligate the aristocracy to share their abundance with their home *póleis* in the form of public benefactions. The aristocratic practice of *megaloprépeia* renders an individual family's wealth a part of the common pool resources of the *pólis* to fund *khoroí* (choruses), public sacrifices, and festivals, to perform diplomatic services such as hosting embassies from abroad, to bolster military resources by raising horses and equipping warships, and to enrich the *pólis* with public works such as *palaístrai* (communal gymnasia). In return for such benefactions, the donator enjoyed *dóxa* (good reputation), *timé* (honor), and even *kúdos* (magical aura). Given the societal conditions that make the period from the late-sixth to early-fifth centuries an era of change and attendant crisis—the emergence of democracy, the threat of tyranny, growth of a money economy, military conflict, most notably with the Persian Empire—*megaloprépeia* was a fraught practice because it could be manipulated to promote the political ambitions of a single individual. In particular, "excessive *megaloprépeia* seems to presage tyranny."[41]

Although the word *megaloprépeia* does not occur in Píndaros *epiníkia*, his alignment of *ploútos* with *areté* (excellence, virtue, prowess) participates in the rhetoric of the practice; for example:

> wealth's [*ploútos*] power is vast P.5.1–4
>   whenever some mortal man
> if destiny grants wealth's gift
>   brings it home
>   tempered
> with undefiled virtue [*areté*]
>   a muchdear escort

This rhetoric communicates to the *pólis* audience that the privileged qualities and achievements of the victorious aristocrat are assets for the entire community and that the athlete's observance of his obligation to share his resources with his *pólis* affirms his civic virtue. Píndaros' poetry controls the public narrative of *megaloprépeia* by casting the athlete's victory as a benefaction to the *pólis*, broadcasting the *dóxa* (good reputation), *timé* (honor), and *kúdos* (magical aura) that accrues to the athlete for this benefaction, and obviating the potentially dangerous perception of personal ambition that may be associated with *megaloprépeia* by confronting the *phthónos* (envy), a form of the blameworthy *éris* (strife) in Hēsíodos' wisdom poetry, that might arise in response to the achievement of victory and its conferral upon the *pólis* as a benefaction. Rather than an asymmetrical dynamic, however, the management of the meaning of victory was an aspect of the mutualistic relationship between poet and athlete.

Monetary compensation for victory commemoration in either medium, statue portrait or the choral performance of song, certainly figured in the dynamics of commissioning these works of art, but the rhetoric of display culture throws into relief the traditional nexus between the *kléos* of the athlete and the *kléos* of the artist. Most typically athletes personally dedicated statue portraits of themselves, though occasionally their families or home *póleis* did so. The prices for a bronze statue and an *epiníkion* composed by Píndaros were comparable and substantial.[42] These facts may suggest that artistic commissions were merely transactional, but it must be remembered that ancient Hellenic society of Píndaros' time was still very much traditional. The available evidence indicates that "no less than 60 per cent of fifth-century victor statues at Olympia were signed" by their makers, uniting athlete and artist in a viewer's encounter with a portrait.[43] In the case of Píndaros' art, if the poet succeeded at projecting the event of victory from the realm of history to the realm of traditional art through the performance and composition of his song—a success signalled by the reperformance of the poet's verse through time (including the present reperformance in the form of this translation)—then the *kléos* of both athlete and poet would abide there and thereafter. The durability of *epiníkion* ensured through reperformance promotes the longlastingness of the athlete's benefaction of his victory to his home *pólis*,[44] as the following passage illustrates:

>   if some god should grant me   P.3.110–15
> sumptuous wealth [*ploútos*]
>   I have hope
>   that I will find
> soaring fame [*kléos*] hereafter
>   we know Néstōr
>   and Lykía's
> Sarpēdón—
>   heroes that people still recall—
> from resounding verses
>   that expert builders [*téktones sophoí*] composed
> virtue [*areté*] endures
>   through the power
>   of famous songs
> an easy feat to achieve for very few

In addition to the collocation of *ploútos* and *areté* that motivate the poet's sense of *khréos* (duty) to requite the athlete's achievement and stature, in this passage Píndaros attributes the enduring fame of figures from Trojan War mythology, Néstōr and Sarpēdón, to the power of song. These lines also exemplify Píndaros' occasional practice of metaphorically presenting his poetry as an *anáthēma* (monument) when he characterizes poets as *téktones sophoí* (expert builders).

Whereas gift exchange pertains to the relationship between poet and athlete in terms of aristocratic affiliation, *megaloprépeia* positions the poet to portray "himself as a craftsman fashioning a precious object to the victor's specifications but for the common good."[45] Píndaros sometimes signals his participation in *megaloprépeia* by representing himself as the builder of a physical monument such as a building or commemorative *stélē* (a stone monument), as in the following lines:[46]

it is a gift	I.1.45–6

easy to give
    for a man of wisdom
        to say
the proper words
    to offer up [*orthósai* (to erect)] a shared beautiful
something in answer to every kind of industry

With the infinitive *orthósai* (to erect), Píndaros metaphorically characterizes his poetry as the erection of an *anáthēma* (monument), which is particularly resonant in light of the statue habit. The dedication of victory statues was an extension of the practice of dedicating votives, including statues, in honor of a god in sacred spaces such as the Panhellenic sanctuaries, and the ancient Hellenic word for such a dedication is *ágalma* (dedication), which appears in the following passages where Píndaros represents his poetry as a communal benefaction:

begin a worthy praisesong	N.3.10–13

    daughter
        for ruler
of cloudthick sky
    I will make it [the praisesong] known to all
with lyre and those singers' voices
        this land's adornment [*ágalma*]
requires delightful toil

as suppliant of Aiakós	N.8.13–16

        I grasp
his holy knees
    on behalf
        of his cherished city

of its citizens here
> I wear my headband

of Lydía
> intricately embroidered
>> with unbridled

music
> Neméa's adornment [*ágalma*]
>> for the double

stádion footraces
> of Deínis
>> and his father

Mégas

In both passages, Píndaros presents the performance of his song as a metaphorical *ágalma* (dedication) to the *póleis* of the athletes whom *Nemean 3* and *Nemean 8* commemorate.

The performance of *epiníkion* has both ideological functions and reciprocal functions in each of these three fields of social practice, *oíkos*, aristocracy, and *pólis*, that confer upon the poet a privileged authority. *Epiníkion* represents athletic victory as a possession of the athlete's *oíkos* in order to reawaken the *kléos* of the family. As the author of the poetry that effects this reawakening, the *kléos* of the poet is implicated in the *kléos* of the *oíkos*. In the field of aristocratic rivalry and prestige, *epiníkion* draws upon the rhetoric of gift exchange to characterize the poet's praise as a duty and as the voluntary fulfillment of a *khréos* (duty), which the word *kháris* (grace, splendor, reciprocity), the conventionally appropriate reciprocation of victory with praise, often expresses. This more interpersonal drama of the *xenía* between poet and athlete serves as a reminder to other members of the aristocracy that they too are obligated to requite the prestige of their fellow victorious aristocrat. To do otherwise would undermine aristocratic claims to supremacy. In the field of the *pólis*, where traditions of gift exchange practices define and regulate the civic duties of aristocratic citizens, the social function of *epiníkion* is to render the achievement of victory a public gift to the *pólis*; the performance of *epiníkion* mitigates the potential threat posed by the newly acquired prestige of the athlete by translating his achievement into a benefaction shared by the community. Thus *epiníkion* reintegrated the athlete and his new status as a victor with all three domains, *oíkos*, aristocracy, and *pólis*. Through the public performance of *epiníkion* "the poet negotiates with the community on behalf of the returning victor. To ease the poet's acceptance by various segments of the audience [*oíkos*, aristocracy, and *pólis*], the poet dramatizes shared representations, portraying the victor as ideal citizen and ideal aristocrat."[47]

In addition to athletic competition as an ordeal that retains vestiges of the rituals of initiation and compensation for death and to the sociological poetics that links together the athelete's *oíkos*, affiliation with the aristocracy, and *pólis*, ancient athletics participated in the "economy of *kúdos*."[48] Although conventionally glossed as "prestige, renown,"[49] upon closer linguistic and anthropological analysis *kúdos* proves to be a "talisman of supremacy," "a magical power" that confers an "advantage at the decisive moment of combat or some competitive activity."[50] As we have already seen, Píndaros characterizes *áethloi* (athletic contests) as *hieroí* (sacred). In the economy of *kúdos*, this definition of games as sacred applies more particularly to crown games, as the testimony of inscriptions and literary sources affirms.[51] The presence of an athlete who was victorious in crown games in battle exemplifies the talismanic power of *kúdos*. The historian Diodorus Siculus (active first century BCE) reports that in the sixth century BCE the military commander Mílōn of Krótōn led the soldiers of his city into battle against the vastly superior forces of Sýbaris (12.9.5–6; cf. 9.14.1).[52] Mílōn's fellow citizens, Diodorus writes, "regarded him with wonder as the reason for their victory," because he wore in battle six victory garlands that he had won in games at Olympía, as well as donning the lion skin cloak of Hēraklés and carrying a club like the hero's. In the eyes of the historian and the people of Krótōn, the victorious athlete festooned with his victory crowns commanded magical power in combat. More specifically and crucially, this anecdote illustrates how the athlete's *kúdos* (talismanic power), symbolized by the victory crown, benefits his city.[53]

The ritual for a victorious athlete's reentry to his homecity upon his return from competing in games dramatizes this link between the athlete's victory crown and the significance of *kúdos* for his city. Drawing upon an episode recorded by Diodorus Siculus (13.82.7–8), Leslie Kurke summarizes the features of the athlete's reentry ritual:

> The crowds invoked blessings, pelted the victor with crowns, and bound *tainiai*, or fillets, about his head. The procession went conspicuously through the main streets to the center of the city, where the victor was announced (just as he had been at the games). The victor's crown was an important part of the ritual ... After the announcement of the victor, the crown was often dedicated at the shrine of a local god or hero.[54]

Píndaros' poetry dramatizes this reentry ritual when he invites an athlete's homecity to welcome the victor's crown.[55] In the opening prayer of *Olympian 5*, the speaker entreats Kamárina, the eponymous *nýmphē* of the homecity of the athlete Psaúmis, to welcome home the athlete and his crown:

> the sweet utmost of soaring talent   O.5.1–8
>   and crowns [*stéphanoi*] at Olympía
> daughter of Ōkeanós
>   accept these gifts
> with laughing heart
>   the mulecart treading tirelessly
> and Psaúmis
>   who magnifies your city that gives people
> life

> Kamárina
> > who honored the six doublealtars
> in lavish festivities
> > for the gods
> > > with cattle
> sacrifice and fiveday athletic contests [*áethloi*]
> with races—chariot mulecart single horse
> when he won
> > he dedicated [*anéthēke*] to you
> his sumptuous magic [*habrón kúdos*]
> > and made a herald
> > > herald
> his father Ákrōn
> > and your newfounded land

The pinnacle of prowess and victory crowns, along with Psaúmis himself, are "gifts" the poetry invites Kamárina to accept. The poetry further commends Psaúmis as increaser of the city's communal abundance. Rather than a matter of contributing to the material prosperity of Kamárina, the verb *anéthēke* (dedicated), which recalls the corresponding noun *anáthēma* (monument), represents Psaúmis' benefaction to his homecity as an offering of the religiously potent *kúdos* that his victory crowns symbolize. The last lines of the passage quoted above include two of the standard elements of the official *angelía* (victory announcement): the athlete's father and his homecity, referred to as "your newly founded land." In addition to the gesture toward the athlete's *oíkos* and *pólis*, the ritual of reentry suggested by these lines solemnizes the athlete's dedication of his victory crown to his homecity and illustrates how the economy of *kúdos* has reciprocal dimensions that align with *megaloprépeia*. Upon the athlete's return to his homecity during the reentry ritual, he dedicates his victory crown to the city and thereby shares with his community the *kúdos* (talismanic power) that he has gained by undergoing an *agón* (ordeal). The city reciprocates the athlete's donation with such rewards as the public reentry ritual, substantial monetary payments, meals in the *prytaneíon* (town hall) at public expense for life, seats of honor during festivals and performances, and in some cases a publicly funded statue erected in the city or at the site of the athlete's victory.[56]

We have already seen how the ritual dimensions of athletic competition are vestiges of the rituals of initiation and compensation for death and how the latter collapses into the former because the ordeal of initiation symbolically enacts the process of death and rebirth, where "death" entails the loss of a former status and "rebirth" the assumption of a new status. The culmination of the initiation process is reintegration into the community, which is analogous to the athlete's ritual reentry into his homecity. The athlete's victory endows him with a new status as someone who possesses *kúdos* (talismanic power). The point I seek to highlight in this recapitulation of the ways in which ritual practices and symbolism are entangled in athletic competition is that the ritual reintegration of the initiate into the community and the ritual reintegration of the athlete into his homecity are analogous. Furthermore, this analogy provides context for understanding the social functions of *epiníkion* and the role of the composer of this performance medium. If the *khorós* that performs *epiníkion* "represents, reenacts, the community of the polis," then we can further observe that "epinician performance is the final realization, the final constitutive event, of the ritual process of athletics."[57]

Whether viewed in ritual terms as the transformation that undergoing an ordeal effects, in terms of the sociological poetics in which *oîkos*, aristocracy, and *pólis* are imbricated, or in the related terms of rendering the victorious athlete's *kúdos* a communal benefaction, "poet and audience conceptualized the poem [i.e. *epiníkion*] as the completion of victory."[58] The reintegration of the athlete is the overarching social function of *epiníkion* and evokes the cultural resonance of primordial rituals of initiation and compensation for death. Such an understanding of the social functions of Píndaros' songs for athletes draws upon contemporary benchmark scholarship that rigorously attends to the referential and metalingual functions of language and enables readers of Píndaros to appreciate the diction, themes, imagery, and performance of *epiníkion* in its indigenous historical and cultural context. But as Hans-Georg Gadamer has written of Píndaros, "someone might explain to us the particular historical context, but this would be only secondary for the poem as a whole."[59] Although Píndaros' poetry undeniably documents context-specific ideologies and cultural practices, the dominant function of his language is ultimately poetic.[60] We find such a distinction among the functions of language in the evidence for meanings of *megaloprépeia*: though the word may connote "munificence" in the context of aristocratic ideology, it means "grandeur" in the context of treatises on poetics written by ancient philologists. Thus Dēmétrios (third or second century BCE?) defines one of the four fundamental types of style that he explores as *tó megaloprepés* (the grand style), which thought, word choice, and decorous composition characterize (*Eloc.* 36–127). Dionýsios of Halikarnassós, a Hellenic writer who resided and taught in Augustan era Rome, identifies Píndaros as the premier practitioner among lyric poets of *austērá harmonía* (austere arrangement), which corresponds to *tó megaloprepés* of Dēmétrios: for Dionýsios *rhythmoí axiōmatikoí* and *megaloprepeís* (dignified and magnificent rhythms) and phrasing that "is balanced, noble, luminous, free, and wants to look more like nature than craft" define *austērá harmonía* (*Comp.* 22).[61] While translation necessarily occludes such poetic features of Píndaros' language as the mélange of Hellenic dialects, the formal patterning of rhythm, poetic line, stanzaic structure, and ring-composition achieved by parallelism of diction or linguistic register, the artful deployment of such rhetorical figures as hypallage or zeugma, and the myriad original-language sound effects of alliteration, consonance, assonance, and homoioteleuton, it is nevertheless possible to discern features of style and compositional design that translation transmits in spite of its erasures.

Although the historical and mythological references in Píndaros' poetry may elude readers, his unbridled metaphors may account more fundamentally for the difficulty of his poetry.[62] A metaphor consists of two elements: (1) the vehicle, such as a word or image, that figuratively represents (2) a field of reference or meaning, the tenor.[63] The passages I have selected to illustrate other aspects of Píndaros poetry are laden with metaphors. We have seen that Píndaros merges two metaphors in one phrase (I.7.18–19, quoted above): poetic skill is yoked—the vehicle, whose tenor is chariot and horseteam— to *rhoaí* (rivers, streams) of poetic verse.[64] The vehicle of "Dorian sandal" refers to some aspect of performance, whether dance or rhythm (O.3.4–9, quoted above). The communally shared munificence of wealth is a companion (P.5.1–4, quoted above). Song is an *ágalma* (votive dedication) (N.3.10–13, quoted above) or a garment with which to adorn the victorious athlete (O.1.100–5, quoted below). The poet is a herald (N.6.57–61, quoted below), and Píndaros metaphorically declares his homeland by claiming to drink the waters of Thébē (O.6.85–6, quoted below). As we have already seen in connection with *megaloprépeia*, Píndaros may metaphorically portray himself as a craftsman (N.5.1–2, P.3.110–15, and I.1.45–6, quoted above).[65]

The category of vegetal metaphors further illustrates the Píndaros' penchant for deploying the device.[66] Píndaros never uses the word *thálos* (shoot) other than metaphorically. Strepsiádas' *pankrátion* victory is a *thálos* shared with his uncle of the same name (I.7.24). Thersándros is the *thálos* of the family line of the hero Ádrastos (O.2.45); Hēraklés, the *thálos* of the Alkäídai (O.6.68); Ortygía, the *thálos* of Syrákousai (N.1.2). We also encounter the *ánthos* (bloom, flower) of praisesong (O.6.105, O.9.48), of youth (P.4.158), of erotic pleasure (N.7.53). The *polyánthemoi Hórai* (fullbloom Seasons) bestow ancient wisdom upon humans (O.13.13–17, quoted above). When authoritative sources present the meaning of the adjective *áphthitos* as "immortal, imperishable," they deaden the vegetal metaphor figured in this and related words,[67] because its root, *phthi*—, means more radically "wilt."[68] Thus the denotation of *áphthitos* is more properly "unwilting," making the word available as the vehicle in vegetal metaphors for immortality. The gods gift Tántalos with ambrosia and nectar, with which they render him *áphthitos* (O.1.62–4). Inó attains an *áphthitos bíotos* (unwilting way of life) by becoming an immortal sea goddess (O.2.29). In an instance of hypallage, the cave where Kheírōn lives is *áphthiton* (I.8.41). The adjective *áphthitos* occurs multiple times in *Pythia 4*: Poseidón is the *áphthitos* Earthshaker, Earthembracer (P.4.33); in a more elaborated vegetal metaphor, the clod of earth that Eurýpylos gives to Eúphēmos as an improvised guest gift is the *áphthiton spérma* (unwilting seed) of Libýē (P.4.42–3); the golden fleece (P.4.230) and Zeus (P.4.291) are each *áphthitos*.

In the mythological narrative of *Olympian 6*, Píndaros portrays the birth and maturation of the prophet Íamos by means of vegetal metaphors. In the understory of a thicket, he suddenly emerges sproutlike from his mother Euádnē's womb into the light (O.6.39–47). As he lies on the ground, serpents nourish him with the *amemphés iós* (blameless elixir) of honey, itself a metaphor for prophecy and poetry (O.6.46–7), so that the wordplay involved in the resonance between *iós* (elixir) and *íon* (violet) sets up a phonic pattern that calls attention to the vegetal metaphor operating in the poem—and aligned with that pattern is the moment when Euádnē names her son Íamos' after the *ía* (violets) (O.6.54–7) that rain (metaphorically) their flowery radiance upon his infant body. When he has grown, Íamos harvests the *karpós* (fruit) of Hébē (goddess of youth) (O.6.58).

In *Olympian 7*, before the island Rhódos had become a *nomós* (terrain) (O.7.33) that the hero Tlēpólemos colonized, the sea covered it like a seed (O.7.57). Hélios saw that it was on the verge of burgeoning plantlike (O.7.62) as a "pastureland for flocks" (O.7.63) even before "the island sprouted from watery sea" (O.7.69–70; cf. N.8.7–8). Given that vegetal metaphors thematically unify *Olympian 7*, does it come as a surprise that in the opening of the poem, Píndaros associates musical dimensions of performance with *zōthálmios* (cf. *thálos* [shoot]) *Kháris* (lifebloom Kháris) (O.7.11)?[69]

It's almost too providentially much, isn't it, the relentlessly kataphatic this-is-that of Píndaros' rampant metaphors that often reduces his audiences to apophatic bewilderment? Which might account for the tale according to which the poet Kórinna of Tánagra (*c.* third century BCE?) one time admonished Píndaros to sow seed with his hand, not the whole sack—an agricultural metaphor for unrestrained artistry (Plut. *De glor. Ath.* 347f–348a).

Another feature of Píndaros' poetics that survives the erasures of translation is a device known as the priamel. As Elroy Bundy, a formidable scholar of Píndaros, defined it, "the priamel is a focusing or selecting device in which one or more terms serve as a foil for the point of particular interest."[70] The opening of *Olympian 1* is a celebrated example:

> best: water   O.1.1–11
>   but gold—
>   like fire brightens night
> gold gives almighty wealth its shine
>   if victory
> crowns inspire your song
>   my heart
>   do not scan
> barren sky
>   for another star
>   more nourishing
> than sun
>   with its daylight brilliance
>   and we will sing
> no trial bolder than Olympía's
>   where praisesong
> worth resinging clothes
>   its shoulders in arts
> of wisemen
>   who sing out
>   for Krónos' son
> parading to Hiérōn's blessed abundant hearth

In these lines, "water, fire, gold, and the sun exist as foil for the introduction of the Olympian games, but the real climax, postponed for effect to the end of the strophe, comes with the mention of Hiérōn."⁷¹ The priamel in the opening lines of *Olympian 2* progresses from general to specific:

> you praisesongs that lord over lyres   O.2.1–6
>   what god
>   what hero
> what man will we sing?
>   yes Písa
>   belongs to Zeus
> Hēraklés founded Olympía's festival
>   his offering
> of war's first yields
>   for victory with fourhorse chariot
> let's shout the name of Thérōn

Píndaros gradually zeros in on the central topic of the song: Písa, the region where Olympía is located, is the first term; the more specific event of Hēraklés' founding of the festival at Olympía (cf. O.10.24–59) is the priamel's second term; after these two foils, we arrive at the topic most specific and most relevant to *Olympian 2*, Thérōn's chariot victory, the priamel's third, climactic term. Priamels occur widely in Píndaros' *epiníkia*.⁷²

According to a common formula for describing the typical discursive design of the victory song, mythological narrative nestles between passages of praise at the beginning and the end of a given poem. This praise-myth-praise formula for the design of *epiníkion* roughly accounts for transitions in the course of a poem from topic to topic and from first-person voice to third-person voice, but many of Píndaros' *epiníkia* spill over this descriptive container and some do not conform to it at all. One reason for the inexact empirical alignment between the praise-myth-praise design formula and actual poems is that this formula is exogenous rather than indigenous to Píndaros' artistic idiom. To use an indigenous Hellenic term for design of *epiníkion*, *poikilía* (embroidery, orchestration) captures the intertextual (cf. Latin *textus* [woven cloth]) quality of his *epiníkia*, in which the poet stitches together both a variety of ancient Hellenic vernaculars—Doric, Aiolic, and Ionic—and multiple registers or styles, each with its conventional stances for speaking voice(s) and addressee(s), conventional topics, and conventional configurations of time and place.⁷³ *Poikilía* also names Píndaros' skill at embellishing his language with rhythm, imagery, metaphor, innovative diction, and a treatment of syntax that privileges soundscape over referential meaning. In the following crucial passage Píndaros characterizes his art as a *poikílos hýmnos* (embroidered praisesong):

>   my mother's mother   O.6.84–7
> was from Stýmphalos
>   Metópē
>   laiden with flowers
> who gave birth to horsedriving Thébē

                 whose lovely
   water I drink
          as I weave elaborate praisesong [*poikílos hýmnos*]
   for warriors

While the syntax, diction, and rhythms of the target-language of translation supplant those of the original Hellenic, Píndaros' intertextual weaving of five stylistic registers is a form of *poikilía* that translation transmits. These registers are the stylistic media for the speech acts that occur in *epiníkion*: proverbs, lyric statements, mythological narrative, a poetically stylized version of *angelía* (victory announcement), and prayers.[74]

    The ancient Hellenic word for a proverb is *gnómē*, and I accordingly refer to the style of proverbs as the gnomic register. Píndaros' *gnómai* (proverbs) are among his most memorable verses. A third-person voice and indefinite addressee characterize the style of *gnómai*, which express appropriate speech or action or claims about the human condition and lack reference to a particular time or place. The following passage is an example of a proverb about the relationship between truth-telling and story-telling:

                 wonders   O.1.28–9
   multiply
       and people's talk strains
           the truth
   their handcrafted stories
       the embroidery of lies
           delude

By couching such ideas about the appropriate uses of speech in the gnomic register, Píndaros portrays them as general wisdom shared between composer-performer and his audiences. The following passage is among Píndaros' most well-known proverbs about the human condition:

we live as if   P.8.95–7
    for a single day
        what is
a someone?
    what is a no one?
        a human creature
is shadow's dream
    but whenever Zeusgiven
        splendor
comes
    daybright radiance
        and a tranquil lifetime
abide among men

The style of *gnómai* represents such thoughts as shared traditional wisdom.⁷⁵

Self-reflexivity is the dominant feature of the lyric register, whose themes are aspects of *epiníkion* or the performance of it, such as poetry, music, dance, and praise. In addition to these self-reflexive themes, a first-person voice, whether singular (referring to the composer) or plural (referring to the *khorós*), speaking in the here and now of performance, actual or rhetorically imagined, characterize the lyric style.

>   to crown that man   O.1.100–5
> with horsestride rhythm
>   and Aiolian song
>   is my duty
> among people today
>   I know of no other host
> so skilled in goodness
>   in command of such power
>   to drape
> with famemaking garments of praisesong

Here we witness a first-person singular voice refer to music, song, meter, praise, and its power to animate *kléos* (renown)—themes that are self-reflexive because they are involved in the composition and performance of *epiníkion*.

The register of *angelía* (victory announcement) occurs in the third-person voice and is the style for describing historical events of the recent past, namely the athlete's achievements in competition. A herald's formal announcement of victory during a festival that hosted games included the name of the athlete, his patronymic, his home *pólis*, the athletic event in which he was victorious, and the site of the games where he won. These same elements appear in the poetically adapted form of *angelía* that occurs in Píndaros' *epinikia*. We see all of these elements, except the athlete's *pólis*, in the following passage:

>   the contest for bronze prizes   N.10.22–8
>   stirs
> the crowd to sacrifice
>   oxen to Héra
>   to judge
> the games
>   where son of Oulías
>   Theaíos
>   forgot
> the toils he bore with poise
>   by winning twice
> another time
>   he overpowered ranks

                of Héllēnes at Pythó
                        and setting out with fortune's
        company
                attained the victory crown
                        at Isthmós
        and Neméa
                he gave the Moúsai
                        soil to plow
        by three times
                taking the garland
                        at the seagates
        three times too
                in the holy plain
                        in Ádrastos'
        rite

These lines exemplify the complexity of Píndaros' *poikilía*: while the poetry evidences features of the *angelía* register, it also includes a self-reflexive reference to performance by way of mentioning the Moúsai. Such hybridizing of registers occurs throughout Píndaros' *epiníkia*. Píndaros often signals his use of the *angelía* register by explicitly naming passages of his poetry *angelía*, using forms of the verb *angéllein* (to announce), or representing himself as an *ángelos* (messenger) or *kéryx* (herald), as in the following lines:

                I took upon   N.6.57–61
        my willing back
                this double burden
                        and came
        as herald [*ángelos*]
                shouting that this
                        is the twenty-fifth
        acclaim in contests
                people call sacred
                        that you
        Alkimídas
                furnished
                        your celebrated family
        with that glory

In this passage we again see a lyric inflection of the *angelía*: Píndaros self-reflexively portrays himself as a herald while performing his song.

Another register that Píndaros threads into his *epiníkia* is that of mythological narrative. Like the register of *angelía*, a third-person voice is a feature of the style of mythological narrative, but the events and figures of such narratives belong to dimensions of time and space that are traditional. When I refer to mythological narrative, I refer to the *style* of Píndaros' mythography rather than to a narrative *per se*. The style of mythological narrative is particular to stories about gods and heroes that are available for reperformance. The stretches of poetry in the register of mythological narrative in Píndaros' *epiníkia* are as brief as one line (for example: O.6.85, O.13.92, and N.8.18) and as long as 179 lines (P.4.68–246). Although many mythological sections of Píndaros' *epiníkia* are abbreviated and allusive, others exhibit a storytelling quality, especially his most fully elaborated mythological account of Médeia, Iásōn, and the voyage of the Argó in *Pythian 4*. We can observe general patterns in the selection of mythological stories: they may focus upon figures associated with the victor's homeland or with the site of victory, figures who are ancestors of the victor's family, or figures whose adventures and trials illustrate a lesson.

The register of prayer comprises several speech acts, such as invocations, entreaties, wishes, promises, vows, and the like, all of which share the features of first-person speaker and second-person addressee, whether the addressee is explicit in the language or implied by the speech act itself.[76] Píndaros' *Olympian 14* (see the translation below) includes multiple prayers, as well as illustrating dynamics of *poikilía* (orchestration) among the registers that occur in the poem. The opening lines comprise two prayers addressed to the Khárites (O.14.1–5 and 5–7), and three discrete sentences at the conclusion of the poem are also in the style of prayers (O.14.13–15, 15–20, and 20–4). The two opening prayers (O.14.1–7) form a ring with the first two of the three concluding prayers (O.14.13–20) by virtue of the fact that all of these prayers are addressed to the Khárites. Since these addressees are particularly associated with song and performance, the prayers addressed to them have a self-reflexive quality, so that features of lyric style inflect these prayers. This ring surrounds a proverb (O.14.8–9) and a brief passage (O.14.9–12) in the register of mythological narrative. Such ring composition is one type of patterning based upon the five recurrent registers of *epiníkion* that occurs in Píndaros' victory songs. Other patterns among these registers may be chiastic or interlocking. The orchestration of such patterns and the integration of them with other poetic features of Píndaros' poetry are aspects of *poikilía*.[77] To return to *poikilía* in *Olympian 14*, the final prayer of the poem, addressed to Ēkhó (Echo) requests the *nýmphē* to relay the *angelía* (announcement) of the athlete Asópikhos' victory to the athlete's deceased father in the underworld. This *angelía* (O.14.22–4) is embedded in the prayer addressed to Ēkhó (O.14.20–4). Such hybridization of registers is another aspect of *poikilía* that occurs in Píndaros' *epiníkia*.

Ancient Hellenic meter is based upon syllabic quantity rather than syllabic stress. Syllabic quantity has to do with the amount of time required to pronounce a syllable. A long syllable (–) requires twice as much time to pronounce as a short syllable (◡). We find three typical metrical rhythms in Píndaros *epiníkia*: (1) dactylo-epitritic rhythm, which combines the dactyl (– ◡ ◡) that occurs in the dactylic hexameter verse of such poets as Hómēros, Hēsíodos, and Parmenídēs, and the epitrite (– ◡ – –); (2) Aiolic rhythm, a composite of such a variety of metrical feet that it is difficult to generalize, but two common meters are the choriamb (– ⌣ ⌣ –) and cretic (– ⌣ –); (3) iambic rhythm, which in ancient Hellenic poetry takes the form of what could be considered in English prosody two iambs (⌣ – ⌣ –), occurs only in *Olympian 2*. Apart from *Olympian 2*, then, Píndaros composed all of his *epiníkia* using either dactylo-epitritic rhythm or Aiolic rhythm, but no two *epiníkia* have the same metrical and stanzaic pattern except *Isthmians* 3 and 4, something so exceptional that some scholars of Píndaros interpret their common meter as evidence that the two songs actually constitute one song. Píndaros often shapes the metrical design of his songs to conform to a triadic structure, which consists of three stanzas: strophe, antistrophe, and epode. To draw upon the original-language terminology, *strophé* "turn" may indicate dance movement in one direction, *antistrophé* "counterturn," movement in the opposite direction, and *epōidós* "aftersong," a moment in performance when the *khorós* members stand or move in place. The on-the-page appearance of Píndaros' *epiníkia* has been an undeniable vector of the poet's reception, but it is crucial to bear in mind that the stanzaic structures of these songs are vestiges of choreography. As William W. Cook and James Tatum write, "with its strophes and antistrophes Greek choral lyric actually has more in common with African dance than it has with our modern printed page."[78] For another illustration of the performative quality of the stanzaic structure of Píndaros' songs, Victoria Moul documents a strain of reception, conditioned by late-sixteenth-century science, in which the strophe represents right-to-left movement in imitation of the cosmos' east to west motion, the antistrophe represents left-to-right movement in imitation of the setting and rising of the planets, and the epode represents Earth's stability.[79] Each strophe and antistrophe in a victory song share the identical metrical pattern. The epode's rhythms differ from, but are analogous to, those of the strophe and antistrophe. Thirty-eight *epiníkia* have this triadic line and stanza structure. When a song includes more than one triad, all triads are metrically identical. Likewise, in the seven *epiníkia* that are monostrophic (O.14, P.6, P.12, N.2, N.4, N.9, I.8)—that is, they have a single strophe without antistrophe or epode—the meter of each strophe is metrically identical. The complex artistry of Píndaros' verbal music is stunning—and completely lost in translation. I indicate the stanzaic structure of each *epiníkion*, as well as line numbers of the original-language text, along the right margin of the page, but do not seek to replicate Píndaros' lines or poetic rhythms in my translation.

The evidence for the choral performance of *epiníkion* is limited to the internal evidence of the text. Píndaros' *epiníkia* refer to three stringed instruments: the *kítharis*, *phórminx*, and *lýra*. While the *kítharis* (=*kithára*) was a seven-stringed instrument with a wooden soundbox, the *phórminx* a stringed instrument that accompanied the performance of Homeric poetry, and the *lýra* a smaller stringed instrument made with a tortoise shell, Píndaros appears to use the terms without differentiation for "lyre."[80] Píndaros also mentions the *aulós*, a wind instrument made of two reeds with finger holes played with each hand simultaneously. Second-person plural direct address to *ándres* (men), *néoi* (youths), and *paídes* (boys) suggests a group of performers, a *khorós* (chorus), who sing and dance. The synesthetic spectacle of performance of such lyric poetry as Píndaros' "tends to create," as Anastasia-Erasmia Peponi so evocatively writes, "a state of consciousness where the concreteness of verbal matter may recede, giving way to less palpable yet wholly pervasive moods or atmospheres that are perceived in various sense modalities."[81] The accident that we possess only textual artifacts of *epiníkia* necessarily consigns us to a diminished experience of the art form that foregrounds the verbal at the expense of the atmospheric. Although we do not have direct evidence for the performance occasion(s) of *epiníkia*, it is conventional to assume they were usually performed at the victor's homecity upon his return, although some scholars argue that they may have been produced at the site of games immediately after the athlete's victory. The occasions for the reperformance of Píndaros' *epiníkia* range from informal recitation from memory by those present at an original performance to solo reperformance of Píndaros' poetry during symposia, semi-ritualized social gatherings for elite males who displayed their cultural competence by performing verbal art, to formal reproductions of the original choral performance.[82]

Selected episodes of Píndaros' afterlives sketch his influence upon the later history of poetry and poetics.[83] While Píndaros was celebrated in antiquity for the dazzling artistry and sobering wisdom of his poetry, soon after his death the comedic playwright Aristophánēs (*c*. 455–386 BCE) had already parodied Píndaros as a sycophantic poetizer, awkwardly overeager to perform their verse in exchange for payment (*Av.* 904–53; cf. *Ach.* 633–40, *Eq.* 1323–30). Such parody of the poet from Thébai in Aristophanic comedy, a popular art form performed before thousands at Athénai, substantiates the posthumous stature of Píndaros: the humor depends upon the fame—or notoriety?—of Píndaros.[84]

In his rhetorical handbook, the Roman scholar Quintilian (*c*. 35–95 CE) ranked Píndaros as by far preeminent among the canonical nine Hellenic lyric poets because of "his grandeur of spirit, proverbs, rhetorical devices, a flourishing bounty of themes and words—like a river of eloquence. Because of such qualities, Horace believed, and deservedly so, that no one can imitate him" (*Inst.* 10.1.61). Quintilian here recalls the Roman poet Horace's (65–8 BCE) mimesis of Píndaros' poetics. In a poem addressed to Iullus Antonius (43–2 BCE), a son of Mark Antony who held political offices of the highest rank and was a family member of the emperor Augustus, Horace declines to compose a Pindaric song in honor of Augustus because his creative powers are too modest, he insists, to write so daringly:

Whoever aspires to rival Pindarus,
Iullus, strives with feathers fused
by the wax of Daedalus' power and surrenders
his name to glassy sea.

Like riversurge plunges down a mountain—
rainstorm feeds it beyond its familiar
banks—Pindarus seethes and crashes down
boundlessly with his deep mouth.

Grant him Apollo's laurel crown,
whether he unscrolls newfound words
in daring dithyrambs and rhythms
freed from law transport him,

27

> or he sings of gods and kings, the bloodline
> of gods ...
>
> Carm. 4.2.1–14

These lines introduce Horace's contrast between grand, Pindaric poetry, the hypothetical project of Iullus Antonius, and Horace's attenuated lyricism, whose model is the Hellenistic poet Kallímakhos (active 285–245 BCE).[85] In the first half of his poem, Horace rejects Píndaros' lofty, exuberant poetics (*Carm*. 4.2.1–32). The second half of the poem dramatizes praise of Augustus in two modes, the more elevated style of Iullus Antonius' projected panegyric poetry (*Carm*. 4.2.33–44), and Horace's own modest, popular, and refined style (*Carm*. 4.2.45–60). Horace's refusal to rival Píndaros proves to be an artistic sleight of hand: in the course of rejecting the Pindaric model, Horace reenacts it.[86] This reenactment of the rejected model surfaces most remarkably both where Horace catalogs Píndaros' poetic genres (*Carm*. 4.2.5–24) and in the encomiastic qualities of the poem's second half. The phrase *laurea* (*corona* implied) *Apollinaris* (Apollo's laurel [crown]) (*Carm*. 4.2.9) solicits multiple associations simultaneously: the celebration of Roman military victors, victors in athletic games at Delphoí, both of which kinds of victors received a laurel crown, and poetry itself, which is the province of the god Apóllōn. Horace reenacts the sublime qualities of the putatively inimitable Píndaros perhaps most strikingly in the final stanza of his catalog of Pindaric genres, where two hypometric lines (*Carm*. 4.2.22–3), with their phrase *viris animumque moresque / aureos* (goldclad strength, courage, and ways), "a perfect tricolon *abundans* [overflowing] (2 + 4 + 6 syllables),"[87] exhibit the torrential exuberance attributed to the model in the lines translated above. Rather than a Píndaros, or the "swan of Dírkē" (*Carm*. 4.2.25), as Horace calls him, the Roman poet would more "humbly fashion his songs ... in the manner and measure of Matinus' bee," words that recall Horace's homeland in southern Italy (*Carm*. 4.2.27–32). Horace's hypothetically cheering voice upon the triumphal return of Augustus to Rome (*Carm*. 4.43–4) may bring to mind the first-person singular voice of Píndaros as the composer-performer of *epiníkion*, given the victory song's role in the athlete's return to his home *pólis* (*Carm*. 4.45–8). The meter of the lines in which Horace imagines himself singing out to Augustus *O Sol pulcher! O laudande!* (Oh lovely Sun! Oh you who must be praised!) (*Carm*. 4.46–7), however, matches the rhythm of popular verses that Roman soldiers sang to their generals, so that the celebration is particularly Roman.[88] Horace translates the rejected Pindaric model into indigenously Roman poetics. Similarly reminiscent of the Hellenic context, where the *khorós* represents the community's welcome of the returning athlete, Horace portrays himself as one member of the first-person plural *omnis civitas* (the whole state) who welcomes the Roman ruler returning in triumph (*Carm*. 4.2.49–52). The chant of this popular chorus, *io Triumphe* (Hurray for the one who triumphs!), is a brief vocal gesture repeated twice (*Carm*. 4.49 and 50), that at once replicates the Roman soldiers' celebratory shout during a triumphal procession and reenacts *dithýrambos*, whether Pindaric or more generally.

Horace's distinction between Píndaros' exuberant, spontaneous, and sublime lyricism and his own carefully wrought, attenuated, and humble poetics often mediates later receptions of Píndaros' poetry.[89] In his collections *The Forest* (published in the 1616 folio) and *Underwoods* (published posthumously in 1640), Ben Jonson (1572–1637) experimented with the ode form and in his later ode *To the immortal memorie, and friendship of that noble paire, Sir Lucius Cary, and Sir H. Morrison* (1630) replicated the triadic structure of stanzas and varied line-length that we observe in Píndaros' *epiníkia*, deployed victory as a metaphor for achievement, and asserted the poet's agency in guaranteeing the celebrated figures' abiding fame, features that also appear in Jonson's masques.[90] While Jonson's engagements with Píndaros and such works as John Milton's *Nativity Ode* (1629), Abraham Cowley's *Pindarique Odes* (1656), and Thomas Gray's *Pindaric Odes* (1758) consolidated the status of the Pindaric ode as a form that would find later, celebrated practitioners,[91] during this period the vogue of Pindarism also came to be synonymous with undisciplined and pretentious versification.[92] For two Romantic poets, the German Friedrich Hölderlin (1770–1843) and the Greek Andreas Kalvos (1792–1869), "Pindar was a source on which to draw in the struggle to re-establish poetry's relation to the absolute: the transcendental dimension lost in the modern world."[93] Receptions of Píndaros' poetry among Romantic poets abound, from the odes of John Keats (composed in 1820) to Percy Bysshe Shelley's synthesis of Platonic thought and Pindaric poetics,[94] to Giacomo Leopardi's poems *All'Italia* (1818), *A un vincitore nel pallone* (1821), and *La ginestra, o il fiore del deserto* (1836).[95] This genealogy extends to Pablo Neruda's *Odas elementales* (1954), *Nuevas odas elementales* (1956), and *Tercer libro de las odas* (1957) and Ross Gay's *Catalog of Unabashed Gratitude* (2015). Robert de Brose masterfully charts the two-hundred-year history of translating Píndaros' poetry as the pursuit of linguistic and cultural autonomy in Brazil.[96] William W. Cook and James Tatum celebrate the African-American poet, scholar, and educator Melvin Tolson (1898–1966) as "the Pindar of Harlem because of his evolution as a poet and critic, because of the circumstances in which he produced his greatest poetry, and because of the enviable reputation his mature work quickly earned for its prodigious learning and baffling obscurity."[97] Merely suggestive of the depth of his creative engagement with Píndaros, the title of a celebrated poetry collection by the formidable poet and translator Reginald Gibbons, *Creatures of a Day* (2008), translates a famous one-word sentence, *epámeroi*, from an often-quoted Pindaric proverb (P.8.95–7). In his poetry collection *Renditions* (2021), Gibbons parodies Píndaros' encomiastic poetics in *Pythian 3*, an ode that draws upon themes of healing to console an apparently aging and ailing Hiérōn, tyrant of Syrákousai. The opening lines of Gibbons' poem, "My Greco-Russian Investigation (after Pindar's Third Pythian Ode)," pick up on the epistolary quality of the Pindaric original and signal who his "Hiérōn" is:[98]

> Dear "Hieron" (I'll call you–not your made-
>   up *lump* of a name),
> A friend came from your tyrannical
>   capital to tell
> me you're ill in spirit and in mind.

In the poem's third epode, the speaker translates Píndaros' original poetry (P.3.63–5) and then transforms the passage, plying the Pindaric themes of healing in contrafactual terms:[99]

> If the centaur were still living in
> his cave, and if I could have sung to
> him some soothing soul-song, honey-sweet,
> I might have persuaded him to teach
> a new healer to cure the love
> of riches and power which so fills you,
> dreadful Hieron.

The receptions of Píndaros that I have selectively surveyed perhaps replicate how *kháris* (splendor, grace) affected the Hellenic poet as a Benjaminian aura, here not as an emanation from art, but as a creative impetus generated by attuned noticing of the world and exceeding its *khréos* (duty), "perceived and acknowledged, turning the strict law into a charming play and becoming visible in the moments of unhoped-for and unmerited success where failure and falling-apart, pointlessness and destruction would seem to be the rule," as Hans Urs von Balthasar writes of Píndaros in his monumental, seven-volume study of theological aesthetics.[100] In the wake of the Second World War and the Holocaust and in the midst of the Cold War, with its very quotidian, indeed domesticated, discourse upon the prospects of nuclear winter and mutually assured destruction, von Balthasar reads Píndaros in ways that may be relevant to another era confronting biological and political precarity. Between the heavenly realm of gods and the earthy realm of athletics, von Balthasar discerns in Píndaros' poetry a Hegelian "dialectic" "in the archaic pendulum swing of a mode of thought which always moves boldly but securely from the perception of a comprehensive totality [moment of understanding] into its opposite [dialectical moment], only to find itself again in the wholeness of both here and beyond [speculative moment]."[101]

The stratigraphy of ancient biographies may include folkloric layers that depict how mystical moments prefigure such speculative insight that esteemed authors exhibit in their compositions. The historian Aelian transmits this anecdote about the ancient Hellenic philosopher Plátōn (Ael. *VH* 10.21):

> Periktiónē [Plátōn's mother] was carrying Plátōn in her arms while Arístōn [Plátōn's father] performed a sacrifice on Mount Hymēttós to the Moúsai or the Nýmphai. Others were on hand for the religious ceremony, and she rested Plátōn among nearby myrtles that were bushy and dense. Bees swarmed upon Plátōn's lips as he slept, and their buzzing sang out as a prophecy of his future eloquence.

In this story, the sympathetic swarming of bees prophetically signals the infant Plátōn's future gifted speech. The symbolic alignment of *méli* (honey), *mélissai* (bees), prophecy, and gifted verbal artistry also appears in anecdotes about Píndaros.[102] When the poet was a boy, he had expended so much effort while hunting in the vicinity of Mount Helikón that sleep overcame him. As he dozed, a bee alighted on his lips and built a honeycomb. This vignette links Píndaros to that other poet from Boiōtía, Hēsíodos, who received his poetic vocation directly from the Moúsai on Mount Helikón, which is sacred to these goddesses (*Op.* 22–35). According to another tale, when he dreamt that honey and beeswax had filled his mouth, the vision epiphanically affirmed that Píndaros was born to be a poet. These anecdotes capture the conventional association between sweetness and song inscribed in adjectives that we find in Píndaros' poetry: *hadyepés* "sweet-voiced" (O.10.93, N.1.4, and N.7.21), *hadymelés* "sweet-versed" (O.7.1, O.11.14, N.2.25, I.7.20), *meliadés* "honeysweet" (P.9.37), and *melígarys* "honeyvoiced" (O.11.4, P.3.64, N.3.4, and I.2.3). The *kháris* (splendor, grace) of honeyvoiced poetry perhaps mimetically replicates the poet's wonder when encountering the transcendent immanent in the sibylline ordinary (cf. P.9.77–9). As if offering an anagogical exegesis of the phrase *zōthálmios Kháris* (lifebloom Kháris) (O.7.11), von Balthasar explains this reciprocity between the observed world and Píndaros' art as follows: "when *charis* shines out as charm and divine favor in the beautiful form, the one who sees it can be inspired as by a flash of lightning and caught up from the realm of the day-to-day where things are obscure and are merely to be made use of and brought to the springs of being."[103]

OLYMPIANS

OLYMPIAN 1

Hiérōn of Syrákousai | Horse Race | 476 BCE

Olympian 1 is Píndaros' most well-known *epiníkion*. The song catalogs features of the ancient sanctuary at Olympía. Písa (O.1.18) was the name for the region surrounding Olympía, which the Alpheiós River (O.1.20 and 92), the largest river in the Pelopónnēsos (the island of Pélops), borders. The Hill of Krónos (O.1.111) overlooks the stadium where non-equestrian athletic events took place. The tomb of Pélops (O.1.90-6), which modern visitors to Olympía may still see, was a cult-site of great antiquity located about fifty meters from the altar (O.1.93) located in front of the Temple of Zeus at Olympía. Píndaros' versions of stories about Tántalos and Pélops "rival / former poets" (O.1.36). First, how did Pélops get his ivory shoulder? According to one interpretation, we may understand the crucial lines, "Klōthó ladled him [Pélops] from a purifying cauldron / his shoulder decked with vivid ivory" (O.1.26-7), as a metaphor for birth, so that Píndaros claims Pélops was born with his ivory shoulder. *Olympian 1* nevertheless reproduces the story that Pélops received an ivory shoulder when he was restored to wholeness after his father Tántalos chopped him to pieces, boiled his flesh in a cauldron, and served this meat to the gods. In that version of the mythology, Dēmétēr unwittingly ate Pélops' shoulder, which an ivory shoulder then replaced when the gods restored the hero to wholeness. The claim that Tántalos deceived the gods by serving them a meal made from the meat of his son, Píndaros tells us, was an awful rumor circulated by a jealous neighbor (O.1.46-51). But if Pélops was born with an ivory shoulder, what crime other than murdering his son and tricking the gods did Tántalos commit? We learn in *Olympian 1* that the gods punished Tántalos for sharing nectar and ambrosia, which they had specially given to him, with his friends (O.1.54-64). Tántalos abused the divine privileges he enjoyed. Tántalos' underworld suffering is the "fourth" in the sense that he joins Sísyphos, Ixíōn, and Tityós in undergoing eternal afterlife punishment (O.1.59-60). Píndaros likens Poseidón's abduction of Pélops to Zeus' abduction of Ganymédēs, so that "that same duty" (O.1.45) refers to Pélops' role as Poseidón's cupbearer and beloved. When Pélops prays for assistance in his chariot race with Oinómaos (O.1.75-85), he couches his entreaty as a request that Poseidón requite "Kypría's warm gifts," that is, the hero's sexual gratification of the god. "That man" (O.1.101) is Hiérōn.

Olympians

best: water   Strophe A (Lines 1–11)
    but gold—
        like fire brightens night
gold gives almighty wealth its shine
    if victory
crowns inspire your song
    my heart
        do not scan
barren sky
    for another star
        more nourishing
than sun
    with its daylight brilliance
        and we will sing
no trial bolder than Olympía's
    where praisesong
worth resinging clothes
    its shoulders in arts
of wisemen
    who sing out
        for Krónos' son
parading to Hiérōn's blessed abundant hearth

in flockrich Sikelía   Antistrophe A (Lines 12–22)
    Hiérōn holds
        the traditional
scepter
    he harvests first fruits
        of every virtue
music's summit bathes him
    in splendor
        such music
as we men often make
    around his table
take the Dorian lyre down from its peg
if the kháris of Písa
    and Pherénikos put
        your mind under
the spell of sweetest worries
    when the horse raced
beside the Alpheiós
    stretched its unwhipped body
along the racecourse

    and delivered its owner
      to dominance

the king of Syrákousai   Epode A (Lines 23–29)
    horselover
      his fame a torchflame
in the braveman settlement
    of Lydía's Pélops
for whom mighty Earthembracer Poseidón lusted
when Klōthó ladled him
    from a purifying cauldron
his shoulder decked with vivid ivory
    wonders
multiply
    and people's talk strains
      the truth
their handcrafted stories
    the embroidery of lies
      delude

Kháris manufactures all   Strophe B (Lines 30–40)
    that comforts
mortals
    Kháris confers esteem
      but so often
renders the incredible
    credible
      days to come
witness most wisely
    it is right
      for human words
to beautify gods
    such speech leaves less
      to condemn
son of Tántalos
    my song of you
      will rival
former poets
    when your father welcomed
the gods to his finely orchestrated feast
to Sípylos
    and requited their kindness
      with a meal

Olympians

the god with glorious trident
    plucked you up

desire punished his guts   Antistrophe B (Lines 41–51)
    the god's goldlit mares
bore you away
    to the sky palace of Zeus
        honored
near and far
    Ganymédēs would go there too
to Zeus
    for that same duty
        when you were nowhere
to be seen
    and people did not bring
        you
back to your mother
    however much they searched
some envysick neighbor
    started to whisper rumors:
they hewed your limbs
    with a knifeblade
        then into water
chugging over open flame
    they shared morsels
of your flesh around the table
    and ate them

I cannot say   Epode B (Lines 52–58)
    that any worshipped god
is a glutton
    I stay away
        loss is usually
the lot of slanderers
    if overseers of Ólympos
honored any mortal man
    it was Tántalos
yet he could not savor
    such a great godsend
his appetites won him
    catastrophic ruin:
the Father hung
    a ferocious bolder

                        above him
for eternity
            desperate
                        to shove it away
from his head
            he wanders far from happiness
                        lost

Tántalos has this helpless   Strophe C (Lines 59–69)
            painbound life
a fourth underworld labor
            because he tricked
undying gods
            and gave ambrosia
                        and nectar
to friends who feasted with him
            those gifts from gods
made Tántalos undying
            if any man hopes
                        his any
deed goes unseen by a god
            he misses the mark
this is why
            the deathless gods sent
                        the son
of Tántalos back
            among men's shortlived kind
when his body blossomed
            and soft hairs sheltered
his chin with dark
            Pélops pondered marriage

to win glorious Hippodámeia   Antistrophe C (Lines 70–80)
            from her father
                        Písa's
son
            near gray sea
                        a lonely night
            he called
to the surfboom trident-wielding god
            who appeared
at his feet
            Pélops spoke

"Poseidón if any
of Kypría's warm gifts
        warrant kháris
            shackle
Oinómaos' bronzesheen spearhead
        truck me to Élis
in the speediest chariot
        and endow me with dominance
he murdered thirteen suitors
        to stall his daughter's

marriage   Epode C (Lines 81–87)
        a daring risk does not find
            a mortal
without might
        death comes
            but why would anyone
abide obscurity
        and namelessly boil away
an empty old age
        no share of anything beautiful?
this contest right before me—
        I hope you grant
the win I want"
        so Pélops prayed
            he worked
no fruitless words
        the god glorified him
            with gifts
a golden chariot deck
        tireless horses
            with wings

Pélops overpowered Oinómaos   Strophe D (Lines 88–98)
        and won
the girl for his bed
        he fathered six sons
            leaders
firm in pursuit of virtue
        Pélops now
enjoys the honor of bloodrich sacrifices
while stretching out
        along the banks of Alpheiós

his often-visited tomb beside the altar
that welcomes many guests
        in races of Pélops
the glory of games at Olympía
        shines far
                when footspeed
and risktaking feats of strength
        compete
                for the life
that's left him
        a winner has honeysweet serenity

because of games   Antistrophe D (Lines 99–109)
        an everdaily
                ultimate
goodness comes to each mortal
        to crown that man
with horsestride rhythm
        and Aiolian song
                is my duty
among people today
        I know of no other host
so skilled in goodness
        in command of such power
                to drape
with famemaking garments of praisesong
        a steward-god
oversees your ambitions
        Hiérōn
                makes them
his mission
        unless he leaves you soon
                I hope

to celebrate an even sweeter victory   Epode D (Lines 110–116)
with swift chariot
        when I find the road
                my ally
for lyrics
        and march to the sunbathed Hill
                of Krónos
Moúsa fuels my mightiest arrow
        with strength

people excel in different ways
        but greatness
attains its highpoint with kings
        no longer search
the far away
        I pray that you walk
                the heights
this hour
        that I am as long
                in the company of champions
that I am known for wisdom
        throughout Hellás

OLYMPIAN 2

Thérōn of Akrágas | Chariot Race | 476 BCE

Olympian 2 and *Olympian 3* celebrate Thérōn's 476 BCE victory in the chariot race. Thérōn ruled as tyrant at Akrágas in Sikelía. Thérōn and his brother Xenokrátēs (O.2.49–51; see also *Pythian 6* and *Isthmian 2*) were members of the Emmenídai family, who claimed Thérsandros, a hero from Thébai, as an ancestor. This genealogy accounts for *Olympian 2*'s attention to the Theban mythology, which provides Píndaros an occasion to forge his affiliation with Thérōn and the Emmenídai, since the poet claimed Thébai as his homeland (cf. O.6.84–6). Thérsandros "rescued Ádrastos' family line" (O.2.45) because, as the son of Ádrastos' daughter Argeía and Polyneíkēs, he is a direct descendant of Ádrastos, whose son Aigialeús, one of the Epígonoi, died. Píndaros merely alludes to a certain suffering without naming Oidípous (O.2.37–42) because he takes it for granted that his audience knows the stories about Oidípous, son of Láïos (O.2.38), his slaying of his father Láïos, his union with his mother, "the warmongering offspring" of Oidípous, Eteoklés and Polyneíkēs (O.2.42), and the Seven Against Thébai.

Píndaros' representation of the underworld and afterlife (O.2.56–83) envisions the transmigration of souls and comments on punishments and rewards in both this-worldly and otherworldly existences. Píndaros refers to Persephónē and Háïdēs as "honored of the gods" (O.2.65–6). It is unclear whether Píndaros' reckons one life and one death as two passages for the soul, so that there are six such passages in all, or reckons one life and one death as one passage for the soul, so that there are three passages (O.2.68–70). Beyond assuming that they are otherworld sites, we do not know what Píndaros means by "Zeus' path" or "Krónos' tower" (0.2.70). The "great father" (O.2.76) is Krónos.

    you praisesongs that lord over lyres   Strophe A (Lines 1–7)
        what god
            what hero
what man will we sing?
        yes Písa belongs to Zeus
Hēraklés founded Olympía's festival
        his offering
of war's first yields
        for victory with fourhorse chariot
let's shout the name of Thérōn
        just in his care
for guests
        loadbearing beam of Akrágas
            the city's
buttress
        among its honored fathers:
            first

they faced their many struggles with heart and won   Antistrophe A (Lines 8–14)
Akrágas River as their sacred home
they were Sikelía's eye
    an era granted
by destiny attended
    this people
        and adorned
their hereditary valor
    with wealth and aura
        son
of Rheía
    son of Krónos
        you who govern
the seat of Ólympos
    competition's summit
and Alpheiós River's flow
    enjoy these songs
and kindheartedly hand
    their ancestral cropfields
        down

to future generations   Epode A (Lines 15–20)
    not even Khrónos
every creature's father
    could make unmade
the outcome of actions
    justly or unjustly done
obscurity might accompany
    an auspicious lot
in life
    a wound that opens
        again and again
dies away when tamed with enduring joys

whenever god's Moíra raises   Strophe B (Lines 21–27)
    good fortune's height
        higher
this proverb applies to Kádmos' royal daughters
who suffered terrible hardships
    deep sorrow withers
when met with mightier goodness
    first Semélē
with rippling hair

                    she died by lightning blast
but dwells among the gods of Ólympos
          Pallás
                    she loves
Semélē always
          the Moúsai love her too
and Father Zeus
          her ivywreathed son adores her

they say the gods decreed   Antistrophe B (Lines 28–34)
          for Inó
                    an unwilting
way of life in the sea
          for all eternity
with saltwater daughters of Nēreús
          the brink
of mortals' death has not at all
          been decreed
not when we will serenely
          finish the day
that child of Hélios
          with blessings uneroded
one river courses toward us
          with elation
another river
          another time
                    with adversity

Moíra   Epode B (Lines 35–40)
          who sustains this people's
                    glad lot
in life from generation
          to generation
in addition to godsent
          good fortune
                    Moíra
also steers them
          toward some sorrow
                    to be
redeemed another time
          because his son
encountered Láïos doomfully
          and killed him

                        he brought
to pass events long-ago
            foretold
                        at Pythó

when sharpsighted Erinýs   Strophe C (Lines 41–47)
            had witnessed
                        his crimes
she caused his warmongering offspring
            to murder each other
Thérsandros
            son of slain Polyneíkēs
                        remained
honored for athletic competition
when young and honored for wartime combat
            the sapling
that rescued Ádrastos' family line
            this is why
it is right for the son of Ainēsídamos
            whose roots reach forth
from that seed
            to clinch a riot
                        of lyrics and lyres

this man collected Olympía's prize of honor   Antistrophe C (Lines 48–54)
and for his brother's same good fortune at Pythó
at Isthmós
            the Khárites they share in common
                        delivered
garlands for the fourhorse chariot's twelve laps
victory soothes inner anguish
            for someone who takes
the risk to win
            if virtue embellishes wealth
then wealth creates
            occasion for any success
by bearing the weight of a deep
            relentless drive—

wealth   Epode C (Lines 55–60)
            star's sheer bright
                        a man's most infallible light
if anyone who possesses wealth

        knows the future
that strengthless phantoms of people
        who have died
here above
        immediately pay their debts
            for wrongdoings
committed in this realm of Zeus
        some judge
below earth pronounces penalties
        with abject authority

good people forever   Strophe D (Lines 61–67)
        enjoying sunlight
            on days
that equal
        the length of nights
            receive a more
untroubled afterlife
        they do not harass
the soil with armstrength
        do not worry seawater
to eke out a livelihood
        whoever was happy
to honor their oaths
        spends an eon
            without tears
beside the honored of the gods
        but wicked
people suffer misery none should see

whoever dwelt three times   Antistrophe D (Lines 68–74)
        on either side
of the divide
        between this life
            and afterlife
whoever has dared to keep
        their souls all
            untouched
by unjust acts
        they travel Zeus' path
to Krónos' tower
        where ocean breezes
            swirl

around the Island of the Blessed
>gold flowers
glisten
>some on the shoreline's bright trees
>>water
waters other blossoms
>they drape their shoulders
and crown their heads with garlands of these flowers

according to the upright decrees of Rhadámanthys   Epode D (Lines 75–80)
whom the great father keeps seated beside himself
the great father
>husband of Rheía—
>>she possesses
the loftiest throne of all
>Pēleús and Kádmos
are reckoned among them
>his mother brought Akhilleús there
when her entreaties won over Zeus' heart

Akhilleús killed Héktōr   Strophe E (Lines 81–87)
>Troía's undefeated
unfaltering pillar
>and delivered Kýknos
>>to death
and Ēós' son from Aithiopía
>in this quiver
under my arm
>a good supply of quick arrows
that resonate in understanding ears
but for the whole truth
>my weapons need translators
the person endowed
>by nature with knowledge
>>is wise
but learners
>with their relentless stream
>>of noise
are like two crowbirds barking nonsensically

at Zeus' holy eagle   Antistrophe E (Lines 88–94)
>now train your bow
on your target—

         guide me my spirit
                    when we shoot
famemaking arrows from the depths of esteem
whom do we hit?
           aiming for Akrágas
with truthtelling intent
           I will voice my story
under oath:
           for one-hundred years
                    no city
has given birth
           to a kinder benefactor
to friends
           or to a hand more inexhaustible

than Thérōn   Epode E (Lines 95–100)
           praise is bloated
                    when unattended
by a sense of balance
           but under the influence
of insatiable men
           ungoverned speech
wants to throw a cover over beautiful
feats of outstanding people
           grains of sand
defy arithmetic
           and who could tell
the number of joys
           that Thérōn bestowed
                    upon others?

OLYMPIAN 3

Thērōn of Akrágas | Chariot Race | 476 BCE

This *epiníkion* depicts the mythological foundation of the Panhellenic festival at Olympía and a rite known as the *theoxénia* (hosting the gods), in which worshippers provide a meal and dining couches for their divine guest(s). *Olympian 3*'s opening prayer (O.3.1–3) names the Tyndarídai, the sons of Tyndáreōs, Kástōr and Polydeúkēs, the twin gods who often featured in the practice of *theoxénia* (O.3.39–41), as well as Helénē. Píndaros incorporates references to Spárta's mythology into a song that commemorates the Sicilian Thérōn's victory at Olympía. In addition to the children of Tyndáreōs, Helénē, Kástōr, and Polydeúkēs, all of whom the people of Spárta specially worshipped, Píndaros mentions Täygétē (O.3.29), the eponym for Mount Täygetos, a prominent feature of Lakōniké's topography, and identifies Ártemis as Orthōsía (O.3.30), her cult-name at Spárta. Gildersleeve explains Täygétē's connection to the land of the Hyperbóreoi (O.3.27–30) as follows: Täygétē is "one of the Pleiades, daughter of Atlas, mother of Lakedaimon and Eurotas. In order to escape the pursuit of Zeus, she was changed by Artemis into a doe, and after she returned to her human form she consecrated a doe to the goddess." Píndaros' geographical references in *Olympian 3* span the ancient Hellenic globe, from the Pillars of Hēraklés (O.3.44), ancient Héllēnes' name for the Rock of Gibraltar, to the Ístros River (O.3.14 and 25–6). The phrase "Dorian sandal" (O.3.5) may refer to the song's meter or to a dance element of choral performance or to both, so that it aligns poetics and performance with *Olympian 3*'s thematic attention to Doric mythology. The "fouryear festival" at Olympía honored Zeus and hosted athletic competitions every four years (O.3.21). *Olympian 3*'s ornate mythology—Zeus, Hēraklés' labors, Hēraklés' establishment of the festival at Olympía, and stories that include Ártemis, Täygétē, Tyndáreōs, Léda, Helénē, and the twins Kástōr and Polydeúkēs—is characteristic of what makes Píndaros' art a challenging one for a modern audience. Yet the play of associations between local and global dimensions of the Mediterranean world, between the particular and the general, whereby an account of human experience undermines the hierarchical ordering of genus and species, type and token—such play conveys much less ambiguously that, for Píndaros, art is an act of devotion, so that his creativity has the same impetus as Hēraklés' desire to adorn Olympía with the olive tree (O.3.13–16 and 32–4). The song concludes with a priamel (O.3.42–4) that recalls the opening lines of *Olympian 1*.

Tyndarídai   Strophe A (Lines 1–5)
    who are generous to guests
        and Helénē
her hair so beautiful
    my prayer to make them
        glad

goes up as prize of honor
    for famous Akrágas
now that I have erected
    Thérōn's praisesong
for victory at Olympía
    the greatest gift
        for horses
with tireless hooves
    the Moúsa must have stood
beside me
    when I minted
        a bright new style
to harmonize with Dorian sandal
    the voice

of this gorgeous parade   *Antistrophe A (Lines 6–10)*
    garlands crowning an athlete's
waves of hair
    give me this godsent duty:
        the lyre's
chordrange
    the shout of auloí
        composing verses—
to blend them beautifully
    for the son of Ainēsídamos
what Písa inspires me to do
    from Písa
these songs
    ordained by gods
        go out among people

for anyone whose head   *Epode A (Lines 11–15)*
    the unerring Hellanodíkas—
the man from Aitōlía
    who keeps the original decrees
of Hēraklés—
    whose curls he decks
        with grayed green
wreath of oliveleaves
    from shadecovered springs
of Ístros River
    once upon a time
Amphitrýōn's son brought

                the olive tree to be
Olympía's most beautiful
            record of athletes' trials

his speech affected the people   Strophe B (Lines 16–20)
        Hyperbóreoi
Apóllōn's worshippers
            with sincere intent
he sought the plant
        for the welcoming grove of Zeus
shade for every person
            crown for victory
the altars for his father were already
consecrated
        and midmonth
                Moon's golden chariot
greeted evening's open eye with brightness

along the holy riverbanks   Antistrophe B (Lines 21–25)
        of Alpheiós
Hēraklés established
            his untarnished standard
for bold competition and founded the fouryear festival
but Pélops's lands alongside the valleys of Krónos'
Hill did not thrive
        with beautiful trees
                Hēraklés
felt that beams of sun
        too harshly punished
the naked garden
        his instincts then spurred him
                to journey

to the land of Ístros River   Epode B (Lines 26–30)
        where Lētó's
horsedriving daughter
        greeted Hēraklés
                when he came
from Arkadía's mountain ridges and zigzagging hollows
when necessity imposed
        by his father
                drove him
to herd back the doe with golden horns

        under the lash
of Eurystheús' injunctions
            the creature that Täygétē
one time consecrated
        for Ártemis Orthōsía

while hunting the doe   Strophe C (Lines 31–35)
        Hēraklés explored that land
beyond the raw gusts
        of chill Boréas
            he stopped
in his tracks
        awestruck by olivetrees
            possessed
by warm desire to plant them
        around the twelve-times-
circled lapmarker of the horserace track
to grace this festival today
        Hēraklés returns
with godlike twins
        sons of Léda
            whose belt rides low

when Hēraklés departed to Ólympos   Antistrophe C (Lines 36–40)
        he trusted
oversight of stunning trials
        in men's strength
and highspeed chariotraces
        to their care
and so passion has a way
        of moving me
to say
        that mysterious power
            comes to the Emmenídai
and Thérōn
        because the horsemen Tyndarídai
            grant
them this
        because more than every
            other mortal
they worship the twin gods
        with hospitable meals

Epode C (Lines 41–45)

they reverently observe
    the rites for blessed gods
and if water is best of all
    but gold
        the most venerated
worldly good
    then Thḗrōn has now arrived
at virtue's boundaryland
    and from his porch
clutches the Pillars of Hēraklés
    for people wise
and witless
    what lies beyond
        is unapproachable
I will not chase it
    I would be a fool

OLYMPIAN 4

Psaúmis of Kamárina | Chariot Race (?) | 452 BCE (?)

References to "driver" (O.4.1), "chariot" (O.4.11), and "horses" (O4.14) corroborate ancient commentators' understanding that *Olympian 4* celebrates Psaúmis' victory in the chariot race in 452 BCE at Olympía. According to another view, *Olympian 4* and *Olympian 5*, which is also addressed to Psaúmis, celebrate victory in the mule and wagon race. In that case, then *Olympian 4*'s representation of the mule and wagon race in terms of the chariot race may be a poetic strategy to amplify the significance of the former, because the chariot race was the most prestigious athletic event. Psaúmis' hometown Kamárina was located in southern Sikelía, and *Olympian 4* accordingly includes topographical references and mythology particular to the island. The opening of *Olympian 4* invokes Zeus (O.4.1) and depicts the composer as an emissary sent forth by the Hórai (O.4.1–3). Píndaros portrays Zeus in his guise as ruler of Mount Aítna, which weighs down the monster Typhós (O.4.6–7). The song's concluding mythological passage (O.4.19–27) features Ergínos, one of the Argonaútai who won a race in armor when the Argó landed at Lémnos, an island inhabited only by women, whose leader was Hypsipýlē. If Ergínos' words (O.4.24–7) may suggest either that Psaúmis had grey hair and looked older than his years or that he was an older competitor than was commonly the case, they certainly articulate the conviction that achievement matters more than appearance.

    skyborne Zeus   Strophe (Lines 1–9)
        driver of tirelessly
                stomping thunder
    your Hórai
        who dance in circles
                to the song
    of polyphonic lyre
        sent me to witness
    supremest games
        good people know
                how to savor
    the sweet news
        when friends succeed
                son of Krónos
    you who hold Mount Aítna
        windworn millstone
    of grim hundredheaded Typhós
        welcome this parade
    inspired by the Khárites
        for the olympiónikos

Olympians

Antistrophe (Lines 10–18)

this longestlasting light
    for feats of sheer strength
this khorós parades
    for the chariot of Psaúmis
        crowned
with Písa's olivewreath
    he rushes to glorify
Kamárina
    I hope a god will be eager
        to answer
his future prayers
    because I praise him
        a man quick
to care for his horses
    who throws his doors wide open
for guests
    who turns to Hēsykhía
        lover of cities
with spotless intent
    I will not stain this claim
with lies
    perseverance proves
        a mortal's worth

Epode (Lines 19–27)

perseverance saved the son of Klýmenos
from dishonor
    among the women
        of Lémnos
he won the footrace in bronze armor
    stepped forward
for his victory crown
    and said to Hypsipýlē:
"I am the man with speed
    strength matches the heart
gray hair grows on young heads in spite of youth"

OLYMPIAN 5

Psaúmis of Kamárina | Mule and Wagon Race | 448 BCE (?)

The manuscript tradition raises doubts about Píndaros' authorship of this song, but *Olympian 5* is certainly pindaric. The opening prayer addressed to Kamárina that occupies the entire first triad (O.5.1–8) suits a song that gestures toward the refounding of Kamárina (461/460 BCE) after Gélōn destroyed the city (*c*. 485 BCE) and to Psaúmis' contributions to this effort (O.5.8 and 14). Given the date of Kamárina's refounding and the fact that the mule and wagon race was an equestrian event in games at Olympía until 444 BCE, this song's composition and performance falls somewhere between those years. The *khorós* represents Kamárina as the eponymous *nýmphē* of the city by singing of her as "daughter of Ōkeanós" (O.5.2) and the "local lake" (O.5.11). According to tradition, Hēraklés founded the six double-altars at Olympía (O.5.5). Each altar was dedicated to a pair of gods: (1) Zeus and Poseidón; (2) Héra and Athēná; (3) Hermés and Apóllōn; (4) Khárites and Diónysos; (5) Ártemis and Alpheiós; (6) Krónos and Rheía. The second triad (O.5.9–16) features Athēná, the third (O.5.17–24), Zeus. The "the lovely home of Oinómaos / and Pélops" (O.5.9–10) is Olympía.

    the sweet utmost of soaring talent   Strophe A (Lines 1–3)
        and crowns at Olympía
daughter of Ōkeanós
        accept these gifts
with laughing heart
        the mulecart treading tirelessly

and Psaúmis   Antistrophe A (Lines 4–6)
        who magnifies your city
                that gives people
life
        Kamárina
                who honored the six doublealtars
in lavish festivities for the gods
        with cattle
sacrifice and fiveday athletic contests

with races—chariot mulecart single horse   Epode A (Lines 7–8)
        when he won
                he dedicated to you
his sumptuous magic
                and made a herald
                        herald

his father Ákrōn
>   and your newfounded land

he arrives here   Strophe B (Lines 9–11)
>   from the lovely home
>   >   of Oinómaos
and Pélops
>   Pallás
>   >   his city's guardian
>   Psaúmis
sings your holy grove
>   your river Óanos

the worshipped local lake   Antistrophe B (Lines 12–14)
>   and riverbeds
places where Hípparis waters your people
>   and builds
in little time a tall forest of steadfast roofs
transports these villagers
>   from hardship
>   >   into sunlight

the toil   Epode B (Lines 15–16)
>   the cost for virtue
>   >   always struggles
toward the feat
>   that danger conceals
>   >   when people
succeed
>   then even their neighbors believe
>   >   they are wise

savior altocumulus Zeus   Strophe C (Lines 17–19)
>   you who dwell
upon Krónos' hilltop
>   who honor the broad flow
>   >   of Alpheiós
and awe-inspiring cave of Ída
>   I come
as your suppliant
>   calling on you
>   >   with Lydía's auloí

        in order to pray   Antistrophe C (Lines 20–22)
                that you decorate
                        this city
with fame for manhood
                and that you
                        olympiónikos
you who take such delight in Poseidón's horses—
that till the end
                you bear your oldage gladly

with your sons beside you   Epode C (Lines 23–24)
                Psaúmis
                        if anyone
nurtures sober happiness
                by being satisfied
with what he owns already
                by making his name worthy
of praise
                let him not seek
                        to become a god

OLYMPIAN 6

Hagēsías of Syrákousai | Mule and Wagon Race | 468 BCE (?)

Hagēsías, son of Sóstratos, was a member of the Iamídai, a family with a history of success in athletic competition (O.6.77–81). Although 468 BCE is a conventionally accepted date for Hagēsías' victory, it may have occurred in 472 BCE. Hagēsías knew Hiérōn at Syrákousai, as suggested by *Olympian 6*, which praises Hiérōn (O.6.93). After he images the commencement of this song's performance as the construction of a building's entryway (O.6.1–4), Píndaros identifies Hagēsías as *sunoikistḗr* (cofounder) of Syrákousai (O.6.6). Ancient commentators explain that Hagēsías' ancestors had migrated to Syrákousai. The mythological narrative of *Olympian 6* presents the story of the birth of the hero Íamos, the Iamídai's mythological eponym, recounting the etiology for the Iamídai's role as priests of the prophetic altar for Zeus at Olympía (O.6.4–5 and 64–70). Píndaros' treatment of the Seven Against Thḗbai myth in this song accordingly features prophets. During the battle of the Seven, the earth swallows Amphiáraos (O.6.14), who is the "eye" of Ádrastos' army (O.6.16). "The god with sungold hair" (O.6.41) is Apóllōn. "The blameless elixir of honeybees" (O.6.46–7) is honey. We learn that Íamos' name derives from the ancient Hellenic word for violets, *ía* (O.6.54–7), which I translate as "heartsease," a common name for *Viola tricolor*. Hēraklḗs' mortal father Amphitrýōn was a son of Alkaíos, and since Hēraklḗs is a hero of Boiōtía, his appearance in the song serves to link Stýmphalos and Thḗbai (O.6.68). The Iamídai, Hagēsías' family, were originally from Stýmphalos in Arkadía, and Píndaros establishes his personal connections with that city: Metópē, mother of Thḗbē, the eponym for Píndaros' homeland of Thḗbai, is from Stýmphalos (O.6.83–7). The phrase "swine of Boiōtía" (O.6.90) refers to the insulting stereotype that the people of Boiōtía were uncultured. When Píndaros calls Ainéas, who, according to ancient commentators, trained the *khorós* that performed *Olympian 6*, a "message stick of the Moúsai" (O.6.91), he refers to a practice of coded communication that his audience would have known: the message-sender inscribed a message on a leather strip that was wrapped around a stick in such a way that the edges of the strip touched and formed a writing surface; when re-wound around a stick with the appropriate diameter, the recipient of the message could decode the inscription. Dēmḗtēr's "whitehorsed daughter" is Persephónē (O.6.95).

    let's build like builders of a stunning palace   Strophe A (Lines 1–7)
    and bolster our structure's sturdy porch
        with columns
  of gold
        when we undertake a feat
            its façade
  must glisten brightly and far
    if someone should be

             an olympiónikos
                       should be steward
                                   of Zeus' prophetic
altar at Písa
             and cofounder of famous Syrákousai
what praisesong would that man escape when he finds
envyless townspeople singing lovely songs?

let the son of Sóstratos know he dresses   Antistrophe A (Lines 8–14)
his inspired foot in such a sandal
            virtue
without risk knows no honor
             in the company
of men
             aboard hollow warships
                        but the memory
of many mortals endures
             if someone pours out
their strength in pursuit of a beautiful something
             praise
is readymade for you
             Hagēsías
                        the praise
that the upright mouth of Ádrastos one time sounded
for the seer Amphiáraos
             son of Oiklés
                        when earth
swallowed both prophet and his skybright mares

after seven funeral fires burned   Epode A (Lines 15–21)
away their corpses
             Talaós' son said at Thébai
something like this: "I miss my army's eye
both worthy seer and worthy fighter with spear"
this also applies to a man from Syrákousai
             commander
of this khorós
             without a quarrel to wage
nor overly in love with winning
             I do
solemnly swear
             to his goodness
                        I testify

freely
> and honeyvoiced Moúsai
> > will endorse me

Phíntis   Strophe B (Lines 22–28)
> yoke for me
> > the might of mules

as quickly as you can
> so that we step

aboard the chariot
> this purified roadway of song

so that I reach the victor's lineage of men
better than other mules, his know how to lead us
on this road
> because they won
> > victory garlands

at Olympía
> and for that we must
> > throw

the gates of praisesong open wide
> for them

today is the day
> we are obligated
> > to go

on time to Pitánē alongside Eurótas River

they tell of her   Antistrophe B (Lines 29–35)
> that after she and Kronídēs

Poseidón braided their bodies together
> Pitánē

gave birth to her daughter Euádnē
> with violet hair

Pitánē hid her unwedded childbirth pains
with folds of her garments
> in the imperious month

she sent her servants off
> with the command to give

the newborn girl to hero Eilatídas to care for
he ruled Arkadía's people
> at Phaisána

and won the lot to make his home beside
the Alpheiós River
> Arkadía raised her

                    and Euádnē
first found
          sweet Aphrodítē
                    with Apóllōn

she did not keep her secret   Epode B (Lines 36–42)
          from Aípytos forever
that she covered up the god's child
          but bitterly
he stomped down in his heart untellable rage
and departed to Pythó
          to consult the god
about this unbearable wound
          she removed her belt
saffron-red
          put down
                    her silver waterjug
and in a nightblue thicket gave birth to a boy
with insight into the divine
          the god with sungold hair sent
to her side
          both understanding Eileíthyia
                    and the Moírai

at the longed-for end of labor pains   Strophe C (Lines 43–49)
          Íamos
sudden came from her womb
          into light of day
worn down by childbirth
          she left him on the ground
two serpents with evergreen eyes—
          he was their worry—
and obedient to the will
          of gods
                    they nourished
the boy with the blameless elixir of honeybees
when King Apóllōn aboard his chariot came
from rocky Pythó
          he asked everyone in that house
about his son
          whom Euádnē mothered
                    he said
the child had been born
          son of Father Phoíbos

that he would be outstanding   Antistrophe C (Lines 50–56)
        among mortals as prophet
for those who walk the earth
        that his family line
would never falter
        Apóllōn made all this known
and they swore
        they neither heard
                nor saw the child
though he had been five days born
        but a drift of rushes
in thick marshland hid him
        yellow and purple
radiance of heartsease rained down
        on his delicate body
so his mother declared
        he would forever be called

by this deathless name   Epode C (Lines 57–63)
        when he harvested the fruits
of goldencrowned Hébē
        giver of gladness
                he waded
midstream the Alpheiós
        and called on mighty Poseidón
his forebear
        called on bowcarrying overseer
of Délos founded by gods
        nightdark
                an open sky
he prayed down upon
        his head
                the honor to tend
the rank and file
        the voice of god
                his father
lucidly sounded
        and sought him out:
                "be quick son
to come here
        land common to all
                in the wake of my voice"

```
          they reached the steep rock                           Strophe D (Lines 64–70)
                    summit of Krónos' Hill
          where he handed down
                    a double storehouse
          of prophecy
                    to hear first
                              the voice ignorant of falsehood
          then later
                    when Hēraklés came with bold plans
          awestriking offshoot of the Alkaḯdai
                    and founded
          for his father both a festival flooded
          with crowds
                    and illustrious rite of games
                              at that time
          Apóllōn ordered Íamos
                    to establish
          an oracle upon the height of Zeus' altar

          since those days                                      Antistrophe D (Lines 71–77)
                    the fame of the family line
          of Iamídai
                    has multiplied among Héllēnes
                              abundance
          followed them too
                    with esteem for virtue
                              they travel
          an open road
                    their every undertaking
          proves this
                    blame that comes
                              from other people
          who envy them
                    looms for those upon whom
                              holy
          Kháris streams a beauty
                    worthy of glory
          while they hurtle around
                    the twelvelap racecourse
          in first place
                    if men in the line of your mothers
                              Hagēsías
```

who dwell in the very shadow
    of Mount Kyllénē

reverently gifted Hermés   Epode D (Lines 78–84)
    herald of gods
with many prayers
    many sacrifices
        Hermés
who controls the daring and destiny of games
    who honors
Arkadía with its wealth of men
    he is
the one
    with his boomingthunder father
        who brings
your good fortune to fruition
    son of Sóstratos
on the tip of my tongue
    the whetstone's glory
its birdcall
    which insinuates itself
        into my will
with lovely gusts of songbreeze:
    my mother's mother
was from Stýmphalos
    Metópē
        laiden with flowers

who gave birth to horsedriving Thébē   Strophe E (Lines 85–91)
    whose lovely
water I drink
    as I weave elaborate praisesong
for warriors
    urge your companions on
        Ainéas
first to sing out praise
    for Héra Parthenía
and then to make it known if we escape
that old insult—
    swine of Boiōtía!—
        with truthful lyrics
you are an upright herald
    message stick
of the Moúsai

        whose hair is beautiful
            and you are
a delicious mixing bowl
        for an uproar of songs

tell them to remember   Antistrophe E (Lines 92–98)
        Syrákousai and Ortygía
which Hiérōn steers with unpolluted scepter
with decisive vision
        he worships
            redfooted Dēmétēr
the festival for her whitehorsed daughter
        the might
of Aítna's Zeus
        our sweetversed lyres
            and song
know Hiérōn
        I pray the creep of time
does not harass his good fortune
        I pray he welcomes
with warmest friendship
        this parade for Hagēsías

which marches from one home   Epode E (Lines 99–105)
        the walls of Stýmphalos
to another home
        leaving behind the mother
of flockrich Arkadía
        it is good to lower
            two anchors
from swift ship
        on a stormy night
            I pray
god grants a destiny of fame
        for people of Stýmphalos
for people of Syrákousai
        searuling Lord
            I pray
you steer their voyage away from struggles
        husband
of goldenspindled Amphitrítē
        that you make
the flower of my praisesongs bloom
        delightingly

OLYMPIAN 7

Diagóras of Rhódos | Boxing | 464 BCE

The temple of Athēná at Líndos on the island of Rhódos housed a copy of the text of *Olympian 7* inscribed with golden letters. Sculpture portraits of Diagóras, his three sons, and his two grandsons, all of whom won contests at Olympía, were still in situ when Pausanias (*c.* 150 CE) saw them (6.7.1–2). Diagóras was a *periodoníkēs* who won boxing matches in all four of the major crown games at Olympía, Pythó, Neméa, and Isthmós. The mythology of *Olympian 7* recounts the settlement of Rhódos by Tlēpólemos. Diagóras' family, the Eratídai, claimed descent from Astydámeia and Tlēpólemos (O.7.20-4). In a pastward inching chronology that forms a ring composition featuring Tlēpólemos, Píndaros narrates a series of events: establishment of a settlement by Tlēpólemos on Rhódos after his exile from Tíryns, a city in the region of Árgos (O.7.20-33); Athēná's birth (O.7.34-8); foundation of cult and festival for Athēná (O.7.39-50); division of spheres of power among Zeus and other gods (O.7.54-60); dedication of Rhódos as a land sacred to Hélios (O.7.61-72); foundation of three major cities of Rhódos, each named for a grandson of Hélios (O.7.72-6); and circling back the beginning of this narrative thread, the establishment of games in honor of Tlēpólemos (O.7.77-80). Likýmnios was son of Ēlektrýōn and Midéa. Ēlektrýōn's wife was Alkménē's mother, Anaxó. As Alkménē's half-brother, Likýmnios was uncle of Hēraklés, father of Tlēpólemos. Thus Tlēpólemos killed a blood relative, which calls for exile from one's community (O.7.27-30). "Grapevine dew" (O.7.2) is how Píndaros images wine. Tlēpólemos is "the settler of this land" (O.7.30). The "seasurrounded pastureland" is Rhódos (O.7.33). "Their future duty" (O.7.40) refers to the cult practices that would honor Athēná. Píndaros portrays statuary that lined the streets of Rhódos as lifelike because so skillfully made (O.7.52). I take the puzzling proverb "to one who seeks it, staggering wisdom is no / deception" (O.7.53) to mean that exceptional creativity can appear to be deceptive because it so far surpasses known possibilities, but to a person who also possesses such creative skill, powerful art motivates appreciation rather than skepticism. Píndaros may be saying something about his own art. The victory prize for games at Árgos was a bronze shield (O.7.83); at Arkadía, works of art, possibly tripods or vessels of some sort (O.7.84); at Thébai, bronze tripods (O.7.84).

    like some man lifts a drinking bowl with rich hand—   Strophe A (Lines 1–6)
    grapevine dew froths inside it—
        and offers a drink
    to bridegroom
        a pledge
            one household to another
    solid gold
        proudest possession

                    he does honor
to celebration's kháris and bonds of kinship
this is how a man makes the bridegroom envied
for marriage harmony
          among friends gathered together

and I deliver liquid nectar   Antistrophe A (Lines 7–12)
          gift
of Moúsai
          the heart's delicious fruit
                    to men
who bring home victory prizes
          I seek god's favor
for those who win at Olympía and Pythó
          fortunate
he is whom worthy acclaim surrounds
          lifebloom
Kháris blesses one person with its look
another time someone else
          but always with sweetsong
lyre and polyphonic gear of auloí

I now step to the sound of both with Diagóras   Epode A (Lines 13–19)
as I sing in praise of seabound Rhódos
daughter of Aphrodítē bride of Hélios
so that I may praise his boxing as it merits—
praise for the fairfighting monster of a man
beside Alpheiós
          and near Kastalía
                    his victory
garlands
          and praise for his father Damágētos
                    who pleases
Díkē
          men who make their home
                    alongside
the spear of Árgos on the triplecitied
island that faces the foreland of spacious Asía

from its origins   Strophe B (Lines 20–25)
          from Tlēpólemos
                    with a herald's voice
I want to set this people's story straight

Olympians

for them
> for the supermighty family line
of Hēraklés
> from their father's side
> > they boast
of being born of Zeus
> from their mother's side
the Amyntorídai
> of being born of Astydámeia
countless failings loom over human hearts
no device exists for discovering this:

what fortune now   Antistrophe B (Lines 26–31)
> and at the end
> > is best
to attain?
> once upon a time
> > the settler of this land
in a state of rage
> struck the bastard brother
of Alkménē
> with his walking stick
> > of ruthless
olivewood
> and killed Likýmnios
> > at Tíryns
as he came from Midéa's bedroom
> troubled minds
cause even a person of wisdom
> to wander off course
Tlēpólemos journeyed to god
> to consult his oracle

from his temple's fragrant innermost chamber   Epode B (Lines 32–38)
the god with sungold hair told him
> go straight by ship
from Lérna's shoreline
> to seasurrounded terrain
where the mighty king of gods
> one time covered
the city with snowflakes of gold
> when Athēná leapt
forth from the height of her father's head

            with the help
    of Héphaistos' craftsmanship
            and his bronzeforged axe
    and she let out a booming warcry
            Ouranós
    and Mother Gaía—
            a chill ran down their spines

    then the god who delivers   Strophe C (Lines 39–44)
            light to mortals
                    son
    of Hyperíōn
            admonished his children
                    to attend
    their future duty
            so they might be the first
    to found for the goddess
            an altar as bright
                    as daylight
    by performing solemn sacrifice
            they might warm
    the hearts of father
            of daughter
                    who thunders her spear
    humility before foresight sows virtue and joy for humans

    oblivion's cloud descends   Antistrophe C (Lines 45–50)
            bewilderingly
                    and drives
    from the mind
            the upright path for endeavors
                    the people
    did not ascend with fuel for firelight
            they built
    the acropolis sanctuary
            with fireless sacrifices
    Zeus herded autumncolored cumulus
            and rained down
    gold
            the goddess with olivegreen eyes
                    endowed them

with every skill   Epode C (Lines 51–57)
        so they outdo others
                who walk
this earth in crafting handmade masterpieces
their roadways carried artwork resembling creatures
that live and stir
        the fame of Rhódos soared
to one who seeks it
        staggering wisdom is no
deception
        in oldtime tales people tell
when Zeus and deathless gods divided up
the lands
        Rhódos was not in sight
                on open
sea
        but salty fathoms covered
                the island

no voice declared a realm for absent Hélios   Strophe D (Lines 58–63)
the sacred god
        they left him with no share
of territory
        after they remembered him
                Zeus
was on the verge of casting lots again
but Hélios would not allow it
        because he said
that with his own eyes
        he saw across spangled sea
a land was about to rise up
        from the seafloor
prolific for humans
        pastureland for flocks

Hélios promptly called on Lákhesis   Antistrophe D (Lines 64–69)
        her headband
made of gold
        to extend her hands
                not to swear
the gods' great oath falsely
        but to nod yes in agreement
with son of Krónos

            that Rhódos
                    when the island
had surfaced under resplendent sky
            then Rhódos
would everafter be
            an emblem of honor
for his godhead
            sown in the soil of truth
a harvest of prayers fulfilled
            the island sprouted

from watery sea   Epode D (Lines 70–76)
            the father who fosters
                    blindingbright
sunbeams
            commander of firebreathing stallions
settled there
            then after he blended
                    his limbs
with the limbs of Rhódos
            he brought up seven sons
to whom he handed down
            the wisdomrichest
knowledge among ancient men
            and one of these sons
was father to Kámeiros
            and Iálysos the eldest
                    and Líndos
they shared their patrimony three ways
            each brother
allotted one town
            each town named
                    for each brother

founded there for Tlēpólemos   Strophe E (Lines 77–82)
            as if for a god
pioneer for Tíryns's people
            a sweet compensation
for mournful misfortune
            a procession
                    sacrifice
and fatsavor of sheepflocks
            awarding prizes for games

Diagóras two times crowned
    with those victory garlands
and four times
    success at famous Isthmós
        one victory
after another at Neméa
    at rocky Athénai

bronze of Árgos knew him   Antistrophe E (Lines 83–88)
    the craftsmanship
of Arkadía
    at Thébai
        contests sanctioned by customs
of Boiōtía
    Pellénē knew him
        Aígina knew him
as sixtime victor
    the record in stone at Mégara
declares no other account
    but Father Zeus
you who rule the ridges of Atabýrion
    honor
the custom of praisesong for victory at Olympía

honor the man   Epode E (Lines 89–95)
    who found mastery
        with his fists
grant him the dignity
    revered by townspeople
        by foreigners
since he follows
    without fail
        the roadway
that despises hubris:
    he is clearly wise
in the ways the upright minds of worthy forefathers
handed downd
    do not cover over
        his family's
shared origins
    from the line of Calliánax
        the city
also celebrates the glory of the Eratídai

HoneyVoiced

    but in the span of a single destiny
            from moment
  to moment
              windgusts veer
                      in different directions

OLYMPIAN 8

Alkimédōn of Aígina | Boys' Wrestling | 460 BCE

Olympian 8 begins by invoking Olympía (O.8.1-2) as a divine personification. Gildersleeve explains the religious practices next described (O.8.3-7): "pyromancy, divination by means of altar flames, was practiced by the Iamídai." Themes of hospitality and fair-dealing, a domain of the goddess Thémis' oversight, as well as the language of commerce (O.8.21-7), document Aígina's importance in Mediterranean trade. The mythological narrative features Aiakós and his descendants, who figure prominently in stories about Troía and the Trojan War. Son of Zeus and the nýmphē Aígina, Aiakós was father of Pēleús (father of Akhilleús), Telamón (father of Aías), and Phókos (grandfather of Epeiós, who built the Trojan horse). Apóllōn's speech (O.8.42-6) encapsulates the mythology of Troía, from its founding with the help of Aiakós, to its capture by Telamón (in the first generation after Aiakós), to its destruction Akhilleús' son Neoptólemos and Epeiós (both in the third generation of descent from Aiakós). Pátara, site of a oracular cult of Apóllōn, was located at the mouth of the Xánthos River (O.8.47). The Amazónes (O.8.47) made their home on the river Thermódōn (modern Terme, in north-central Turkey). Píndaros portrays Aígina as the site, actual or dramatic, of *Olympian 8*'s performance: "here" (O.8.51) refers to the island. The phrase "such kháris / at Neméa" (O.8.56-7) juxtaposes Alkimédōn's achievement with his trainer Melēsías' victories at Neméa as a boy and later as adult in the pankrátion (O.8.54-9). In the sentence, "dirt does not hide / from their sight the treasured aura of their kin" (O.8.77-8), both occurrences of "their" refer to deceased family members. The news of Alkimédōn's victory reaches the athlete's deceased father Iphíōn, who in turn transmits this report to Kallímakhos, another deceased relative (O.8.81-4).

mother of goldgarlanded games   Strophe A (Lines 1-7)
    Olympía
matriarch of truth
    site where seers
        decipher
the code of altar flames
    to test the mind
of lightningbright Zeus
    whether he has any report
of people who passionately strive to attain
outstanding virtue
    to catch their breath after toil

when men pray   Antistrophe A (Lines 8-14)
    an answer requites

HoneyVoiced

      their reverence
but you
    the beautifully wooded grove
       of Písa
beside Alpheiós
    welcome this song
       this dance
this victory coronation
    renown is evergreat
for whomever your splendid prize
    of honor escorts
good fortune visits different people differently
with god's help
    many pathways lead
       to happiness

Timosthénēs   Epode A (Lines 15–22)
    the roll of destiny's dice
      allotted
your family to your forefather Zeus
    who made you
the talk of Neméa
    made Alkimédōn olympiónikos
beside the Hill of Krónos
    he was so beautiful
to see
    his performance did not disprove
      his body
by winning his wrestling match
    he declared longoared Aígina
his homeland where more than other people do
they worship their guardian Thémis
    her throne beside Zeus

lord of hosts and guests   Strophe B (Lines 23–29)
    if any weight sinks
and sways the scale
    it is hard to tackle
      the task
of judging with strict attention
    and not unfairly
some decree by deathless gods erected
this seasurrounded land

                    as a wonderous pillar
for guests from every country—
          I hope the billows
of time do not grow weary of this work—

the land that Dorian people tend   Antistrophe B (Lines 30–36)
          since the days
of Aiakós
          when the son of Lētó and Poseidón
                    who rules far
and wide
          were on the verge
                    of crowning Ílios
with walls
          they called on Aiakós
                    to be a coworker
in their construction
          because this garland of stone
was fated to exhale raging smoke
in citydestroying battles
          when warfare flared up

three greenbright serpents   Epode B (Lines 37–44)
          launched themselves upon
the newly founded fortress
          two went down:
immediately dreadstruck
          they relinquished their last breath
but the one still living battlecried and attacked
then quick to read the ominous sign Apóllōn
declared "here where your hands have labored
          hero
Pérgamos is taken
          this the phantasmic sight sent
from Kronídēs
          thunderboom Zeus
                    reveals to me—

not without your sons   Strophe C (Lines 45–51)
          but destruction will reign
in their first and third generations"
          after the god
had made his blunt predictions

    onward he drove
to Xánthos
    to Amazónes
      women who cherish horses
onward to Ístros
    but toward the seashored Isthmós
the Tridentlauncher aimed
    his chariot's speed
and with his golden mares
    delivered Aiakós here

on his way to behold   Antistrophe C (Lines 52–58)
    the Kórinthos ridgeline
renowned for festivity
    humans will equally enjoy
no one thing
    if I ascend in song
      Melēsías'
mysterious power over unbearded rivals
let no rancor strike me with its jagged
stone
    and I will likewise tell
      such kháris
at Neméa
    as well as that of men
      who battle

in the pankrátion   Epode C (Lines 59–66)
    yes the craft
      of teaching
is easier for one with knowledge
    and lack of learning
beforehand is reckless
    emptier are the minds
of those who never dare
    Melēsías would
outreach all others
    in telling those tests of strength
would tell what training propels
    a man who intends
to carry home
    from holy games
      the glory

most coveted
> today his prize of honor
>> is
Alkimédōn
> who claimed Melēsías'
>> thirtieth victory

who with godsent good fortune　　　　　　　　　　Strophe D (Lines 67–73)
> his bravery unfaltering
in the face of four opponents' bodies
shoves aside a hateful homeward return
demeaning gossip
> the hidden alleyway
and inspires in his father's father
> the strength
to wrestle against old age
> a man who does
what locks tightly together harbors
> no thought of Háïdēs

but I must reawaken　　　　　　　　　　　　　　Antistrophe D (Lines 74–80)
> memory and proclaim
the height of victory
> attained by hands of Blepsiádai
whom a sixth crown from games
> that give the prize
of garlands now adorns
> those who have died
they too enjoy some share
> in sacred rites
performed in accord with tradition
> dirt does not hide
from their sight
> the treasured aura
>> of their kin

when Iphíōn hears　　　　　　　　　　　　　　　Epode D (Lines 81–88)
> the daughter of Hermés
Angelía
> he might tell to Kallímakhos
>> the story
of the glistening honor
> at Olympía

    that Zeus awarded their family
        my every wish
is that this god may willingly
        gift them one worthy
feat upon another
        that he may stave off
caustic illness
        I pray he does not make
their share in the measure of beautiful hours waver
but that he brings them a lifetime free from affliction
and magnifies this family and its city

OLYMPIAN 9

Ephármostos of Opoús | Wrestling | 466 BCE

This song begins with a reference to "the Arkhílokhos melody sung at Olympía" (O.9.1–2), possibly a gesture toward these lyrics attributed to the iambic poet Arkhílokhos (*fr.* 324 West):

> *ténella* oh beautifully victorious [*kallínike*]
> *khaíre* to ruler Hēraklés
> you and Iólaos, warrior duo

Ancient commentators explain that the opening lines of *Olympian 9* acknowledge Arkhílokhos (7th c. BCE) as composer of a traditional *hýmnos* "praisesong" addressed to Hēraklés. The untranslatable word *ténella* echomimetically vocalizes the sound of a plucked lyre's strings; in the absence of musical accompaniment, the *khorós* leader vocalized the sound *ténella* while other members of the *khorós* sung the lyrics of this *hýmnos*, which seems to have been improvised on the occasion of an athletic victory. Ancient commentators further explain Píndaros' words "'o beautifully victorious' three times ringing out" (O.9.2), where Píndaros names Arkhílokhos' song simply as *kallínikos* (beautifully victorious), as a reference to the thrice-repeated refrain *ténella kallínike*. Píndaros' namechecking of Arkhílokhos perhaps additionally contrasts the spontaneous cry of celebration for a victory with his more singular and ornate choral song.

The mythological narrative recounts the origins of Opoús, the homecity of Ephármostos. Human injustice—though Píndaros omits these details in his mythological narrative, perhaps in order to honor the injunction (O.9.40–1) to leave the gods out of (stories about) war and battle—motivated Zeus to destroy humans and their communities by means of a worldwide flood. The only humans to survive were the pious couple Pýrrha, daughter of Epimētheús, and Deukalíōn, son of Promētheús. As the father of Epimētheús and Promētheús, Iapetós (O.9.55) is the great-grandfather of Prōtogéneia, daughter of Pýrrha and Deukalíōn. This genealogy explains why Píndaros calls Opoús "the town / of Prōtogéneia" (O.9.41–2): she is a mythological ancestor of the city's people. Pýrrha and Deukalíōn refounded the human race by correctly interpreting an oracle from Thémis that instructed them to throw the "bones" of their "mother" behind their backs: they understood their "mother" to be Gaía and her "bones" to be stones. Heeding the oracle's instructions, the couple recreated humanity without sexual reproduction and "founded / a lineage born of stone" (O.9.45). In addition to the city, the name Opoús also belongs to two figures. The elder Opoús is king of the Epeioí in Élis and grandfather of the younger Opoús, son of Zeus and an unnamed daughter of the boy's grandfather (O.9.57–9). Lokrós, the adoptive mortal father of the younger Opoús, named the boy "Opoús" in honor of Opoús the elder (O.9.63–4) and handed rule of the city over to his adopted son (O.9.66), effectively establishing the younger Opoús as the eponymous refounder of the city Opoús, a city of the Lokroí in Boiōtía near Mount Parnassós.

"The holy height of Élis" (O.9.6–7) is the Hill of Krónos. In the phrase "the son and his city" (O.9.14), "the son" is Ephármostos and "his city" is Opoús. "The farknown splendid-treed mother of the Lokroí" (O.9.19–20) is again Opoús. Píndaros shuns (O.9.35–6) tales according to which Hēraklés fought against the gods Poseidón, Apóllōn, and Háïdēs (O.9.29–35). As descendants of the younger Opoús, Ephármostos' family claims an illustrious ancestry that includes Iapetós and Zeus (O.9.53–6). Píndaros briefly narrates Zeus' rape of the unnamed daughter of the elder Opoús (O.9.57–9) in a disturbingly breezy manner. The son of Menoítios (O.9.69–70) is Pátroklos (O.9.75). The "muscletaming spear" (O.9.78) belongs to Akhilleús, son of Thétis (O.9.76). "Both men" (O.9.84) are Ephármostos and his relative Lamprómakhos. Píndaros catalogs Ephármostos' impressive record of victories in crown games at Olympía (O.9.5–10), Delpoí (O.9.12), Isthmós (O.9.86), and Neméa (O.9.87) and in local games at Árgos (O.9.88), Athénai (O.9.88), Marathón (O.9.89), Arkadía (O.9.95–6), Pellénē (O.9.97–8), where the prize was a woolen cloak, Thébai, which held games in honor of the hero Iólaos (O.9.98–9), Eleusís (O.9.99), and, Opoús, which held games in honor of the hero Aías, son of Oïleús (O.9.112–13).

```
        the Arkhílokhos melody                                Strophe A (Lines 1–10)
                sung at Olympía
                        "o beautifully
victorious"
                three times ringing out
                        was good
        enough to lead the way
                for Ephármostos
                        when he
sang and danced
                alongside Krónos' Hill
        with his closest friends
                but now
                        from the farshooting bowstrings
of the Moúsai
                aim with unerring arrows
        for Zeus
                with redglow lightning
                        and for the holy
height of Élis
                where Pélops
                        Lydía's hero
        one time won Hippodámeia's regal dowry
```

Olympians

    and launch a sweetwinged arrow   Antistrophe A (Lines 11–20)
        toward Pythó
in no way will you latch
        onto words that crash
into the dirt
        when you make the lyre thrum
for wrestling bouts of the man from renowned Opoús
my wish is that you praise
        the son and his city
               which destiny
awards to Thémis
        and her savior daughter
illustrious Eunomía
        that city teems with achievement
beside your waters
        Kastalía
               near rippling Alpheiós
where the most esteemed victory garlands dignify
the farknown splendid-treed mother of the Lokroí

but I—   Epode A (Lines 21–28)
        by setting this beloved city
alight with torchlit songs
        I broadcast this dispatch
more swiftly than headstrong stallion
        or wingfleet ship
if I tend the Khárites' extraordinary garden
with the help of some providential artistry—
they are the ones
        who grant us pleasure's
                transports
men become worthy and wise
        through god's decree

or how would Hēraklés   Strophe B (Lines 29–38)
        wield his club
                with armstrength
against the trident
        when Poseidón resolutely
                faced him
down at Pýlos
        when Phoíbos cornered him
                waging
war with his silver bow

               or when Háïdēs did not
stay his staff
               with which he ushers mortal
bodies of the dead
               to his cavernous village?
reject this story
               mouth
                              because blasphemy against
the gods is venomous wisdom
               and tactless boasts

are the musical accompaniment of mania   Antistrophe B (Lines 39–48)
do not rattle on now about such nonsense
leave the undying gods out
               of warfare and battle
I hope instead
               you bring your tongue
                              to the town
of Prōtogéneia
               to where Pýrrha and Deukalíōn
                              descended
from Parnassós
               and built their first home
                              as lightningbolt Zeus
ordained
               without a marriage bed
                              they founded
a lineage born of stone
               that they named "the people"
awaken for them
               a birdsong path
                              of lyrics
praise aged wine and the flower of newer songs

they tell that water's might   Epode B (Lines 49–56)
               engulfed the whole earth's
dark
               but that thanks to Zeus' engineering
suddenly the flood withdrew
               from that beginning
came your family's forebears
               with bronzecast shields
evermore the kings native to your land

sons descended from daughters
        in the line
of Iapetós
        descended from Krónos' bravest offspring

until the commander of Ólympos   Strophe C (Lines 57–66)
        tore the daughter
of Opoús from the land of Epeioí
        he blithely mixed
his wine with her water
        in Maínalon's mountain valleys
then brought her to Lokrós
        so that the hero's
course of life might not doom
        him to a fate
deprived of children
        his new wife carried
                fertile
seed
        and he was overjoyed
                to behold
his adopted son
        Lokrós then named the boy
after his mother's father
        he grew into a man
whose body and feats defied description
        Lokrós
conferred upon him both city
        and people
                to helm

guests from other lands visited him   Antistrophe C (Lines 67–76)
        from Árgos
and Thébai
        visitors from Arkadía
                from Písa
too
        beyond all other settlers
                he honored
the son of Áktōr and Aígina
        Menoítios
                whose son
joined the Atrëídai

    and ventured to the plain
of Teúthras
   he was the only one
     who stood
beside Akhilleús
   when Télephos drove back
     the other
dauntless Danaoí
   and battered their seaborne shipsterns—
for someone with a mind
   a display in how
to comprehend the resolute will of Pátroklos
after that battle
   Thétis' son urged him
     again

and again   Epode C (Lines 77–84)
   to never take up position
     in lethal
warfare far from his muscletaming spear
may I find the lyrics
   and properly pilot
the Moúsai's chariot
   may daring and capacious power
arrive
   as friendship's emissary
     and for the sake
of victory
   I come to honor
     Lamprómakhos' woolen
ribbons at the Isthmós
   when both men prevailed

two wins in one day   Strophe D (Lines 85–94)
   and after that
     two further
victory thrills
   at the gates of Kórinthos
     then still
more joy for Ephármostos
   in Neméa's hollow
he held men in awe at Árgos
   and at Athénai

as a boy
      though deprived of competing
           with beardless opponents
at Marathón
      he weathered the trial
           against older men
for silver cups
      without a single fall
he trounced his rivals
      with cunning maneuvers
           and passed through
the crowd that cheered
      so loudly
           because he performed
formidable feats
      when full of youth
           and beautiful

his appearance astounded   Antistrophe D (Lines 95–104)
      the rank and file
           of Parrhasía
at the festival for Zeus
      Lykaíon's lord
and when he brought home
      from Pellḗnē
           a warm
antidote to cold winds
      the barrow of Iólaos
testifies to his splendor
      as does seaside
Eleusís
      nature's gifts are supreme
           but many
strive to claim renown
      for talent acquired
by learning
      when god is absent
           each event is
no fouler if it remains
      untold
           some pathways

Epode D (Lines 105–112)

      run farther than others
           no single devotion
                  will nourish
every one of us
        wisdom's slopes
              are steep
when you deliver this prize
           shout boldly skyward
that this man was born
           under divinity's care
with powerful hands
         with legs as agile
               with strength
in his eyes
       as victor in your festival
              he decked
your altar with garlands
         Aías son of Oïleús

OLYMPIAN 10

Hagēsídamos of Epizephyrian Lokroí | Boys' Boxing | 474 (?) BCE

Olympian 10 and *Olympian 11* commemorate the 476 BCE victory of Hagēsídamos in boys' boxing. *Olympian 10* is conventionally dated to 474 BCE because the song's opening lines (O.10.1–12), invested with the idiom of commerce, suggest that Píndaros was slow to fulfill his commission for the ode. As an often-recited hypothesis has it, since Píndaros had also composed songs for the tyrants Hiérōn of Syrákousai and Thérōn of Akrágas in 476 BCE, after completing the shorter *Olympian 11* (20 lines) immediately upon the occasion of Hagēsídamos' victory that year, the poet produced the longer, lusher *Olympian 10* two years later.

Olympian 10 recounts the mythological foundation of the festival at Olympía and its games—feats performed by Hēraklés to commemorate his father, Zeus (O.10.43–77). The difficulty of Hēraklés' battle with Kýknos (O.10.15–16) is an obscure detail that serves to telegraph the song's central mythological narrative and perhaps communicates the unavoidability of adversity. We then see Hēraklés' labors bring him to the region of Olympía (O.10.24–42). One of the Herculean labors represented in the twelve metopes of the Temple of Zeus at Olympía is the uncertainly heroic task of cleaning the stables of Augeías, King of the Epeioí (O.10.35), inhabitants of Élis, the region where Olympía was located. Hēraklés diverted the Alpheiós River in order to flush horse manure from Augeías' stables. *Olympian 10* simply depicts Augeías as Hēraklés' adversary (O.10.28). His other adversaries are the Molíones Ktéatos and Eúrytos, sons of Poseidón (O.10.26–8, 30–4). Hēraklés dedicates the spoils he gained after defeating his enemies (O.10.56–9) to founding Olympía's festival. *Olympian 10* describes six double-altars dedicated to the twelve Olympian deities, crediting Hēraklés with the creation of these monuments (O.10.24–5), where, Píndaros suggests (O.10.48–9), the hero includes a place for the Alpheiós River. The discus was made of stone (O.10.72). Dírkē (O.10.85) is the name of a spring and stream in Thēbai and recalls Píndaros' home *pólis*.

The language of *Olympian 10* is erotically charged. The word *kháris* (splendor, grace) (O.10.12, 17, 78, and 94) is a case in point. Its first occurrence entails reciprocity, at the same time that *kháris* refers both to the attractiveness of the athlete and to his achievement: "we promise that this performance / we share will pay the balance due for splendor [*kháris*]" (O.10.11–12). Píndaros' victory song is an act of *kháris* that requites athletic achievement, but the word *kháris* also taps into the code for male-male erotic relationships. The related verb *kharízesthai* (to gratify), for example, may refer to a boy-beloved's sexual requital for his older lover's attention and esteem. Píndaros plays upon the double entendre of *kháris* when he sings of the boy-athlete Hagēsídamos, "let him render his thanks [*kháris*] to Ílas, / as Pátroklos did Akhilleús" (O.10.17–19). Some ancient Héllēnes interpreted the relationship between Pátroklos and Akhilleús as erotic, so that Píndaros stages the relationship between the athlete and his trainer Ílas in erotic terms. The wordplay in the first two occurrences of *kháris* establishes the expectation that reciprocity and an erotic double entendre are in play in the second two occurrences, which I translate as "splendor" (O.10.78 and 94). The adjective *eratós*, whose radical meaning is "sexually desirable," underscores the erotic tenor of *Olympian 10*; it occurs in two phrases, "moon's seductive [*eratón*] light" (O.10.75) and "the alluring [*eratón*] son of Arkhéstratos" (O.10.99), who is Hagēsídamos. The last lines of the song refer to Zeus' abduction of Ganymédēs (O.10.104–5), who became the god's boy-beloved, and suggest that Ganymédēs' beauty and Aphrodítē's enhancement of his erotic appeal spared the boy the mortal's fate of death. *Olympian 10*, like evening moonlight, illuminates the erotic appeal of ancient athletics.

    read out loud the olympiónikos   Strophe A (Lines 1–6)
        son of Arkhéstratos
    his name is etched upon my heart
        my debt
    to him
        the melody I owe
            is overdue
    Moúsa!—
        and I call on you too
            Alétheia
        daughter
    of Zeus
        with your rectifying hands
            fend off any
    charge of wrongfully lying to a friend

    the once longdistant hour has now passed   Antistrophe A (Lines 7–12)
    and shames my deep duty
        and yet the dividends
    of delay have power
        to remedy the gall
            of blame
    just look:
        as churning seawave
            overwhelms
    a stranded pebble
        we promise that this
            performance
    we share
        will pay the balance due
            for splendor

    rectitude shepherds the city of Western Lokroí   Epode A (Lines 13–21)
    they attend to Kalliópē and bronzeclad Árēs

                battle
against Kýknos routed
        even hypermighty
Hēraklés
        Hagēsídamos won
                as boxer at Olympía's
festival
        so let him render his thanks
                to Ílas
as Pátroklos did Akhilleús
        with the helping hand
of god
        a man might hone
                a natural talent
and launch him toward
        the dizzying height
                of renown

few are those   Strophe B (Lines 22–27)
        who obtain
                a toilless joy
life's ray of light, brighter than every feat
        the laws
of Zeus incite our songs
        for his unmatched
athletic trials
        which Hēraklés once founded
                with six
double-altars
        near Pélops's ageold tomb
after he slew blameless Ktéatos
        son of Poseidón

and slew Eúrytos   Antistrophe B (Lines 28–33)
        in order to stubbornly claim
                the slave's wage
that imperious Augeías withheld
        near Kleōnaí
                Hēraklés
lurked in a tangle of brush
        then vanquished those brothers
on an open road
        because the scornful

Molíones had one time slaughtered
    the hero's soldiers

from Tíryns   Epode B (Lines 34–42)
    as they bivouacked
        in the shallow valleys of Élis
the guest-deceiving king
    of the Epeioí
        soon saw
his luxury-laden homeland
    bend its neck
to merciless torch and clanging iron
    saw
his city lay in doom's deep pit
    avoid
a clash with stronger foes?
    there is no way out
his judgment faltered
    and when he finally faced
his capture
    Augeías did not escape
        clifffall death

Zeus' brave son afterwards   Strophe C (Lines 43–48)
    gathered his whole
army and all his plunder at Písa
    and mapped
the godtended grove
    for his almighty father
he enclosed the Áltis
    to articulate
the space
    then made the surrounding field
        a place
for mealtime rest
    he honored the course
        of Alpheiós

alongside the twelve gods   Antistrophe C (Lines 49–54)
    who rule Ólympos
        Hēraklés
declared the outcrop there
    the Hill of Krónos
for in times past it was nameless

                    when Oinómaos
held sway
                    when heavy snowfall drenched it
                                the Moírai
stood nearby for this rite
                    these firstborn games—
and so did Khrónos
                    that one and only
                                touchstone
for the truth
          of what abides
                    unforgotten

as Khrónos bounded ahead   Epode C (Lines 55–63)
          it openly broadcasted
how Hēraklés handpicked
          his worthiest warprizes
to give and consecrated them
          how he founded
the fouryear festival
          Olympía's first games and victories
who took the new olivecrown
          for speed
                    for feats
of strength
          for chariot race?
                    and who envisioned
a champion's glory
          then seized it
                    in competition?

Oiōnós   Strophe D (Lines 64–69)
          son of Likýmnios
                    bested the footrace
his sprintstride taut
          he came commanding an army
from Midéa
          Ékhemos' wrestling glorified
                    Tegéa
Dóryklos
          who dwelled in Tíryns
                    brought off boxing's
finish
          as did Sámos

                        son of Haliróthios

from Mantíneia   Antistrophe D (Lines 70–75)
        in the chariot race
                next Phrástōr
speared the target with his javelin
        Nikeús
wound his arm back
        then launched the stone
                farthest
his troop of friends fueled
        a joyous uproar
                lovely
moon's seductive light
        illuminated evening

as victory parades do   Epode D (Lines 76–84)
        the sacred site echoed
                all
around with song
        with festivity's pleasures
                we follow
those early origins
        and vow to celebrate
that splendor named for exalted victory
        to sing
of thunderclap and firehanded weapon
of thunderstoking Zeus
        to sing of flamewashed
lightningbolt
        the emblem of every show
of strength
        the surge of songlyrics will match
                the reedpipe

lyrics finally revealed   Strophe E (Lines 85–90)
        at famous Dírkē
and yet
        a longed-for son
                born to his wife
warms with deep affection
        the heart of a father
who has reached the age
        when youth is a memory—

for wealth whose lot
> is an alien keeper
>> brought
from abroad is abhorrent
> to a dying man—

in the same way   Antistrophe E (Lines 91–96)
> whenever a man
>> who achieved
something beautiful
> without a single song
Hagēsídamos
> enters Háïdēs' abode
>> his lungs spent
for nothing
> in exchange for his ordeals
he garners
> only some fleeting pleasure
>> but you—
the lyre's delightful verse and aulós with sweet notes
shower you in splendor
> the Pierídes
>> Zeus'
daughters
> nourish your unbounded renown

I hasten to stretch my arms   Epode E (Lines 97–105)
> and embrace
>> the honored
Lokroí by drenching their city of good men
> with honey
I praised the alluring son of Arkhéstratos
> whom I
witnessed win with armstrength
> near Olympía's
altar
> beautiful to behold then
>> a mixed drink
of youth that once guarded Ganymédēs
> against impenitent
death
> by the grace of the goddess
>> born on Kýpros

OLYMPIAN 11

Hagēsídamos of Epizephyrian Lokroí | Boys' Boxing | 476 BCE

Olympian 11 commemorates the same 476 BCE victory of Hagēsídamos in boys' boxing as *Olympian 10*. The first strophe of *Olympian 11* contains a priamel in which sailors' need for winds (O.11.1–2) and farmers' need for rain (O.11.2–3) are foils for the victorious athlete's need for praisesongs (O.11.4–6). The referent of the first-person plural "our" (O.11.8) is the *khorós*.

    people's deepest need is sometimes   Strophe (Lines 1–6)
    for wind
        but other times
            it's skysent
    waters
        stormy children
            of raincloud
    if some achievement should reward
    hard work
        then honeyvoiced praisesongs
            prove
    to be a feedstream
        for future stories
    a trustworthy pledge for virtue's cadence

    I dedicate this envyless praise   Antistrophe (Lines 7–12)
    to Olympía's champions
        our tongue wants
            to shepherd
    some remarkable thing—
        and yet it
    is thanks to god
        a man likewise
            flowers
    with inner wisdom
        know this now
            son
    of Arkhéstratos:
        your fistfighting
            Hagēsídamos

    moves me to add   Epode (Lines 13–20)
        this adornment of delightful

lyrics to your garland of goldbright olive
in admiration of the Epizephyrian Lokroí
join this victory parade
    you Moúsai
        I swear
that you visit no people
    who spurn a guest
        or who are
unschooled in beauty
    but only the utmostly wise
and the warrior
    we know that neither
        flamered fox
nor roaring lions
    may change
        their inborn ways

OLYMPIAN 12

Ergotélēs of Himéra | Dolikhós | 470 (or 466?) BCE

Ergotélēs, son of Philánōr, won in the *dolikhós*, a distance running event (about 4,800 meters), two times at each of the crown games, becoming a double *periodoníkēs* (Pausanias 6.4.11). Ergotélēs' original homeland was Knōssós on Krétē (O.12.16), from where he emigrated as a result of political turmoil to Himéra in northern Sikelía. The modern town Termini Imerese derives its name from "The warm springs of Nýmphai" (O.12.19) at Himéra.

    daughter of Liberator Zeus   Strophe (Lines 1–6)
        I beseech
you
        Savior Týkhē
                watch over widemighty Himéra
you pilot ships
        that sweep across sea
                on land
you steer flammable wars
        and gatherings that bestow
advice
        men's hopes pitch on breakers
                then plunge down into
troughs as they slice through the surf
        of listless lies

    no one who treads the earth   Antistrophe (Lines 7–12)
        has yet found a trustworthy
sign from god
        for what will happen next
knowledge of what will come to pass
        is blind
humankind undergoes
        many things
                that defy
our expectations
        that deny us joy
                and those who
meet with merciless gales
        trade their pain
for the depths of goodness
        in the blink of an eye

Olympians

Epode (Lines 13–19)

son of Philánōr
    like a rooster battling
inside its coop
    your footspeed's honor
        would have
shed its leaves
    beside your ancestral hearth
without renown
    if strife that makes men clash
had not robbed you
    of your homeland Knōssós
        but Olympía
crowned you
    as twice Pythó did and Isthmós
        Ergotélēs
and now you dignify
    the warm springs of Nýmphai
while keeping company
    with your homestead's cropfields

OLYMPIAN 13

Xenophón of Kórinthos | Stádion and Péntathlon | 464 BCE

Xenophón's victories in two competitions during the same games at Olympía is an extraordinary feat, as Píndaros acknowledges (O.13.30-1). In the original Hellenic, the first word of this song, *trisolympioníkan* (threetimes *olympiónikos*), slots into the entire first poetic line, an artistic feat that complements Xenophón's two victories and the victory of his father, Thessalós, in the stádion, all at Olympía. *Olympian 13*'s mythology celebrates the creativity of the people of Kórinthos, who invented *dithýrambos*, a form of lyric poetry associated with Diónysos (O.13.19), the bridle and bit (O.13.20), the use of *akrōtéria*, architectural ornaments affixed to a temple pediment's apex or corners (O.13.21-2).

Píndaros' genealogy of the Hórai (Seasons) (O.13.6-8) corresponds to Hēsíodos' (*Theog.* 901-2): Thémis and Zeus parent Eunomía, Díkē, and Eirénē. Each of the Hórai align with a phase of the agricultural cycle: Eunomía "Adherence to Custom" with planting; Díkē "Justice" with harvest; Eirénē "Peace" with celebration of yields. Píndaros personifies *hýbris* (overbearing pride, violence, outrage) and *kóros* (satiety, too-much, indulgence) (O.13.10). The "sons of Alétēs" are the people of Kórinthos (O.13.14). As one of the Hērakleídai, Alétēs, who overpowered the descendants of Sísyphos to become king of Kórinthos, is Dorian. His name invokes the Dorian heritage of Kórinthos. The *dithýrambos* is "cattledriving" (O.13.19) in the sense that the poetry and music is associated with animal sacrifice. "The twin kings of birdrealms" (O.13.21) are *akrōtéria*. Píndaros informs us that Xenophón had already been victorious in games at Isthmós and Neméa (O.13.32-4). The Hellótia (O.13.40) were local games held at Kórinthos in honor of Athēná. Ptoiódōros (O.13.41) was father of Thessalós, father of Xenophón. Terpsías (O.13.42) was Ptoiódōros' brother and Thessalós' uncle. Erítimos (O.13.42) may have been the son of Terpsías. Where Píndaros writes of the function of "songs more / expansive" (O.13.41-2), he rhetorically renounces the task of celebrating the relatives of Xenophón, a gesture that simultaneously implies the ineffability of their achievements and affirms the poet's intention to praise Xenophón above all. The "lion's meadow" (O.13.44) refers to Neméa; one of Hēraklés' labors was to kill a lion at the site. Píndaros' word-choice for the crew of the Argó, *própoloi* (servants, ministers) (O.13.54) entails a religious metaphor that I seek to capture with the word "sextons." Píndaros notes that heroes from Kórinthos fought on both sides of the Trojan War (O.13.58-60). "Peirénē's town" (O.13.62) is Kórinthos, where the spring was located. The father of Glaúkos, in Píndaros' account, is Bellerophóntēs (O.13.61-2). The "horsetaming father" (O.13.69) is Poseidón. Sleeping overnight in a temple was a form of divination in certain cult practices (O.13.75-6). The people of Kórinthos worshipped Athēná as "horsegoddess" (O.13.82). "The fenced grove sacred/ to Aiakídai" (O.13.109) refers to a sanctuary at Aígina, which hosted local games. "The cities beautified by abundance below Aítna's / lofty ridges" (O.13.111-12) are Aítna and Syrákousai.

Olympians

threetimes olympiónikos   Strophe A (Lines 1–8)
       this house I praise
              gentle
toward townspeople
       and devoted to guests
              from abroad
I will make known
       this fortunate Kórinthos
              forecourt
of Poseidón
       who rules the Isthmós—
              Kórinthos
       the splendor
of its youth
       where Eunomía dwells
              and her sister
Díkē
       unfaltering bedrock for cities
              and Eirénē
raised together with them
       she stewards men's
abundance—the goldgleam daughters
       of prudent Thémis

they are determined   Antistrophe A (Lines 9–16)
       to stave off Hýbris
              the braggart
mother of Kóros
       I have beautiful things
to declare
       and plainspoken boldness
              incites my tongue
to tell them
       burying inborn ways
              is futile
but for you
       sons of Alétēs
              the fullbloom Hórai
often bestowed victory's radiance
       when you went
beyond with towering talent in holy games

    they plant in men's hearts   Epode A (Lines 17–23)
        the origins of many discoveries
every feat belongs to its inventor
from where did the charms of Diónysos come to light
with cattledriving dithýrambos?
        who added temperance
to horsetack
        or twin kings of birdrealms
                to temples for gods?
the Moúsa's sweetairs flower among you
        among you
Árēs flowers in deadly spears of young men

most high Father   Strophe B (Lines 24–31)
        you who rule
                Olympía's
reaches
        for as long as time exists
                may you know
no spite for my lyrics
        Zeus
                herd this people
away from harm's path
        and steer the wind
                of Xenophón's
destiny
        welcome on his behalf
                this ritual
parade for victory garlands
        that he leads home
from Písa's plains
        as winner in stádion footrace
together with péntathlon
        no mortal man
has ever shared in such achievement before

two wreaths of wild celery   Antistrophe B (Lines 32–39)
        sheltered his head
when he appeared
        in festivals
                at the Isthmós
and Neméa does not deny him
        the footspeed luster

of his father Thessalós
> is offered up
near the waters of Alpheiós
> at Pythó
he owns the honor
> for stádion and díaulos
>> two wins
in one sun's circuit
> in the very same month
on Athénai's rocky terrain
> a single swiftfooted
day adorned his hair
> with tree lovely garlands

and the Hellótia crowned him   Epode B (Lines 40–46)
> seven times
>> in Poseidón's
festival nestled between two seas
> songs more
expansive will have to attend Terpsías and Erítimos
along with his father Ptoiódōros
> so far did your family
best your rivals at Delphoí
> and in the lion's
meadow
> that I contend
>> with too many voices
over the profusion
> of your beautiful feats
I would not know at all how to reckon beyond
a doubt the number
> of pebbles in the sea

each endeavor finds   Strophe C (Lines 47–54)
> its proper measure
to heed this
> is the most harmonious symmetry
as a private person
> put out to sea
for a communal undertaking
> when I voice
the genius of its forbears
> voice its warfare

and heroic bravery
        I will not lie about Kórinthos:
Sísyphos was an incomparably canny schemer
like a god
        and Médeia
               who defied
her father's wishes
        and arranged her own wedding
delivered that ship
        the Argó—and its sextons

they once upon a time   Antistrophe C (Lines 55–62)
        displayed their might
before the walls of Dárdanos
        on both sides
carving up the conflict's outcome
        those warriors
allied with Atreús' cherished son
        who tried
to bring Hélénē home
        and the warriors
               who fiercely
drove them back
        the Danaoí trembled
               in dread
of Glaúkos
        who came from Lykía
               they heard him boast
that his ancestral domain
        his fathomless portion
of land
        his palace
               were in Peiréné's town

beside Peirénē   Epode C (Lines 63–69)
        it was his father
               Bellerophóntēs
who one time suffered
        a painful urge
               to harness
Pégasos
        son of the serpentclad Gorgó—
but that was before the unwedded goddess Pallás

brought him a bridle
   with golden straps
      from dream
a sudden sober vision
   and she spoke:
"you sleep
   heir of Aíolos and king?
      behold this elixir
for horses—it's yours
   sacrifice a sunbright
bull and show this
   to the horsetaming father"

the virgin with cornflower aigís   Strophe D (Lines 70–77)
      seemed to speak
such words to him
   while he slumbered
      through murky night
Bellerophóntēs then sprang
   immediately to his feet
he took in his hands
   the magical thing that lay
before him and elatedly sought out the land's
own soothsayer
   he revealed to Koiranídas
      the entire
outcome of the ritual
   how he slept
upon the goddess's altar
   in accordance
with the seer's insight
   how the daughter
of Zeus—
   his weapon is a thunderbolt—
      brought him

the gold that tames a horse's temper   Antistrophe D (Lines 78–85)
      the seer
ordered Bellerophóntēs
   to right away
      obey
her dreamscape presence
   and, when he had sacrificed

103

a stronghoofed bull to Earthembracer,
        whose might
is vast,
        to build without delay
               an altar
for horsegoddess Athēná
        what gods can do
brings to light
        even a simple invention
               beyond vow
or hope
        rugged Bellerophóntēs rushed forth
               to stretch
the soothing elixir over its muzzle
        and caught

the winged horse   Epode D (Lines 86–92)
        cloaked in his armor's bronze
                he swung
right up onto the creature's back
        boyish with warfare
astride the horse
        from the frigid pleats
                of deserted
ether
        Bellerophóntēs hurled down upon
the women's bowandarrow army
        of Amazónes
firebreathing Khímaira
        the Sólymoi
                and slew them
I will be silent about his doom
        but Pégasos—
Zeus' ageold mangers on Ólympos welcome him

I must not forcefully wield too many weapons   Strophe E (Lines 93–100)
with my two arms
        and fire the directhit whirl
of javelins off target
        I readily came as ally
to both the brightthroned Moúsai
        and to the Oligaithídai
with this small word

Olympians

      I will render brightclear
          all
that happened at the Isthmós and Neméa
     from both
those lands the infallible
      sixtyfold sweettongued voice
of a worthy herald will endorse my praise

it seems that we have already sung   Antistrophe E (Lines 101–108)
     their victories
at Olympía
     I would declare
          their future
feats when they happen
     I am hopeful today
yet the outcome doubtlessly lies with god
if birthright fortune should wend its way forth
     we will yield
its fruition to the care of Zeus and Árēs
six victories below the brow of Parnassós
     those many
in Árgos and Thébai
     and to so many more
among Arkadía's people
     will the allruling
royal altar of Zeus
     lord of Lykaíon
          bear witness

Pellénē Sikyón and Mégara   Epode E (Lines 109–115)
     the fenced grove sacred
to Aiakídai
     Eleusís
          fatgleam Marathón
the cities beautified by abundance
     below Aítna's
lofty ridges
     Eúboia—
          if you seek further
than eyesight reaches
     you will find
          their glory
throughout Hellás

HoneyVoiced

      and now
              to swim away
with agile feet
     Zeus accomplisher
         grant us
reverence and fortune's sweet taste of delight

OLYMPIAN 14

Asópikhos of Orkhomenós | Boys' Stádion | 488 BCE (?)

Olympian 14 honors the three Khárites, Agláía, Euphrosýnē, and Thalía. This reverence is fitting both for the performance of this choral song, an art form with which the Khárites are associated, and for the victory the song commemorates: the Khárites had a cult site at Asópikhos' hometown of Orkhomenós, along the Kēphisós River (cf. Paus. 9.35.1 and 3). Orkhomenós is also associated with Minýas, the eponym of the Minýai (O.14.4), a legendary Hellenic people. The concluding prayer addressed to Ēkhó (O.14.20–4), whom Píndaros dispatches to convey the news of Asópikhos' victory to his deceased father Kleódamos, emblematizes the power of song in the face of death.

    waters of Kēphisós—   Strophe A (Lines 1–12)
        you who earned
    their lot
        who live in a land
            beautified
    by foals
        royalty of fatgleam Orkhomenós
    you whom songs sing
        Khárites
            you
    who watch over the Minýai
        born long ago
    hear when I pray
        you ripen our every
    mortal delight
        our every sweetness
    if a man is wise
        if beautiful
    if full of splendor
        without the holy
    Khárites
        not even gods compose
    their dances and feasts
        these midwives of every
    feat in the firmament set their thrones
    beside Apóllōn
        goldenbowed
    god of Pythó

             and revere the eternally
flowing grandeur of Ólympos' father

majestic Agläía and Euphrosýnē   Strophe B (Lines 13–24)
who delights in dance and music
daughters of the mightiest god
hear me now—
            and Thalía
                        whose pleasure
is song—
            you behold this victory parade
that strides on air because fortune is kind
I have come devotedly singing
of Asópikhos in Lydía's
melody—
            all because you made
Minýeia victorious at Olympía
journey now
            Ēkhó
                        to Persephónē's
home with walls of gloom
            and cart
this glorious report to Asópikhos' father
so that when you see Kleódamos
you may tell him
            how his son crowned
his young man's hair
            in Písa's illustrious
hollows with a winglike garland
from games that bestow their magical aura

PYTHIANS

PYTHIAN 1

Hiérōn of Aítna | Chariot Race | 470 BCE

Pythian 1 suggests that the official victory announcement on site at the Pythian Games identified Hiérōn's home as Aítna, a city founded by Hiérōn in 476/5 (P.1.30-3). If this is correct, the poem records the public proclamation at a Panhellenic venue for Hiérōn's founding of Aítna, broadcasting that event along with athletic victory. The ancient historian Diodorus Siculus reports (11.49) that Hiérōn displaced the people of Katánē, a city at the base of Mount Aítna, and refounded it as the new city of Aítna with 5,000 settlers from Syrákousai, where Hiérōn reigned as a tyrant, and 5,000 from the Pelopónnēsos. The newly founded city of Aítna is the "neighbor" (P.1.32) of Mount Aítna. *Pythian 1* also honors Deinoménēs, Hiérōn's son, whom the latter installed as ruler of the new city (P.1.58-60).

The opening lines of the song (P.1.1-4), with their reference to the lyre's music, dancers' movements, and lyrics, depict epinician performance, whether figuratively or literally. The sweetness of song overcoming Zeus' thunderbolt, soothing Zeus' warrior bird, pacifying Árēs' martial bent, and generally delighting the gods, along with onomatopoetic (in the original Hellenic) depiction of the eruption of Mount Aítna (P.1.5-28)—this is one of Píndaros' most compellingly poetic passages in all of his works. Aítna, the city, is "this land" (P.1.40). Hiérōn is "that man" (P.1.42), as well as the referent of the possessive adjective "his" (P.1.46) and of the pronoun "he" (P.1.51). In 474 BCE Hiérōn defeated the Tyrsanoí in the Battle of Kýmē, a city on the western coast of Italy near Naples (P.1.72-5). The unspecified conflict to which Píndaros alludes earlier in the poem (P.1.47-51) may be this same Battle of Kýmē. If the pronoun "they" (P.1.48) refers to Hiérōn, Gélōn, and their military forces, then this passage may also recall that in 480 BCE Hiérōn and Hiérōn's older brother Gélōn allied with Thérōn, tyrant of Akrágas, against a large Carthaginian force, which they defeated, in a battle at Himéra near the northern coast of Sikelía (P.1.79). Píndaros envisions the reception his praise will enjoy at Athénai and Spárta (P.1.75-8), where he alludes to events of the Hellenic war against the Persians, in which the navy of Athénai led the defeat of the Persian fleet in the Battle of Salamís in 480 BCE and Spárta defeated the Persian army at the 479 BCE Battle of Plátaia, near Mount Kithairón in Boiōtía. Deinoménēs (P.1.79), after whom Hiérōn's son is named, is the father of Hiérōn and Gélōn. Kroísos (P.1.94) was a king of Lydía (*c.* 560-546) famous for his wealth. Phálaris (P.1.96) of Akrágas was a tyrant in Sikelía (*c.* 570-549) known for his extreme cruelty, as evidenced by the story that he roasted enemies alive in a bronze bull.

The mythological content of *Pythian 1* is relatively spare for a longer ode. Philoktétēs, son of Poías (P.1.50-5) was a Hellenic warrior known for his skill as an archer. He inherited Hēraklés' bow and arrows. At the beginning of the Trojan War, in which he fought on the Hellenic side, a snake bit Philoktétēs' foot. The wound festered and became so foul-smelling that the Héllēnes abandoned Philoktétēs on Lémnos. Later in the Trojan War, Odysseús and other heroes went to Lémnos to persuade the rejected Philoktétēs to rejoin the Héllēnes because an oracle stipulated that the hero and his bow were required to defeat the Tróes. Ancient commentators explain that Hiérōn suffered an illness during his campaign at Kýmē, but fought, "following Philoktétēs' rectitude" (P.1.50), despite his infirmity. The mythological foundation of the Dorian race (P.1.61-6) compliments Sikelía, which claimed Dorian heritage. As noted above, Hiérōn settled his new city of Aítna with people from the Pelopónnēsos, where Spárta is located. Three Dorian tribes descended from Hēraklés' son Hýllos and the two sons of Aigimiós, Support Pámphylos and Dýmas. The song's conclusion (P.1.87-100) is an appeal, brazen or amusing, to Hiérōn's largesse when it comes to compensating Píndaros for this song.

golden lyre of Apóllōn and the Moúsai   Strophe A (Lines 1-6)
with hair dark as violets
    you are their possession
        you plead
their case
    dancesteps inaugurate splendor
        and hear
your melody
    singers heed
        your phrasing when
your strings tremble
    when your overtures
        launch the khorós
you quench the warrior thunderbolt of flame
that everflows
    the eagle dozes on Zeus'
scepter
    drains its swift wings
        down its flanks

the commander of birds   Antistrophe A (Lines 7-12)
    you pour a cumulonimbus
darkness over its sinking brow
    a gentle
latch for eyelids
    in thrall to your tremors
        the eagle

slumbers
>raises and lowers
>>its liquid mantle
violent Árēs leaves his heartless spearpoint
far away
>rest mellows his heart
>>your weapons
even spellbind gods' minds through their artistry—
Lētó's son
>the Moúsai
>>dressed in robes with thick folds

to hear the voice of the Pierídes terrifies all   Epode A (Lines 13–20)
that is unloved by Zeus
>on land
>>and relentless
sea
>and the one who lies in grim Tártaros
>>he warred
against the gods
>one-hundred-headed Typhós
the cave in Kilikía
>known by many names
once raised him
>but now at Kýmē
>>the cliffs enclosed
by sea and Sikelía
>crush his woolly chest
the skyward pillar
>snowcapped Aítna
>>confines him—
Aítna
>yearround nurse
>>to whetstoned winter

sanctified springs of pitiless fire   Strophe B (Lines 21–26)
>chug up
from the mountain's belly
>by day
>>lavaflows discharge
flaming streams of smolder
>but with night's darkness

swells of crimson fireflame dump
  boulders into
sea's deep sprawl with a boom
  that creature spews
harrowing fountains of Héphaistos
  the monster a wonder
to see—
  to hear of it from those who were there
    a wonder

Aítna's blackleafed heights and foreland shackle   Antistrophe B (Lines 27–32)
such a creature
  whose bed cleaves
    his whole stretched out back
and lashes him
  I hope
    Zeus
      I hope to please you
you whose presence haunts this mountain
  this fruitful
land's brow
  the founder's renown endowed
    Aítna's
neighbor
  the city that shares its name
    with aura:
at the racecourse
  during games at Pythó
the herald called out
  Aítna
    when he publicly
proclaimed Hiérōn's beautiful chariot victory

the first godsend   Epode B (Lines 33–40)
  when seafaring men
    begin
their journey
  is for a following wind
    to come
their voyage is likely then
  to also end
by clinching a happier return
  for today's good fortunes

this proverb conveys the hope
    that fame for victory
crowns and horses
    will be Aítna's future
that Aítna will become a byword for feasts
and music
    god of Lykía
        Phoíbos
    you
who rule Délos
    who cherish Kastalía's spring
on Parnassós
    I hope it is your will
        to acknowledge
such promise
    to make this land abound
        in good men

all the machinery for mortal achievement comes   Strophe C (Lines 41–46)
from gods
    the wise
        those with powerful bodies
            gifted
speakers—
    they are born like this
        I am so eager
to praise that man that I hope
    I do not hurl
my bronzecheeked javelin of poetry out of bounds
as I wield it in my hand
    but by launching it far
I aspire to outthrow my rivals
    I only wish
that in this way
    alltime may straighten
        his path to happiness
and prosperity's gifts
    may soothe the memory of toil

and alltime would yes   Antistrophe C (Lines 47–52)
    remind him
        in what great battles
Hiérōn stood firm with resolute soul

                in warfare
when through the gods' maneuvers
                they gained such honor
a stately garland for wealth
                as no one in Hellás
gathers at this moment
                by following Philoktétēs'
rectitude
                he has entered battle
                                one man
despite his vanity
                even flattered Hiérōn
as a friend when pressured by necessity
they tell that godlike heroes came
                to escort
the man tormented by his wound
                from Lémnos

the son of Poías   Epode C (Lines 53–60)
                bow-and-arrow marksman
who destroyed the city of Príamos
                and brought
an end to toils for the Danaoí
                Philoktétēs'
wound weakened his walk
                but this was all according
to fate
                so too as time edges onward
                                I hope
that Hiérōn has a god as his keeper
                who grants him
a proper share of what he desires
                heed me
Moúsa
                and for Deinoménēs
                                reward the fourhorse
chariot with song
                a father's victory is
a joy belonging to
                no stranger
                                so let us
compose a praisesong that Aítna's ruler loves

Pythians

for whom Hiérōn founded   Strophe D (Lines 61–66)
    that city with godbuilt
freedom
    according to Hýllos' benchmark traditions
descendants of Support Pámphylos
    and the Herakleídai—
        they dwell
beneath the slopes of Mount Taÿgetos—
    wish
to evermore remain Dorians
    under the laws
of Aigimiós
    down Mount Píndos
        those fortunate
warriors charged
    and seized Amýklai
        as neighbors
of the Tyndarídai with bright foals
    their glory
reached the sky
    their fame for war's weapons
        bloomed

Zeus the fulfiller   Antistrophe D (Lines 67–72)
    decree such unbroken destiny
for the citizens and rulers
    beside Aménas'
waters
    so that others know
        their true worth
through your power
    a man who leads
        who instructs
his son
    would magnify his people's
        honor
by steering them toward harmonious tranquility
I entreat you
    son of Krónos
        nod your head
yes that Phoiníke and Tyrsanoí
    may keep their warcry
peacefully at home
    now that they have witnessed

their swollen pride bring them shipwreck grief at Kýmē

witnessed what they endured   Epode D (Lines 73–80)
    when Syrákousai's commander
overpowered them:
    he scattered their young men at sea
overboard their swiftsailing ships
    and delivered
Hellás from wretched slavery
    for Salamís I will earn
the wage of gratitude
    from Athénai's people
then gratitude at Spárta too
    the battle
before Mount Kithairón—
    these conflicts defeated the crescent
bow of the Médoi—
    after I render praisesong
to Deinoménēs' sons along Himéra's
watery banks
    the song they received
        to requite
their courage
    when their enemies
        bitterly suffered

if your voice should match the moment   Strophe E (Lines 81–86)
    by drawing
the tackle of many words tightly together
    then less
condemnation comes from the crowd
    endless tedium
blunts the edge of impatient hopes
    to hear
of another's goodness
    secretly crushes the hearts
of townspeople
    and yet since envy is better
        than pity
do not neglect the things of beauty
    steer
the people with a straightsighted rudder
    forge
your tongue's bronze on an undeceitful anvil

if you are the source of some scant spark　　　　　　　　　　Antistrophe E (Lines 87–92)
　　　a bonfire
catches flame
　　　you steward many endeavors
and there are many
　　　believable witnesses to praise
and blame
　　　unwavering
　　　　　　in your everblooming
spirit
　　　if at all you love to always
hear people speak admiringly of you
do not agonize over how much you spend
like a shipcaptain
　　　let your sail billow
out
　　　do not be seduced
　　　　　　by shameful gains
my friend
　　　the afterlife acclaim
　　　　　　of glory

is the only thing that reveals departed　　　　　　　　　　Epode E (Lines 93–100)
men's way of life to writers and singers
　　　Kroísos'
capacity for kindness to friends
　　　does not wither
　　　　　　but loathsome
reputation surrounds Phálaris
　　　in every land
his ruthless brimstone schemes
　　　his bronze bull
　　　　　　lyres
in dining halls do not welcome him as gracious
company for the lovely song of boys
success is life's foremost prize
　　　to hear admiring
speech about us
　　　is the secondplace share
of fortune
　　　any man who comes upon both
and keeps them
　　　has received the loftiest crown

PYTHIAN 2

Hiérōn of Syrákousai | Chariot Race (?) | 475 BCE (?)

The year when and the site where Hiérōn achieved the chariot victory *Pythian 2* celebrates are uncertain. Ancient commentators saw in Píndaros' reference (P.2.18–20) to events at Epizephyrian (Western) Lokroí, a colony of Opountian Lokrís located in modern Calabria, an allusion to Hiérōn's intervention to defend the Lokroí against Anaxílas of Rhégion in 477 BCE. If that is correct, Píndaros could not have composed this song earlier than that date. I understand Píndaros' phrase "the girl of the Western Lokroí" (P.2.18–19) as metonymy for the city's people. Píndaros identifies two gods only by their qualities: "the virgin who pours her arrows out" (P.2.9) is Ártems and "the tridentthrowing god" (P.2.12) is Poseidón. Ixíōn killed Deioneús (P.2.32), father of Día, his wife, by digging a pit, filling it with livid coals, and covering it, then luring Deioneús into the trap. Kástōr is associated with horses. *Pythian 2* celebrates a victory in an equestrian event. Kástōr was particularly revered at Spárta, a Dorian community. Hiérōn's Syrákousai identified as Dorian, and the Doric dialect features in choral poetry such as *epiníkion*. Perhaps for these reasons, Píndaros calls his current composition, or some part of it, a "Kástōr song" (P.2.68–9). Based upon another interpretation, the verses before "khaíre" (P.2.67) constitute "this song" (P.2.67–8), so that the Kástōr song includes everything that follows (P.2.69–96). The phrase "both alike" (P.2.74) may refer either to the slanderer and the slandered or to a slandered person and those who hear the slander.

    city of greatness   Strophe A (Lines 1–8)
        Syrákousai
                sacred ground
    of warsteeped Árēs
        divine caretaker of men
    and horses
        whose joy is iron
            I have come
    from fatsleek Thébai bringing to you these lyrics
    this proclamation
        for the earthshaking fourhorse
    machine in which Hiérōn triumphed
        victorious
    in his chariot
        he adorned Ortygía's head
    with farshining garlands—
        Ortygía
            abode of Ártemis
    goddess of rivers

        thanks to whom
                he tempered
those fillies
        their leatherworked reins
                in his coaxing hands

since with both hands   Antistrophe A (Lines 9–16)
        the virgin
                who pours her arrows
out
        and Hermés
                the overseer of games
attire his horses
        with a splendid harness
whenever Hiérōn yokes horsemight
        to the smoothplaned
cockpit
        to the chariot
                that heeds his reins
as he calls upon the tridentthrowing god
whose might is unbounded
        one man pays a tribute
of echoing song to some kings
        to reward their virtue
another man
        celebrates other kings
                the voices
of Kýpros' people often chorus for Kinýras
whom goldenhaired Apóllōn
        utterly adored

Aphrodítē's favored priest   Epode A (Lines 17–24)
        gratitude delivers
its answer
        when humbled
                before another's gracious
gestures
        and you
                son of Deinoménēs
        the girl
of the Western Lokroí
        entreats you
                outside her home

in the thick of war's exhausting futility
    thanks
to your strength
    she eyes the horizon
        unflinchingly
they tell that Ixíōn
    who endlessly turns
        and turns
upon his winged wheel
    imparts these words
to mortals
    by the gods' decree:
        "approach
your benefactor
    and answer their kindness
        with kindness"

Ixíōn learned this lesson   Strophe B (Lines 25–32)
    although he garnered
an easy existence beside the generous Kronídai
he was not long content
    with their blessings
        but went
mad with eros for Héra
    whose destiny was pleasure
in Zeus' bed
    violent pride flung Ixíōn
into spectacular ruin
    that man
        whose suffering
soon matched his gall
    won incomparable misery
his two crimes inflicted agony upon Ixíōn
first because the hero not uncunningly
tainted mortalkind with family bloodshed

and then because he   Antistrophe B (Lines 33–40)
    one time crossed
        a boundary
with Zeus' wife
    in her cavernous bedroom
        we must
always see the scope of every possibility

according to one's own measure
> forbidden beds
plunge a person
> into utter wickedness
such troubles visited Ixíōn
> because the man
unwittingly stalked
> an enticing lie
>> and lay
beside a cloud
> whose appearance mirrored
>> the most
distinguished goddess
> Krónos' daughter
>> Zeus
devised the treacherous cloud
> a beautiful source
of sorrow
> but Ixíōn rendered
>> the fourspoked prison

his own doom   Epode B (Lines 41–48)
> when cast down
>> into unshakeable shackles
Ixíōn received a proclamation common
to all
> the Khárites' blessing withdrawn
>> this singular
cloud creature gave birth
> to a singular
>> and insolent child
who found no honor
> among men
>> nor in unwritten
laws of gods
> as his mother nursed him
>> she called him
Kéntauros
> he coupled with Magnēsía's
>> mares
in Pélion's foothills
> an awestoking breed was born
from them

                with features of both parents
                        legs
and flanks of mother
            the father's
                    arms and shoulders

a god achieves   Strophe C (Lines 49–56)
        the full reach
                of his aspirations—
the god that overtakes
        even strongwinged eagle
outswims sea's dolphin
        makes any overproud mortal
cower
        and bestows upon others
                an ageless aura
I must flee slander's tenacious teeth
        with hindsight's
help I see
        that Arkhílokhos
                ever ready
to blame
        so often faltered
                and fattened himself
on oppressive words of hatred
        to enjoy abundance
through destiny's good fortune
        is wisdom's
                best reward

you are clearly able to display such   Antistrophe C (Lines 57–64)
wealth with a lavish spirit
        lord and ruler
of many streets wreathed with fortifications
        ruler
of your city's people
        if someone now claims
that any other man of former times
throughout Hellás is your superior
        when property
and honor are at stake
        with an empty grasp
of things he wrestles

                the void
                            I will embark
upon a ship
            adorned with flowers
                        and sing
in celebration of your prowess
            bravery
in terrifying warfare
            benefits youth
I therefore tell
            how you found
                        unbounded fame

by fighting among both horsedriving cavalry ranks   Epode C (Lines 65–72)
and footsoldiers
            your guidance
                        venerable beyond your years
allows me to praise you
            in light of every reason
to do so
            in verse that risks no protest
                        khaíre
this song traverses
            blindingbright sea
                        like cargo
shipped from Phoiníke
            and when you greet it
                        behold
with kindness the Kástōr song
            its Aiolic chords
the sevenstrum lyre's splendor
            I pray that you
become who you are
            now that you have learned it
                        yes
an ape is noble
            in the eyes of children—
                        always

noble   Strophe D (Lines 73–80)
            Rhadámanthys prospered
                        because his lot
in life was the blameless yield

                of insight
                            and he takes
    no heartfelt pleasure in the sort of deceit
    that always follows a mortal
                    when slandermongers
    invent their rumors
                those who whisper scandal
    are an invincible wickedness
                to both alike
    their character stubbornly matches
                the ways of foxes
    what does this wiliness gain?
                while other shipgear
    toils in the depths of open sea
                I am
    unsinkable
                like cork on the surface
                            of saltwater

    a scheming citizen   Antistrophe D (Lines 81–88)
                has no power
                            to scatter
    convincing words
                among good people
                            in spite
    of groveling before everyone
                he weaves the entire
    fabric of his ruin
                I do not share
    his brashness
                I want to be
                            a devoted friend
    but in the face of a foe
                as his enemy
                            stalking
    my prey in any direction on winding paths
    I will ambush him
                with the wolf's sense
                            of right
    and wrong
                the straighttongued man stands forth
                            in every
    form of government:

        under a single ruler
or when the reckless crowd
        when wise men
                watch over
a city
        it is irreverent to clash
                with a god

who furthers the designs   Epode D (Lines 89–96)
        of schemers one moment
                but then
bestows a brilliant aura
        upon other people
even such observations
        do not console
the minds of those
        who are plagued
                with envy
because they stretch
        the plumbline beyond
                its reach
some humans plant
        a painful wound
                in their hearts
before they attain
        all that their thoughts
                envision
it is best to take
        the yoke upon
                our necks
and bear it lightly
        to kick against
                the whip
becomes a hazardous path
        I hope to be
a source of delight in the company of worthy people

PYTHIAN 3

Hiérōn of Syrákousai | Horse Race (?) | 474 BCE (?)

As consolation and counsel to Hiérōn during his illness, the mythology of *Pythian 3* centers upon Korōnís and her son Asklēpiós, the healer hero-god. Although the song does not commemorate an athletic victory, ancient editors may have included it among Píndaros' Pythian songs because it mentions the Pythian victory of Hiérōn's horse Pherénikos (P.3.73–4), probably in 478 BCE (Píndaros' *Olympian 1* celebrates Pherénikos' victory at Olympía in 476 BCE). Since Píndaros calls Hiérōn "my friend who lives in Aítna" (P.3.69), the poem's date falls somewhere between Hiérōn's foundation of the city of Aítna in 476 BCE (see the introduction to *Pythian 1*) and his death in 467 BCE. Some commentators hypothesize that *Pythian 3* is a literary letter to Hiérōn and was, therefore, not intended for performance. But the poetics of the song, such as its artistic mélange of varieties of Hellenic language and stanzaic structure, are generic features specific to the occasion of choral performance. The "stranger" from Arkadía (P.3.25–6) is Ískhys. The "wooden tower" (P.3.38) is Korōnís' funeral pyre. The unborn child Asklēpiós is necessarily in danger of dying in his mother's womb (P.3.40–4). "Lētó's grandson" is Asklēpiós and the "son of the Father" (that is, of Zeus) (P.3.67) is Apóllōn. Both are healers. "Sky's own star" (P.3.75) is the sun. It is unclear who the "Mother" (P.3.78) is, but Rheía, Dēmétēr, and Kybélē (Cybele) are possibilities. Píndaros represents the Moúsai as performing at the weddings of Thétis and Pēleús on Mount Pélion and of Harmonía and Kádmos at Thébai (P.3.89–91). The mythology of Pēleús and Kádmos conveys the lesson that Hiérōn should bear the adversity of his illness with composure and gratitude because on the one hand, even such illustrious heroes who communed so directly with the gods suffered misfortune, and on the other hand, despite his hardships, Hiérōn has enjoyed a very fortunate life. Kádmos is the father of Agaué, Autonóē, Inó, and Semélē. His "three daughters" are the first three (P.3.97–8), all of whom suffered the death of a son. Thyónē (P.3.99) is another name for Semélē. "An easy feat to achieve for very few" (P.3.115) is either the attainment of "virtue" or the composition of "famous songs" (P.3.114); the ambiguity is more productive than problematic.

    my wish would be   Strophe A (Lines 1–7)
        that Kheírōn
                Philýra's son—
if we need our tongue
        to speak this prayer
                on every
mind—
        that the departed healer
                were living now
the widely ruling child of Krónos Ouranídēs

that the wilderness creature
      endowed with a mind
           devoted
to men
      still held sway in Pélion's valleys—
          as alive
as he once was
      when he raised
           the softtouch worker
of limbstrengthening relief
      from pain
           Asklēpiós
the hero bulwark
      against every sort
           of sickness

before the daughter   Antistrophe A (Lines 8–14)
      of horseman Phlegýas
           gave birth
to him with the help of midwife Eileíthyia
      the golden
arrows of Ártemis defeated her in her bedroom
she entered the house of Háïdēs through Apóllōn's
plans
      the fury of Zeus' children
           is not
fruitless
      with wayward judgment she mocked it
           and approved
another marriage without her father's knowledge—
although she had already blended her limbs
with those of Phoíbos
      god with uncut hair

and while she carried the purified seed of that god   Epode A (Lines 15–23)
she did not wait
      for the bridal table to arrive
for an outburst of exuberant wedding songs
like the affectionate words of evening songs
that unmarried girls
      agemates of the bride
are fond of singing to their friend
      but her—

she desired what was far away
    many
mortals suffer from such illusions
    there is
a bitterly aimless branch of humankind:
whoever disdains the earth beneath their feet
and gazes upon distant horizons
    on the hunt
for windblown things
    with hollow aspirations

clothed in her lovely robes   Strophe B (Lines 24–30)
    defiant Korōnís
succumbed to such dangerous delusion
    when a stranger
arrived from Arkadía
    she slept with him in his bed
Korōnís did not escape Apóllōn's sight
although the temple's lord found
    himself just then
in Pythó where sheepflocks are welcome
    Loxías
        he knew
affirming his verdict according to that most
plainspoken ally
    his allknowing mind
he entertains no falsehood
    no god
        no mortal
misleads him
    neither their actions
        nor their schemes

the instant he knew about the foreign bed   Antistrophe B (Lines 31–37)
of Ískhys Eilatídas and her unholy betrayal
he dispatched his sister
    who seethed with unyielding strength
to Lakéreia
    because the unmarried mother-to-be
was living near the banks of Lake Boibiás
a fortune more cruel escorted Korōnís to misery
and overwhelmed her
    many neighbors shared

her ruin and perished as well
>   flame struck from a single
spark wipes away whole tracts of mountain forest

but when her closest kin laid the girl out   Epode B (Lines 38–46)
upon a wooden tower
>   and voracious flames
of Héphaistos raced around it
>   Apóllōn spoke:
"I will no longer endure the anguish of killing
my son
>   a sorrowful death
>   >   knitted to his mother's
mournful plight"
>   the god spoke
>   >   then suddenly there
a single stride
>   he snatched his son
>   >   from her corpse
the funeral pyre parted
>   its flames for him
Apóllōn took the child in his arms
>   and entrusted
him to Magnēsía's Kéntauros
>   from whom he would learn
how to heal the sicknesses that people suffer

and all who came harassed by sores not caused   Strophe C (Lines 47–53)
by injury
>   or those with limbs wounded
>   >   by sunglint bronze
by slingstone launched from afar
>   or those with flesh
racked by fever's summery heat
>   or wintery
chills—
>   he freed one person
>   >   after another
from their different pains and rescued them
curing some with healing spells
>   while others
he served with elixirs
>   or coated their bodies with balms
and he brought still others back to health with surgery

profit fetters even wisdom   Antistrophe C (Lines 54–60)
        a handful
of gold appeared
            and seduced that healer
                to bring
a finished man back
        from death
                for an almighty wage
the son of Krónos
            shot through both men's breastbones
and swiftly extinguished their last breath
            Zeus' thunderbolt
flame
            rained down doom upon them
                we must seek
from gods what behooves a mind that dies:
        to know
what is beneath our feet
        what destiny is ours

do not my soul   Epode C (Lines 61–69)
            strive for deathless life
                but drain down
every drop of your ready-to-hand invention
if enlightened Kheírōn still dwelled in his cave
if our honeyvoiced songs cast any spell
upon his heart
            I would persuade him
                to provide
for upright men
        a healer of feverish sickness
someone called Lētó's grandson
            or son of the Father
slicing the Ionian Sea on ship
        I would travel
to Aréthousa's spring
        to my friend
            who lives in Aítna

who watches over Syrákousai   Strophe D (Lines 70–76)
        as ruler
            kind
to common people

                without envy
                        toward worthy
men
        an astounding father
                to his guests
for him a double kindness
        if I were to come
with goldsmithed good health
        with a victory parade
for games at Pythó
        to brighten the splendor
                of garlands
that Pherénikos
        once upon a time had won
at Kírrha
        when he bested other horses
then yes
        I would cross deep sea
                and come as a light
shining farther for him than sky's own star

me—I want   Antistrophe D (Lines 77–83)
        to pray to the Mother
                the worshipped
goddess whom
        along with Pan
                the girls often
sing at night near my doorway
        if you are skilled
Hiérōn
        at understanding the truths
                art tells
then you know this proverb
        because you learned it
from elder poets:
        the undying gods dispense
to mortals two sorrows for each joy
        thoughtless
people cannot weather this burden with dignity
but good ones do
        by turning their admirable gifts
                outward

    good fortune follows you   Epode D (Lines 84–92)
        remarkable destiny
looks upon
        if any human
                the people's
sovereign leader
        an untroubled life did not
exist for Pēleús Aiakídas
        for godlike Kádmos
though storytellers say that they enjoyed
mortalkind's utmost happiness
        that they heard
the Moúsai in golden headbands sing
        on the mountain
at sevengated Thébai
        when Kádmos married
coweyed Harmonía
        when Pēleús married
Thétis
        glorious daughter
                of sage Nēreús

the gods attended wedding feasts for both heroes   Strophe E (Lines 93–99)
who witnessed the majestic children of Krónos on goldcast
thrones
        and accepted wedding gifts
                from them
through Zeus' kindness
        they traded former trials
for uplifted hearts
        but his three daughters
later left Kádmos
        bereft of his share
                of happiness:
they suffered bitterly
        but Zeus the Father visited
the seductive bed of Thyónē with sunbright arms

and son of Pēleús   Antistrophe E (Lines 100–106)
        the only child
                to whom
undying Thétis gave birth in Phthía
        wounded

by arrows
        he left his soul behind
                in warfare
and as he burned on the funeral pyre
        he stirred
a mournful dirge from the Danaoí
        if any mortal
discerns truth's path
        he must flourish
                with whatever
fortune the gods grant
        gusts of steeply climbing
winds blow one way
        one instant
                then shift the next
men's happiness
        does not come unbroken
                for long
whenever it follows them and falls with its full weight

I will be a small man   Epode E (Lines 107–115)
        in small moments
great in greater moments
        I will always
revere with my art
        the fortune that finds me
                devoted
to it with all my skill
        if some god should grant me
sumptuous wealth
        I have hope
                that I will find
soaring fame hereafter
        we know Néstōr
                and Lykía's
Sarpēdón—
        heroes that people still recall—
from resounding verses
        that expert builders composed
virtue endures
        through the power
                of famous songs
an easy feat to achieve for very few

PYTHIAN 4

Arkesílas of Kyrḗnē | Chariot Race | 462 BCE

Pythian 4 and *Pythian 5* commemorate the chariot victory of Arkesílas IV, king of Kyrḗnē, a north African polis, in the Pythian Games of 462 BCE. The site of ancient Kyrḗnē is near modern Shahhat in northern Libya. Emigrants from the island of Thḗra (modern Santorini), led by Báttos, founded Kyrḗnē as a Hellenic colony around 630 BCE. The original colonists identified as Dorian Héllēnes. Arkesílas' rule began some time prior to his chariot victory and lasted until about 440 BCE, when democracy supplanted the Battídai dynasty. The themes of magic, medicine, and healing in *Pythian 4* recall that Kyrḗnē exported silphium, a medicinal plant. Victory in an equestrian event is commensurate with Kyrḗnē's renown for horses (P.4.2, 6–8, 117). After the song's opening declares its celebratory mission, Píndaros pitches us into mythology with a speech by Médeia, followed by a flashback to the motivations and preparations for the voyage of the Argó and to Médeia and Iásōn's cooperation in winning the Golden Fleece. This storytelling is an elaborate backdrop for the mythological genealogy of Báttos. *Pythian 4* commemorates Arkesílas' victory by celebrating—and legitimizing—the leadership of the Battídai in Kyrḗnē: the song recounts that Báttos, a descendant of Eúphēmos, one of the Argonaútai, fulfilled Médeia's prophecy (P.4.4–56) that he would leave Thḗra in order to found Kyrḗnē. Médeia's speech, Iásōn's prayers at the prow of the Argó, the seer Mópsos cheering the heroes on at their rowing, those heroes shouting for joy when Iásōn succeeds at successfully plowing furrows with fire-breathing oxen—the performative possibilities of such passages offer a counterstatement to the more prosaic hypothesis that this piece would have been too long or too narrative for choral performance. An original choral performance of *Pythian 4* would have been an outstandingly grand gesture and, thus, a compelling appeal for the reconciliation that a certain Damóphilos appears to have sought (P.4.277–99).

Thḗra is the "holy island" (P.4.6–7) and the "seabattered land" (P.4.14). The "chariotrich city" (P.4.7–8) is Kyrḗnē. The daughter of Épaphos is Libýē (P.4.14). *Pythian 4*'s mythology explains the traditional connections between Thḗra and Kyrḗnē. Médeia's speech (P.4.13–56) predicts events that lead to the future founding of Kyrḗnē, a future that belongs to the mythological past relative to the present of *Pythian 4*'s performance and its audiences. "This island" (P.4.42) is again Thḗra, the site where Médeia performs her speech. The "whole continent" (P.4.48) is Libýē. The "mortal to rule / the nimbostratus plains" (P.4.52–3) is Báttos. Gaía is "the forested Mother" (P.4.74). "Aphrodítē's / husband who drives a bronzecast chariot" (P.4.87–8) is Árēs. The "cow" (P.4.142) is Enarétē, wife of Aíolos and mother of Krētheús, an ancestor of Aísōn, his son Iásōn, and Pelías. Although contemporary pejorative connotations of referring to a woman as a "cow" are not in play here, the sexist and otherizing husbandry metaphor for birth and mothering entailed in the word is salient. Inó (P.4.162) is Phríxos' stepmother. Poseidón is "the lord of ships" (P.4.207). The "rockfaces that crash together" (P.4.208) are the Symplēgádes. The goddess who assists Iásōn by providing him with a magical device with which he incites Médeia's love for him (P.4.213–17) is Aphrodítē. By calling Médeia "slayer of Pelías" (P.4.250), Píndaros refers to passages of Médeia's story beyond the voyage of the Argó: when Pelías refuses to yield to Iásōn the rule of Iōlkós, as promised (P.4.165–6), Médeia tricks the daughters of Pelías into killing their father. In the conclusion to the mythological narrative, the second-person addressees (P.4.254–62) are the Battídai, Arkesílas' family. The "oaktree" in the parable-riddle (P.4.263–9) appears to be Damóphilos. The word "pebble" (P.265) introduces a voting metaphor to represent the "oaktree" advocating on its own behalf; officials tallied votes in ancient Hellás based on the number of pebbles deposited by voters in a voting box. Píndaros adopts the language of healing (P.4.270–6) to appeal to Arkesílas to reconcile with Damóphilos, whom the poet represents as a devoted citizen who longs to return to his homeland (P.4.279–99). "Apóllōn's fountain" was in Kyrḗnē (P.4.294). The last line of the poem, which depicts Damóphilos—"that Átlas" (P.4.289)— as the beneficiary of guestfriendsthip at Thḗbai, Píndaros' homecity, suggests that the young exile from Kyrḗnē commissioned *Pythian 4*. The length of the song testifies to the intensity of Damóphilos' appeal; at 299 lines, *Pythian 4* is by far Píndaros' longest *epiníkion*.

today you ought to stand beside a man Strophe A (Lines 1–8)
we cherish
    beside the king of horsetending Kyrḗnē
so that as Arkesílas parades in glory
    Moúsa
you amplify the airstream of praisesongs owed
to Lētó's children
    owed to Pythó
        where one time
when Apóllōn happened not to be abroad
the coworker of Zeus' golden eagles
    the priestess
prophesied Báttos would settle in fruitbearing
Libýē
    that after he immediately
departs from the holy island
    he should found
the chariotrich city on the gleamingbright hilltop

that in seventeen generations Antistrophe A (Lines 9–16)
    Báttos would
fulfill the word Médeia
    once spoke at Thḗra
        the word
Aiḗtēs' formidable daughter
    an eminence among

>   the Kólkhoi
>   breathed forth from immortal lips
>   she addressed
>   spearman Iásōn's demigod sailors like this:
>   "hear me
>   you sons of strongwilled humans and gods
>   for I declare
>   that from this seabattered land
>   the daughter of Épaphos will one day plant the taproot
>   of towns
>   that mortals treasure
>   in Zeus Ámmōn's temple

when they exchange shortfinned dolphins for swift horses   Epode A (Lines 17–23)
reins for wooden oars
        they will steer stormfooted
chariots
        that omen will make Théra become
mothercity of great cities
        the omen that Eúphēmos
once received when he jumped down from the ship's prow
at the outflows of Lake Tritōnís
        and met
a god with a man's appearance
        who gave him a clump
of earth as a gift of friendship—
        Father Zeus
                son
of Krónos
        clanged providential thunder
                for him—

when he came upon us   Strophe B (Lines 24–31)
        as we were hanging
against the ship the bridle of swift Argó
the anchor's bronze jaw
        before that encounter
                we
had hauled the Argó ashore
        on my advice
and portaged the seaborne timber from Ōkeanós
across the land's lonely back
        for twelve long days

at that moment
> the companionless spirit approached us
taking on the radiant look of a man
to be revered
> he began with friendly speech
like charitable people
> who unhesitatingly
offer a meal to strangers when they arrive

the homeward journey's sweeter cause   Antistrophe B (Lines 32–39)
> however
prevented us from staying longer
> he
declared himself Eurýpylos
> son of unwithering
Earthembracer Earthshaker
> he knew that we
were eager to sail
> quickly grabbed some soil
with his right hand
> and sought to offer this
as an improvised guestgift
> Eúphēmos did not refuse
the hero instead leaped to the shore
> extended his hand
to Eurýpylos' hand
> and accepted the divine dirtclod
I have learned that this clump of soil went
seaborne when saltwater washed it overboard

at twilight   Epode B (Lines 40–46)
> and swept it away in the current
> > how often
I urged the rowers
> who ease our travel's toil
to guard that dirtclod
> but their vigilance faded
now on this island is poured out before
its time
> the undying seed
> > of boundless Libýē
if Eúphēmos
> son of Poseidón Hípparkhos

                        and king
had returned home to holy Taínaros
            and thrown
the dirtclod into the underworld mouth
            of Háïdēs—
Eúphēmos
            to whom Eurṓpē
                        the daughter of Tityós
once gave birth
            on the banks
                        of Kēphisós River—

then his bloodline's fourth generation of children   Strophe C (Lines 47–54)
would have controlled the whole continent
            with the Danaoí
because those people are then to move abroad
from great Lakedaímōn
            from the Gulf of Árgos
and Mykénai
            but now in beds
                        of foreign women
he will find a distinguished people
            who come to this island
esteemed by the gods
            and beget a mortal
                        to rule
the nimbostratus plains
            and one day Phoíbos
will give him oracular advice in his house awash

with gold   Antistrophe C (Lines 55–62)
            in later days
                        when Báttos visits
his temple at Pythó
            to lead a multitude
                        on ships
to Kronídēs' fruitful sacred ground
            near the Neílos"
yes this was Médeia's battalion
            of oracular verses
wonderstruck motionless silenced
            the godlike heroes
heard her prophetic vision

                    fortunate son
of Polýmnēstos
          with those words
                    prophecy exalted you
through the unbidden voice of Delphoí's bee
          calling
out to you
          "khaíre! khaíre! khaíre!"
                    the priestess
proclaimed you Kyrḗnē's fate-appointed king

when you inquired how the gods will atone   Epode C (Lines 63–69)
for your faltering speech
          and evermore
                    to this very
day
          like the peak of spring's fullbloom purple
                    Arkesílas
blooms as eighth in the line of Báttos' children
through their emissaries
          Apóllōn and Pythó
bestowed upon him
          a talismanic aura
for horseracing
          Arkesílas and the ram's
allgolden fleece
          are the debt I owe
                    the Moúsai
when the Minýai sailed
          in quest of that prize
their voyage sowed the seeds of their godsent glory

what outset greeted their ship's journey?   Strophe D (Lines 70–77)
          what danger bound them
to a board with tough nails of adamant?
          a god
decreed that Pelías would die
          by the might
                    or unyielding
will of Aíolos' august sons
          there came
an oracle
          uttered at the omphalós

                    of the forested
Mother that chilled the blood of his scheming heart:
Pelías must in every way fully guard
against the onesandaled man
        whether a stranger
or someone from town
        when he comes from his steep dwelling

to the sundrenched land of illustrious Iōlkós   Antistrophe D (Lines 78–85)
then after some time
        a daunting man
                who held
twin spears
        arrived
                he wore both kinds of clothes:
Magnēsía's local garments conformed to his stunning
body
        and leopard skin sheltered him
                from shivery
rainstorms
        his splendid strands of hair
                were not cut
but drained down his back's breadth
        in waves
                subjecting his fearless
judgment to the test
        he quickly stepped forward
then stood there
        as people crowded into the agorá

they did not recognize him   Epode D (Lines 86–92)
        but one of those
astonished people nevertheless said this:
"he is not at all an Apóllōn
        not Aphrodítē's
husband
        who drives a bronzecast chariot
                they tell
the story that Iphimédeia's sons perished
        on gleaming Náxos
Ótos and you
        brash Ephiáltēs the king
                yes Ártemis'

arrow
        quick from her unconquerable quiver
tracked down Tityós
        so that mortals desire
                to touch
the loves within their realm
        of what
                is possible"

back and forth like this   Strophe E (Lines 93–100)
        they muttered to each
other
        then hurtling recklessly
                in his well-planed
mule wagon
        Pelías arrived
                the sight
of the visitor's unmistakable single sandal
on his right foot
        immediately shocked him
                Pelías
hid fear beneath a veneer of resolve
        and shouted:
"what country
        stranger
                are you proud
        to call your homeland?
what earthborn human ejected you from her old
woman's womb?
        without defiling your bloodline
with offensive falsehoods
        declare your origins"

he confidently answered with these gracious words: Antistrophe E (Lines 101–108)
"I promise to display the teaching of Kheírōn
I return from the cave
        abode of Kharikló and Philýra
where the kéntauros' holy daughters cared
for me
        I completed my twenty years
                without shame
for some wrong deed or word toward them
        and have come

to recover my father's time-honored power
    held now
in violation of destiny
    which Zeus once granted
the people's leader Aíolos and his sons

I have learned that Pelías trusted the bright glare   Epode E (Lines 109–115)
of his delusion
    and lawlessly tore Zeus' gift
from the hands of my parents the legitimate rulers
    in dread
of this tyrannical usurper's violence
    the moment
I first saw daylight
    they staged in our home a show
of gutwrenching grief
    as if for a stillborn child
and women keened
    but secretly
        they sent me off wrapped
in purple
    making night
        the journey's companion
and entrusted me
    to Kronídēs Kheírōn
        to raise

you know the crux of my history   Strophe F (Lines 116–123)
    now show me the straightest
way
    my cherished fellow citizens
        to the home
of my fathers
    who tended snowbright horses
        as son
of Aísōn
    born in this place
        I come to no foreign
land of strangers
    that godly animal addressed me
by the name of Iásōn"
    he spoke
        then his father

recognized at sight the man
>who had come
tears spilled from the careworn corners of Aísōn's eyes
his spirit overcome with joy at seeing
his son so distinguished
>the most magnificent of men

both of Aísōn's brothers came   Antistrophe F (Lines 124–131)
>when news
of Iásōn spread
>>Phérēs left behind
>>>the nearby
Hyperian Spring
>>Amytháōn departed Messénē
Ádmētos and Melámpous were also quick to arrive
and shower their cousin with kindness
>a feast fit or such
a reunion
>Iásōn greeted them all
>>with warm words
prepared a decorous welcome
>and prolonged their lavish
enjoyment
>for those five crowded nights
>>and days
Iásōn harvested the good life's sacred height

but on the sixth day   Epode F (Lines 132–138)
>Iásōn set forth
>>his whole
urgent story
>from the beginning
>>and entrusted
his plight to his kinsmen
>who sided with him
>>he rose
to his feet
>and they too were quickly up
>>from their couches
Pelías' palace
>they hurried there
>>and stood firm
inside

        when the son of Tyró
            whose long hair cast
a spell
        heard the heroes' arrival
            he confronted
them
        allowing his language
            to ripple along
with a gentle voice
        Iásōn laid the groundwork
for words of wisdom
        "son of Poseidón of the Rock

the judgment of mortals is very quick to praise   Strophe G (Lines 139–146)
stolen profit instead of justice
        while they
veer toward the next day's ruthless reckoning
but you and I must govern our passions and weave
the fabric of a lasting abundance
        I
will say what you already know
        that one cow
mothered Krētheús and Salmoneús
        whose mind dared greatly
seeded from them in this third generation
        we gaze
upon sun's golden might
        may the Moírai turn
their faces away
        if any enmity
            arises
to bury mutual esteem
        among family members

it is wrong that we two   Antistrophe G (Lines 147–154)
        divide our forebears' wealth
and power with bronzewrought swords or javelins
        to you
I surrender sheepflocks
        the russet cattleherds
and all the cropfields
        that you have seized from my parents
by force

        and cultivate
             making your wealth grow fat
it does not rankle me
        if your house exploits
the livestock and farmland
        but the ruler's scepter
the throne where the son of Krētheús
        once used to sit
as he straightened the course of justice
        for this horserearing
nation—
        with no anguish for either of us

relinquish these   Epode G (Lines 155–161)
        so that no newborn wrong
arises between us"
        Iásōn spoke
              and Pelías
very quietly replied
        "I will be the kind
of man you seek
        but I already break bread
with the old man's stage of life
        while your youth's bloom
begins to oceanwave
        you can remove
the wrath of underworld spirits
        Phríxos
commands us to go
        to Aiétēs' palace
              to bring
his soul back home
        and to retrieve
              the ram's
plushfleeced hide
        which once saved him
              from the sea

and from his stepmother's godless arrows   Strophe H (Lines 162–169)
    a dream
of wonder came to tell me these things
        at Kastalía
I asked the oracle

                if I must obey them
it urges me to ready
                a journey by ship
as quickly as possible
                agree to complete this trial
I vow to allow you
                to be sole ruler and govern
as an unbreakable oath
                let Zeus
                            our shared
ancestor
                be witness"
                            they approved this pact
                and went
their separate ways
                but Iásōn
                            with no delay

dispatched heralds to make known everywhere   Antistrophe H (Lines 170–177)
that there would be a voyage
                and right away
they came
                unwearied in battle
                            three sons of Zeus
Kronídēs
                one whose mother was Alkménē
                            with arcing
eyebrows
                two whose mother was Léda
                            next
two men
                their hair in waves
                            the Earthshaker's offspring
doing honor to their courage
                from Pýlos
from the headland of Taínaros
                they proved the worth
of their worthy reputation—
                Eúphēmos' and yours
Periklýmenos with imposing might
                from Apóllōn
the lyrestrummer
                father of songs
                            acclaimed

Orpheús—he joined the expedition too

Hermés   Epode H (Lines 178–184)
      who carries a wand of gold
            sent off
his twin sons for the unabating work
Ekhíōn and Érytos
      who brimmed with youth
            and swiftly
they travelled
      the natives of Pangaíon's foothills—
swiftly the ruler of winds
      their father Boréas
eager and moved by the thrill
      he armed Zétēs and Kálaïs
men whose backs flexed
      with purple wingfeathers
            Héra
kindled in these god-descended heroes
the delightful flame of irresistible yearning

for the ship the Argó   Strophe I (Lines 185–192)
      so that no straggler
might stay beside his mother
      and pamper a life
unventured
      but even unto death
            discover
in the company of peers
      his own most sublime
elixir for daring
      when this crew beyond
compare arrived at Iōlkós
      Iásōn took stock
and approved them all
      after Mópsos consulted
the gods through birdflight and sacred lots
      the seer
was happy to have the sailors board their ship
when they hoisted anchors over the prow

at the ship's stern   Antistrophe I (Lines 193–200)
      the leader of their quest

took in his hands a golden drinking bowl
and called on Zeus
      the father of Ouranídai
            whose weapon
is thunderbolt
      called on seawave surges
            and windgusts
to be fleet travelers
      called on nights
            and searoads
and days
      to be kindhearted
            to their voyage
called on them
      that their homeward journey's fate
might be a friend
      from the clouddeck
            thunder's voice answered
Iásōn propitiously
      bright lightning flashes
broke forth
      the heroes obeyed the god's signs
            their sense
of purpose galvanized
      the wonder-watcher

Mópsos spurred them on   Epode I (Lines 201–207)
      to lean into their oars
reminding them of their aspirations
      ceaseless
rowing issued from their quickchurning arms
escorted by gusts of Nótos
      they reached the mouth
of Áxeinos
      where they founded a sanctuary
sacred to Poseidón of the Sea
      a herd
of Thrákē's umber-colored bulls
      was there
as well as the hollow
      of a newbuilt altar of stone
plunged into thick danger
      they entreated the lord of ships

Pythians

    to escape the stubborn movement   Strophe J (Lines 208–215)
        of rockfaces
                that crash
together
        they were living creatures
                those twin rocks
they geared together more swiftly
        than brigades
of booming winds
        but the heroes' journey finished them
the Argó then landed at Phásis
        where the crew
showed its strength among the darkfaced Kólkhoi—
before the very eyes of Aiétēs
        her eminence
with the sharpest arrows
        joined a spotted
wryneck to an unyielding fourspoked wheel

    and for the first time   Antistrophe J (Lines 216–223)
        the goddess born at Kýpros
conveyed from Ólympos to humanity
        the madness
of this birdcharm
        she taught the son of Aísōn
to be skilled at incantatory prayers
so that he might remove
        Médeia's daughterly deference
to her parents
        so that seductive Hellás
might unsettle her
        make her burn inside
under the lash of Peithó
        and she immediately
revealed how to master her father's trials
Médeia mixed a potion with olive oil
an antidote to unrepentant pain
and gave it to Iásōn to apply to his skin
they mutually agreed to marriage's mutual joy

but when Aiétēs planted before those gathered   Epode J (Lines 224–230)
the untameable plow and oxen
        that were exhaling

flame of stoked fire from russet muzzles
        each one
pounding the ground with bronze hooves
        by himself
                he herded
these oxen forth
        and led them
                to the yokestrap
he steered the plowteam
        and lined out straight furrows
                clove
the back of cloddense earth
        as deep
                as the length
of outstretched arms
        he spoke:
                "if the ruler
        whoever
commands this ship
        completes for me this labor
let him carry off the imperishable bedcover

the ram's fleece   Strophe K (Lines 231–238)
        radiant, so goldbright its fringe"
                when Aiétēs
finished
        Iásōn threw off his saffron cloak
obedient to the god
        he attacked his task
fire did not engulf him
        thanks to her
to instructions from the sorceress
        who welcomed him
Iásōn grabbed the plow
        strapped the harness to oxnecks
as the trial demanded
        and struck the strongribbed creatures
with relentless treeswitch
        the man's sheer might
powered the plow
        the required distance
                Aiétēs
silenced his distress

       but could not suppress
a cry because Iásōn's ability astounded him

the Argó's crew stretched   Antistrophe K (Lines 239–246)
       their loyal arms
              to the strong man
decked him with leafgreen garlands
       and embraced him with warm
congratulations
       at once the astonished son
of Hélios told next
       of the shining ram's fleece
              the place
where Phríxos' knifeblades
       had stretched it out
              Aiétēs
still did not believe
       Iásōn would accomplish
such dreadful toil because the fleece was lying
in dense woods
       guarded by a serpent's ravenous
jaws
       in thickness and length this beast
              surpassed
a fifty-oared battleship
       that hammerstikes built

too long the distance to travel by wagonroads   Epode K (Lines 247–253)
time is closing in
       and I know
              a short footpath
I lead many others along the ways of song
Iásōn deftly killed
       Arkesílas
              the quartzeyed
serpent with lacework dorsal scales
       and abducted
Médeia
       murderer of Pelías
              with her own help
they reached the seatracts
       of Ōkeanós
              the Red Sea

the land of the husbandslayer women of Lémnos
on that island the Argonaútai flaunted their brawn
in athletic contests
    a cloak for the one
        judged winner

and slept with those women   Strophe L (Lines 254–261)
    that was when Moíra's day
or Moíra's nights
    welcomed in foreign cropland
        your seed
of sunlit abundance
    the line of Eúphēmos took root
in Lémnos
    and fruited forth evermore
        they shared
the hearths of Lakedaímōn's men
    then eventually peopled
the island once called Kallísta
    where Lētó's son granted you
Libýē's plains to tend
    because the gods
esteem you—
    and granted you
        the holy town
of goldenthroned Kyrénē to oversee

because you discovered the art of upright government   Antistrophe L (Lines 262–269)
know now the wisdom of Oidípous
    if someone should chop
a soaring oaktree's branches off with a sharpedged
axe and disfigure the breathtaking symmetry of it
although its acorns are wasted
    it would cast
a pebble on its own behalf
    if it ever
ends its journey in a winter fire—
or if supported by some powermonger's
towering columns
    the oak performs deplorable
toil inside a foreign city's walls
after leaving its native soil exposed

you are the timeliest healer   Epode L (Lines 270–276)
    and Paián extols
the light in you
    it is right to apply a mild
hand to mend a wound's hurt
    it is too easy
even for weaker citizens
    to convulse their city
but a grim fight to reestablish its foundations
unless a god immediately shipcaptains
cityleaders
    good fortune finishes its splendid
fabric for you
    be bold enough to expend
every effort for godfavored Kyrḗnē

among the words of Hómēros   Strophe M (Lines 277–284)
    grasp and follow
this saying
    he said a worthy messenger
        adorns
every action with the lushest honor
an honest message also magnifies the Moúsa
Kyrḗnē and the most illustrious house
of Báttos acknowledged Damóphilos' just intentions
a young man among boys
    but like an elder
        with wise
advice
    as if he found
        a one-hundred-year lifetime
he bereaves a wicked tongue of its clamor
he has learned to despise a violent man

he does not spar against respected people   Antistrophe M (Lines 285–292)
and delays no exploit
    timeliness has a brief window
in human matters
    Damóphilos knows that truth
he observes it with care
    not like a hired
laborer
    they say that this

                        is the greatest grief:
to force someone who knows
            what is worthy
                        to keep their feet
outside their city
            at this moment
                        that Átlas
grapples with sky
            removed from his homeland
                        from what
belongs to him
            undying Zeus set the Titánes
free
            and shipsails eventually shift
                        when winds

subside   Epode M (Lines 293–299)
            now that Damóphilos has drained
                        his cup
of wretched sickness
            he prays to someday see
his home
            while drinking wine with friends
                        at Apóllōn's
fountain
            prays to freely surrender
                        his heart
to youth's exuberance
            in his hands the finely
crafted lyre
            before an audience of wiser
citizens
            he prays to taste tranquility
                        causing
no anguish to anyone
            free from harm at the hands
of neighbors
            and he would tell the tale
                        Arkesílas
of what a spring of heavenly lyrics
            he found
when recently welcomed as a guest in Thébai

PYTHIAN 5

Arkesílas of Kyrēnē | Chariot Race | 462 BCE

A remarkable feature of *Pythian 5* is that Píndaros commends the skill of Kárrhōtos, Arkesílas' chariot driver (P.5.23–53). Original Hellenic texts capitalize the noun *próphasis* (excuse), signaling that Píndaros personifies the word (P.5.27–9). Próphasis is fittingly the daughter of Epimētheús, whose name means "afterthought." "Kyrḗnē's steward" (P.5.62) is Báttos, whom Píndaros depicts as an agent of Apóllōn's colonization of Libýē. The catalog of Apóllōn's domains of divine power, healing, music, and prophecy (P.5.63–9), aligns with this song and its audiences: Kyrḗnē was known for medicine and was the site of an oracle of Apóllōn. Píndaros then (P.69–73) celebrates the role of Apóllōn's prophetic power in the fortunes of Dorian people, with whom he links his family, the Aigeídai (P.3.74–6). Hellenic immigrants settled Kyrḗnē in two stages: first came those who survived the fall of Troía (P.5.82–5), who welcomed the colonists from Thḗra, led by Báttos, also called Aristotélēs (P.5.85–93). These latter settlers imported to Kyrḗnē the Kárneia, an originally Spartan festival held in honor of Apóllōn (P.5.77–81). *Pythian 5* concludes with Píndaros' prayer (P.5.124) that Arkesílas might enjoy victory in the most prestigious games. Ancient sources report that Arkesílas did in fact attain victory at Olympía.

    wealth's power is vast   Strophe A (Lines 1–11)
        whenever some mortal man—
    if destiny grants wealth's gift—
        brings it home
            tempered
    with undefiled virtue
        a muchdear escort
    godfavored Arkesílas
        from the towering threshold
    of your celebrated life
        you have sought it
    along with glory
        by the will of Kástōr
    with chariot of gold
        who streams down tranquil skies
    upon your blessed hearth
        after a winter's rainstorm

    yes the wise abide more gracefully even   Antistrophe A (Lines 12–22)
    godgiven power
        abundance surrounds you
            as you

walk uprightly
>first because you
>>are king
of cities that flourish
>your birthright fortune claims
this venerated honor enriched by your insight
now too you are blessed
>because you won the vaunted
prize for horses
>in the illustrious festival
at Pythó
>and have welcomed
>>this victory parade of men

Apóllōn's joy   Epode A (Lines 23–31)
>and so as they sing of you
throughout Aphrodítē's
>fragrant garden
>>in Kyrénē
do not forget to exalt the god
>as each thing's
reason
>and cherish Kárrhōtos far beyond
your other friendships
>he did not bring along
Próphasis
>daughter of latelearning Epimētheús
when he arrived at the home of the Battídai
>whose rule
tradition sanctions
>but as guest at Kastalía's waters
he decked your hair
>with the bestplaced chariot's glory

its reins unbroken   Strophe B (Lines 32–42)
>in the sacred grove
with twelve swiftfooted circuits
>he shattered none
of the chariot tackle's strength
>then Kárrhōtos hung
as a votive offering
>all the equipment crafted
by skilled hands of artisans

             that he plied
                   when he skirted
the Hill of Krísa
             bound for the god's woodland nestled
in the valley
             cypress roofbeams shelter
his harness
             near the statue carved from a single
treetrunk
             that archers of Krḗtē dedicated
inside a temple cella on Mount Parnassós

it is therefore the graceful thing to do   Antistrophe B (Lines 43–53)
to face a benefactor with ready kindness
Alexibiádas
             Khárites with flowing hair
                   fuel your glory's
flame
             you are blessed:
                   after such adversity
you possess monuments of durable words
while forty other drivers fell
             you delivered
your chariot cockpit safe with undaunted skill
from the splendid games
             you have now come
to Libýē's plains
             and your ancestral city

no one is   Epode B (Lines 54–62)
             nor will be
                   without their share
of toil
             if it deals this outcome or that
Báttos' ancient good fortune
             the city's fortress
and brightest beacon for foreigners
             nevertheless
persists
             lions—the ground trembles
                   when they roar—
fled in fear
             when he unleashed

                        his strange speech
from across the sea
            the city's founder Apóllōn
afflicted the creatures with terror
            so that his oracles
might not fail for Kyrénē's steward

Apóllōn delivers cures for dreadful sickness   Strophe C (Lines 63–73)
to men and women
            furnished the kithara
                        and gifts
the Moúsa to whomever he wishes
            filling minds
with warless harmony
            he shields his oracular sanctuary
from where he settled
            the brave descendants of Hēraklés
and Aigimiós in Lakedaímōn
            in Árgos
                        in godtended Pýlos
my poetry sings out Spárta's admired fame

where those mortals were born   Antistrophe C (Lines 74–84)
            the Aigeídai
                        my forefathers
who sailed to Théra
            not without the gods
but some Moíra led them
            from that island
                        we welcomed
the yearly festival
            thick with sacrifices
and in the feast that honors you
            Apóllōn
Karnéios
            we worship the firmly
                        founded city
Kyrénē
            which foreigners who relish
                        bronzeclad battle
Tróes Antēnorídai
            possess
                        they came with Helénē

after they witnessed their homeland
    reduced to smoke

under the lash of Árēs   Epode C (Lines 85–93)
    giftbearing men,
whom Aristotélēs led there
    on swift ships
        when he clove
the open way of sea's deep,
    met the horsedriving
people and welcomed them openheartedly
with sacrifices
    he founded lusher treegroves
for the gods and established
    an avenue laid straight
        level
paved
    and echoing with horsehooves
        in processions
for Apóllōn that safeguard mortals
    an avenue where
at the edge of the agorá
    he now lies apart
        in death

Báttos lived his blessed life among men   Strophe D (Lines 94–104)
and upon his death
    became a hero his people
revere
    set apart from him
        before the palace
lie the other sacred rulers
    who reaped
the lot of Háïdēs
    though the earth shrouds
        their senses
I imagine they hear about unrivaled
achievements sprinkled
    with gentle dewdrops
        through rippling
victory celebrations
    hear that their happiness
is the justly earned splendor

    they share with their son
Arkesílas
   it is clear that to call upon
     goldsword Phoíbos
with song performed
   by young men
     is proper for him

because he takes from Pythó   Antistrophe D (Lines 105–115)
   the graceful melody
that beautifies victory
   and redeems the cost of contests
people who know
   acclaim that man
     I only
tell the story
   they tell
     he nourishes his speech
and mind more capably
   than his years admit
he soars in boldness
   an eagle among birds
     the strength
of his competitive spirit
   like a fortress
wingborne among the Moúsai
   because of his mother
he has displayed his chariot racing skill

he ventured every path to stunning victory   Epode D (Lines 116–124)
in local games
   a god readily brings
     his power
to fruition
   at this moment
     and in the future
blessed Kronídai
   may you grant
     that he
enjoys the same results
   in action
     in foresight
in case the wintery windgusts

               that make fruit rot
overwhelm his hour
               the vast mind of Zeus
helms the destiny of his favored men
I pray that he endows the family line
of Báttos
               with such distinction
                          at Olympía

PYTHIAN 6

Xenokrátēs of Akrágas | Chariot Race | 490

Xenokrátēs was the younger brother of Thérōn, ruler of Akrágas (c. 489–473 BCE; see *Olympian 2* and *Olympian 3*). *Pythian 6*, like *Isthmian 2*, ostensibly composed in honor of Xenokrátēs, praises Thrasýboulos, son of Xenokrátēs and nephew of Thérōn (P.6.46). The ambiguous "it" (P.6.19) is either Xenokrátēs' victory or Kheírōn's teaching. "The godlike man" is Antílokhos (P.6.38). The rhetoric of the poem's last lines (P.6.44–54) is that Thrasýboulos' outstanding honor toward his father extends to his generous compensation for the composition and performance of this *epiníkion*; such generosity would rival his powerful uncle's and display Thrasýboulos' refinement, exemplified by his appreciation for the Moúsai and honeybees' work—song and music, that is. Win-win.

    hear us as we plow again   Strophe A (Lines 1–9)
        the cropfield
    of Aphrodítē with darting eyes
        plow the Khárites' cropfield
    hear as we process to the temple-adorned
    omphalós of roaring earth
        where a storehouse of praisesong
    for victory at Pythó is built—
        built in Apóllōn's
    goldwashed valley
        for the prosperous Emmenídai
    for riverside Akrágas
        for Xenokrátēs

    neither wintery rainstorm   Strophe B (Lines 10–18)
        a heartless battalion
    of roaring cloud driven from abroad
        nor wind
    will carry that storehouse
        pounded by siltthick torrents
    down into sea's beneath
        but in purified sunlight
    that building's façade will herald
        Thrasýboulos
            the chariot
    victory won in the clefts
        of Krísa's slopes
    and shared by your father

        by your family line
a thing of glory for the talk of mortals

you clutch it in your right hand   Strophe C (Lines 19–27)
        and follow his teaching
the lessons people say
        Philýra's son
once gave in his mountain home to mighty Pēleídēs
when he was deprived of his parents:
        revere beyond
all other gods Kronídēs
        booming lord
of lightningflash and thunderbolt
        and never
deny the allotted lifespan of parents
        such reverence

in former times too   Strophe D (Lines 28–36)
        fierce Antílokhos embodied
this learning
        he perished in place of his father
                when he
stood face to face against the mortalslaying
commander of Aithíopes, Mémnōn
                the horse wounded
by Páris' arrows snarled Néstōr's chariot
and Mémnōn aimed his powerful spear
        the panicked
heart of Messénē's old man cried out
        "my boy!"

he did not launch a plea   Strophe E (Lines 37–45)
        that crashed into the dirt
the godlike man held his ground
        and bought his father's
salvation at the price of his own death
with this formidable feat
        in the eyes of that distant
generation's young men
        he proved himself best
in the practice of filial duty
        those events
are past but more than the sons of today

             Thrasýboulos
approaches that benchmark for honor toward a father

rivaling his uncle in shows of every splendor   Strophe F (Lines 46–54)
he oversees his wealth with thought
          the yield
of his youth is
          neither unjust
                    nor overbearing
but he harvests wisdom in the valleys
of the Pierídes
          to you Earthshaker
                    who rule
horserace entryways
          Poseidón
                    with every
intention to delight
          he devotes himself
to you
          kindhearted in the company
                    of fellow
drinkers
          he requites the honeycombed toil
                    of bees

PYTHIAN 7

Megaklés of Athénai | Chariot Race | 486 BCE

Megaklés' victory at Pythó provides occasion to commemorate the lavish donation that the Alkmaiōnídai made to Delphoí by funding the restoration of Apóllōn's temple after a fire (Hēródotos *Histories* 5.62). Píndaros' concluding thoughts about how envy undermines achievement critically evaluate Megaklés' ostracism (487 BCE) from Athénai.

the flourishing city of Athénai is	Strophe (Lines 1–8)
the loveliest overture—	
the groundwork for chariot	
songs—to lay down	
for the powerful	
house of the Alkmaiōnídai	
in what homeland	
in what home	
could you dwell	
and call	
more illustrious for Hellás to learn?	
all cities share the same esteem	Antistrophe (Lines 9–16)
for the people of Erekhtheús	
Apóllōn	
they built your astounding temple	
at sacred	
Pythó	
five victories at the Isthmós	
move me	
and one distinguished victory	
at Zeus' Olympía	
two at Kírrha	
Megaklés	Epode (Lines 17–21)
your family's	
and your ancestors'	
I bask in your new achievement	
but bitterly	
grieve when envy answers beautiful	
feats	

HoneyVoiced

        and yet they say
             that this is
how good fortune's abiding bloom
yields a man some good—
        and some bad

PYTHIAN 8

Aristoménēs of Aígina | Wrestling | 446 BCE

If the date of Aristoménēs' victory is correct, *Pythian 8* is the last *epiníkion* that Píndaros composed. Aristoménēs' uncles were victorious at crown games, Theógnētos at Olympía (P.8.36), Kleitómakhos at the Isthmós (P.8.37). Aristoménēs himself had an impressive record of victories in games at Mégara, Marathón, and Aígina (P.8.78–80). Porphyríōn (P.8.12) is the "king of Gígantes" (P.8.17). Prophetic language, as Píndaros acknowledges when he labels Amphiáraos' speech as "enigmatic prophecy" (P.8.39–40), is often coded. Where Amphiáraos says that Alkmaíōn "drives / the serpent with marbled scales on his gleaming shield" (P.8.46–7), the serpent is a decoration embossed on Alkmaíōn's shield; the metonymy focalizes the audience's attention on the visual art. The "former loss" (P.8.48) is Ádrastos' first, failed expedition to Thébai, the subject of the Seven Against Thébai mythology. Prophets interpreted bird flight to divine the gods' will, so that "a better bird of omen" (P.49–50) signals better fortune for Ádrastos in his second campaign against Thébai. Although he leads his forces safely back to Árgos after the battle, he suffers the loss of his son Aigialeús (P.8.51–5). Píndaros claims to have encountered the son of Amphiáraos, Alkmaíōn, whom the poet embraces as his neighbor and protector of his property (P.8.56–60). Unless the mythological hero's epiphany actually occurred, this meeting is imaginative, aligning the poet and poetics of *Pythian 8* with a tradition of prophetic poetry. Píndaros sings of Alkmaíōn's "hereditary art of prophecy" (P.8.60), a gift inherited from his father Amphiáraos, whom the god of prophecy, Apóllōn, cherished. Píndaros attends (P.8.61–6) to Apóllōn's central importance at the religious sanctuary of Delphoí and his contribution of the péntathlon to games at Aígina ("here at home"). The second-person plural possessive adjective in the phrase "your festivals" (P.8.66) refers to the siblings Apóllōn and Ártemis, in honor of whom Aígina held a festival called the Delphínia. In the subsequent prayer (P.8.67–9), Píndaros again links his art with Apóllōn, a god of music, poetry, and prophecy. The poet invests the conclusion of *Pythian 8* with existential contemplation.

    kindhearted Hēsykhía   Strophe A (Lines 1–7)
        daughter of Díkē
            you
who amplify cities
        who hold the powerful keys
for deliberation and warfare
        welcome the honor
of Aristoménēs' victory at Pythó
        you know
how to both engender and enjoy gentleness
with unerring attunement to the moment

but whenever someone lodges relentless rage　　　　　Antistrophe A (Lines 8–14)
deep in their heart
　　　you ruthlessly confront the force
of fierce enemies
　　　　　and plunge their violence
　　　　　　　　into the bilge
Porphyríōn failed to grasp your might
　　　　　when his hostile
provocations trespassed against destiny
　　　　　gain
would be most gladly gotten
　　　　　if we obtain
it from the home of a giver ready to share

strength eventually brings　　　　　　　　　　　　Epode A (Lines 15–20)
　　　　　even the loudest
braggart down
　　　　　Kilikía's hundredheaded
Typhós did not escape it—
　　　　　nor the king
of Gígantes
　　　　　thunderbolt
　　　　　　　　and Apóllōn's arrows
destroyed them
　　　　　and it was Apóllōn
　　　　　　　　who warmly welcomed
from Kírrha Xenárkēs' son crowned with leafgreen
from Parnassós
　　　　　with a Dorian victory parade

the island home　　　　　　　　　　　　　　　　Strophe B (Lines 21–27)
　　　　　of a lawful city
　　　　　　　　that latches
onto the illustrious character of the Aiakídai
its lot did not fall out far from the Khárites:
　　　　　Aígina
possesses perfected glory from its origins
and is a thing of song
　　　　　because it fostered
heroes who prevail in untold victory-
awarding competitions
　　　　　in hectic battle

Aígina's greatness is also due to its men   Antistrophe B (Lines 28–34)
I have no idle hours to pledge a prolix
sermon to lyre and liquid voice
      for fear
that tedium may set in
      and rankle listeners
but let my present duty to you go speeding
ahead
      my boy
            this latest of your beautiful
endeavors wingborne with my poetry machine

tracking the wrestling trail blazed by your mother's   Epode B (Lines 35–40)
brothers
      you do not tarnish Theógnētos' victory
at Olympía
      do not discredit the limbbold
victory of Kleitómakhos
      at the Isthmós
by making the house of the Meidylídai thrive
      you prove
the enigmatic prophecy
      that the son of Oiklés
once revealed
      when he saw the sons stand
            their ground
with spears in hand at sevengated Thébai

when the Epígonoi journeyed from Árgos   Strophe C (Lines 41–47)
      to launch
a second campaign
      as they clashed he said this:
            "sons
display by nature the birthright resolve
      of their fathers
I behold him clearly
      Alkmaíōn—
            he drives
the serpent with marbled scales on his gleaming shield
at the battle's front
      before the gates of Kádmos

he who struggled in the face of former loss—   Antistrophe C (Lines 48–54)
a better bird of omen's declaration
now entangles him
    the hero Ádrastos
his family's affairs will turn out otherwise:
although the only one among the band
of Danaoí to gather his dead son's bones
    through godwilled
fortune
    he will return with his troops
        unscathed

to Ábas' broad streets"   Epode C (Lines 55–60)
    these were the predictions
        Amphiáraos
chanted
    I happily deck Alkmaíōn
        with garlands
and shower him with praisesong
    because as neighbor
and watchman of my belongings
    he met me when I
travelled toward earth's often sung omphalós
then summoned his hereditary art
    of prophecy

you   Strophe D (Lines 61–67)
    Farshooter Apóllōn
        who oversee
the celebrated temple
    in Pythó's valley
        that welcomes
all of Hellás—you
    bestowed there
        the greatest joy
and here at home
    you one time brought
        the gift
that people yearn to relish
    during your festivals
the péntathlon
    lord
        with reverent mind I pray

to set my sights
        upon the bonds
                between us
in every verse I venture
        Díkē stands
beside the melodious victory parade
        I seek
the gods' ungrudging goodwill
        for your family's
fortunes
        Xenárkēs
                if someone gains good things
without persistent toil
        they seem to many
people to be wise among the mindless

                                                Antistrophe D (Lines 68–74)

seem to arm their life with
        shrewd forethought
                but good
things are not ready to hand for men
        a god
provides
        one moment with a takedown
                another
with a stronghold—
        a god makes a mortal
                submit
to moderation
        at Mégara
                you have glory's
prize
        in lowlands of Marathón
                and with three
victories
        Aristoménēs
                you prevailed in Aígina's
games in honor of Héra
        thanks to your grit

                                                Epode D (Lines 75–80)

plotting their downfall
        you pounced on four bodies
                to whom
the games at Pythó

                                                Strophe E (Lines 81–87)

    did not award a homeward
return as sunny as yours
    and when they reached
their mothers' sides
    no warm laughter kindled gratitude
bitten by misfortune
    they keep their distance
from rivals and slink
    along the alleyways

whoever lights upon the lot   Antistrophe E (Lines 88–94)
    of some beautiful
new thing
    in a moment rife
      with luxury
soars on the strength of hope with virtue's wings
because they aspire for something that surpasses
wealth
    the pleasure mortals enjoy
      will instantly
grow
    but just as quickly
      pleasure jolted
by wayward judgment crashes
    into the dirt

we live as if   Epode E (Lines 95–100)
    for a single day
      what is
a someone?
    what is a no one?
      a human creature
is shadow's dream
    but whenever Zeusgiven
      splendor
comes
    daybright radiance
      and a tranquil lifetime
abide among men
    beloved Mother Aígina
protect this city on its voyage toward freedom—

you
>together with Zeus
>>and regal Aiakós
and Pēleús and worthy Telamón
>and with Akhilleús

PYTHIAN 9

Telesikrátēs of Kyrḗnē | Footrace in Armor | 474 BCE

Píndaros composed this song for another athlete from the North African city Kyrḗnē (see *Pythian 4* and *Pythian 5*). In Píndaros' geography (P.9.7–8), the earth's three "roots," or continents, are Europe, Asia, and Africa, which is the "third root" (P.9.8). Ancient Héllēnes were unaware of other continents. I translate *ápeiros* as "land with no limit" (P.9.8) in order to capture the radical and metaphorical connotation of a word that is reasonably translated as "continent" or "mainland": a landscape neither crowded with mountains and nor hemmed by seashores is unbounded compared to the lands of Hellás, which are craggy and never far from the sea. The main mythological narrative (P.9.5–69) and the shorter, concluding narrative about Telesikrátēs' ancestor Alexídamos (P.9.105–25) establish marriage as a dominant theme.

The nýmphē and eponymous heroine Kyrḗnē prefers weapons with which she might kill wild predators harassing her father's livestock to weaving indoors and enjoying gatherings with other young women (P.9.18–25). These qualities captivate Apóllōn. Kheírōn playfully points out the irony of omniscient Apóllōn inquiring of him whether to pursue Kyrḗnē or not, but the kéntauros willingly reveals the future to the god of prophecy. Kheírōn thus predicts the foundation of the city Kyrḗnē when Apóllōn brings the nýmphē Kyrḗnē from Pélion in Thessalía to Libýē—future events relative to the mythological past, relative to the present of *Pythian 9*'s performance, past events. A denizen of mountain wilderness, Kheírōn lived in a cave, which Píndaros calls (P.9.29) a *mégaron* (palace), the term Hómēros regularly applies to a hero's impressive house. Zeus' garden (P.9.53–5) refers to the cult site in Libýē where Zeus was honored as Zeus Ámmon. Píndaros names the populace of Kyrḗnē "people from the island" (P.9.55) to recall the colonization of Libýē by emigrants from Thḗra (cf. *Pythian 4*). Aristaíos, son of Apóllōn and Kyrḗnē, is a hero of the land (P.9.63–5). According to various accounts, the Moúsai taught him healing, prophecy, agriculture, apiculture, and viticulture. His relationships with the Moúsai, the Hórai (P.9.60), and Gaía (P.9.60) mirror Píndaros' conflation of Aristaíos with his father Apóllōn: Agreús (the hunter) and Nómios (the herder) (P.9.65) are epithets of Apóllōn that also capture the rural quality of Aristaíos' kind of heroism. The "most beautiful city" is Kyrḗnē (P.9.69–70). Ancient sources report that Telesikrátēs was victorious in local games at Thḗbai held in honor of Iólaos. This may explain why the mythology of Thḗbai (P.9.79–88) appears in this song. Another explanation for Píndaros' attention to this mythology is that to thread stories about Kyrḗnē's foundation and Theban stories into the same poem forges links between the poet, who claimed Thḗbai as his homeland, and athlete. Iólaos (P.9.79) was the grandson of Amphitrýōn (P.9.81), natural father of Iphiklés, father of Iólaos, and adoptive, mortal father of Hēraklés. Amphitrýōn emigrated from Árgos to Thḗbai, so that he was "the guest of the Spartoí" (P.9.82) in the sense that the people of Thḗbai, descendants of the Spartoí, welcomed him. Alkmḗnē slept with Zeus and Amphitrýōn on the same day, conceiving Iphiklés with Amphitrýōn and Hēraklés with Zeus (P.9.84–6). Aígina (P.9.90) hosted local games, where it seems Telesikrátēs enjoyed success. Nísos (P.9.91) was a legendary king of Mégara, and the "hill of Nísos" is a toponym for the site at Mégara where local games were held. Nēreús is the Old Man of the Sea (P.9.94). The games cited next in the poem (P.9.101-3) are local to Kyrḗnē, including the "Olympian games" (P.9.101), which are not to be confused with the crown games at Olympía. The person—"some man" (P.9.103)—who inspires Píndaros to compose poetry is Telesikrátēs.

The compelling explorations of the power of art (P.9.76-9) and other luminous moments in *Pythian 9* do not mitigate the disturbing mythological representations of Apóllōn's desire to seize Kyrḗnē (P.9.36-7)—is Kheírōn not coyly admonishing the god, particularly with the oxymoronic phrase "gentle fury" (P.9.38-43)?—and of the daughter-bride as a prize and as ripe fruit ready for harvest, a violent sexual metaphor (P.9.105-25), for the man who out-competes other men. We might understand athletic competition from an indigenous Hellenic point of view as a legitimate means for a father to discern the nobility and promise of wealth and communal prominence of a prospective son-in-law, but since such legitimacy entails traumatizing suppression of female agency, it incriminates the prestige of nobility, wealth, and leadership. Although mythological and, therefore representational, this depiction of patriarchal ideology is nearer to rather than distant from historical reality. The poem concludes with celebration rendered as at once victory parade and marriage procession. By broadcasting the marriage-ready qualities of Telesikrátēs, *Pythian 9* is an *epiníkion* that dovetails with epithalamion.

I herald the bronzeshield victor at Pythó—   Strophe A (Lines 1–8)
    beside me
the Khárites with belts slung hipheight—
    and readily sing
for Telesikrátēs a man whom fortune favors
    the crown
of horsedriving Kyrḗnē
    whom the son of Lētó
his hair in waves
    abducted from Pélion's windthroated
ridges
    he carried the wilderness virgin off
on his golden chariot deck
    to where he installed her
as sovereign of flockrich and cropthick country
        to inhabit
the third root
    an abundant
        alluring land with no limit

but silversandaled Aphrodítē   Antistrophe A (Lines 9–16)
    welcomed the lord
of Délos as her guest
    guiding his godwrought
chariot with her deft touch
    she instilled in them
a reverent desire
    for the wedding bed's sweetness
and joined them in intimate mutual marriage
    god
and girl
    daughter of mighty Hypseús
        a hero
second in descent from Ōkeanós
    at that time
the king of overproud Lapíthai in Píndos'
famous valleys
    after the naiad basked
in the bed of Pēneiós,
    Kréousa daughter of Gaía

mothered Hypseús   Epode A (Lines 17–25)
    he cared for his child Kyrḗnē
whose arms were graceful
    she loved
        neither the back-and-forth
trudge of loomwork
    nor the delights of dining
with her female companions indoors
    but bronzetipped
javelins and sword in hand
    she fiercely slaughtered
wild game and furnished her father's cattle
with steady untroubled peace
    briefly sharing sleep's
sweet company
    that settles upon the eyelids
        at sunrise

Farworker Apóllōn   Strophe B (Lines 26–33)
    who carries a hefty quiver
happened to find her
    wrestling a ferocious lion

alone
        without a weapon
                and straight to Kheírōn
Apóllōn called him from his palace and spoke:
"leave your holy cave
        son of Philýra
                and let
the wonder of a woman's
        bravery and prowess
possess you
        such a battle she wages
                her nerve
unshaken
        a girl with heart unbent by adversity
wintery fear has not stormed her mind
        what human
fathered her?
        broken off from what family tree

does she come to know the secluded nooks   Antistrophe B (Lines 34–41)
of shadedrenched mountains
        to savor unbounded fortitude?
does it conform to laws of gods to lay
my glorious hand upon her
        to pluck lovemaking's
honeysweet foliage?"
        the mantic kéntauros laughed
as tenderly as a sapling
        with a face
of kindness and was quick to answer the god
with insight
        "wise Peithó's keys to sacred love
Phoíbos
        are hidden away
                both gods and humans
hesitate to clinch the sweetness of another's
bed for the first time before the eyes of all

gentle fury drove you—   Epode B (Lines 42–50)
        and it defies
gods' laws for you to breach the truth—
        to pose
your questions slyly

                    you ask about the girl's
family origins
            do you Lord
                        you who know
the established end of everything
            know every pathway?
how many springtime leaves the earth sends up
how many sandgrains surf and windgusts swirl
in ocean currents and rivers
            what the future
brings
            from where it will come to be—
                        you behold
all this
            if I must match the god of wisdom

I will speak   Strophe C (Lines 51–58)
            you came to this wooded valley
to be her husband and are going to carry her
across the sea to the breathtaking garden of Zeus
there you will establish her as a city's
ruler after you assemble people
from the island on the hill surrounded
by fields
            majestic Libýē with sweeping meadows
will soon—and gladly—welcome your glorious bride
in her goldwashed home
            she will immediately endow
Kyrénē with an allotment of land to keep
as her traditional domain
            a land neither without
its bounty of flora bearing every sort
of fruit
            nor unknown to wild creatures

in her new homeland   Antistrophe C (Lines 59–66)
            Kyrénē will give birth
to a boy
            whom glorious Hermés
                        will take from the arms
of his beloved mother
            and bring to the Hórai
with stately thrones

                    and to Gaía
                              what a sight
that newborn on their knees—
          they will trickle nectar
and ambrosia on his lips
          and make him deathless
a Zeus a holy Apóllōn
          a joy to men
he cherishes, the most nearby companion of sheepflocks
called by some Agreús or Nómios
          by others
Aristaíos"
          Kheírōn spoke and urged Apóllōn
to bring his marriage to delightful fruition

the action of gods who move with purpose is swift   Epode C (Lines 67–75)
their journeys brief
          that one day was decisive
they stirred their bodies together in Libýē's bedroom
made all of gold
          where Libýē tends a most beautiful
city famous for athletic contests
now in sacred Pythó
          the son of Karneiádas
unites it with fortune that flowers forth
          his victory
there proclaimed Kyrénē
          who will happily
welcome him to his homeland with lovely women
because he brought from Delphoí yearned-for glory

outstanding achievements are   Strophe D (Lines 76–83)
          always worthy
                    of wordlush
stories
          it is a spectacle of sound
                    when poets
adorn the everyday
          with transcendent art
attunement to the moment
          likewise attains
the height of every terrain
          sevengated

Thébai knew
> that Iólaos did not
>> disdain
this creed
> after he slew the head of Eurystheús
with swordedge
> they buried Iólaos
>> beneath the earth
in chariotdriving Amphitrýōn's tomb
> where his father's
father reposed
> guest of Spartoí
>> when he moved
abroad to the streets
> of Kádmos' brighthorse people

Alkménē with a mind of fire stirred   Antistrophe D (Lines 84–91)
her limbs with him and Zeus
> then in a single
bout of birthpangs
> she bore the battleready
strength of two sons
> any man
>> who does not
throw his voice around the shoulders of Hēraklés
who fails to always remember Dírkē's waters
which fostered him and Iphiklés—
> such a man lacks
attunement
> I vow to sing in celebration
of those heroes
> when I enjoy the fulfillment
of some good thing in answer to my prayer
may the purified brightness of the echoing
Khárites not leave me
> I tell how three times
>> at Aígina
on the Hill of Nísos
> Telesikrátēs exalted
>> this city

and by my act of song   Epode D (Lines 92–100)
> I evade a forlorn

silence
> let no one therefore
>> whether a friendly
neighbor or some adversary
> bury
the fruit of toil on behalf of the common good
by wounding the Old Man of the Sea's injunction:
he said praise even an enemy
> if he performs feats
of beauty with passion and uprightly
> they watched you
win commandingly in annual festivals
for Pallás
> and each girl silently prayed
>> that you
might be her beloved husband or son
> Telesikrátēs

victorious in Olympian games   Strophe E (Lines 101–108)
> in games
for deeply rippled Gaía
> in every local
contest
> some man renders me
>> dutybound
to quench the thirst for songs
> to awaken once more
the ancient glory of his forebears
> like those
who traveled to the city of Írasa
> a woman
in Libýē their aspiration
> suitors for marriage
to Antaíos' distinguished daughter with lovely
hair
> whom many honored kinsmen sought
and many foreigners too
> her beauty
>> a wonder

to behold   Antistrophe E (Lines 109–116)
> they longed to harvest
>> the ripe fruit

of her goldcrowned Hébē
	sowing the seeds
of a more illustrious marriage for his daughter
her father heard
	that Danaós in Árgos one time
discovered how to settle hurried marriages
for forty-eight virgin daughters
	before midday
he hastily arranged the whole khorós of them
at the finish line for a competition
	and ordered
the many would-be grooms
	who came
		to decide
by footrace
	which daughter each hero
		would have as his wife

with the same manner of matchmaking   Epode E (Lines 117–125)
	Antaíos
of Libýē gave his daughter a husband
	he clothed
her in lovely garments
	stood her at the finish
line as the lofty goal
	and told the gathered
men that whoever sprinted fastest and touched
her robes first would bring her
	home as his wife
		and then
Alexídamos—
	he outsped the flying racers—
		her hand
in his
	he took the admired maiden
		and led her
through a crowd of horseriding Nomads
	they rained down
upon them armfuls of leaves and garlands
	heaps
of winglike victory crowns he had won before then

PYTHIAN 10

Hippokléas of Thessalía | Boys' Díaulos | 498 BCE

Pythian 10 is Píndaros' earliest extant *epiníkion* if the song's 498 BCE date is correct. Hippokléas' father Phrikías twice won at Olympía in the race in armor, once at Delphoí (P.10.12–16). The unnamed god (P.10.33) is Apóllōn. Perseús, son of Zeus and Danáē, killed Médousa, whose head he carried back to Sériphos, his island home, to punish Polydéktēs who had detained Danáē by force. Píndaros also treats Perseús' murder of Médousa (P.10.44–8) in *Pythian 12*. "The islanders" (P.10.47) are the people of Sériphos. Hospitality, harnessing the Pierídes chariot, friendship (P.10.64–6)—this is how Píndaros images the role of Thórax, member of the Aleuádai from Lárisa in Thessalía, in commissioning *Pythian 10* on behalf of Hippokléas. The brothers Thórax, Eurýpylos, and Thrasydaíos (P.10.69–72) joined Mardónios of Persia at the Battle of Plátaia in 479 BCE (Hēródotos 9.58).

Lakedaímōn abounds   Strophe A (Lines 1–6)
    and blessed is Thessalía
        from one
father
    the line of battlebest Hēraklés rules
both lands
    why do I boast
        without restraint?
but no
    Pythó and Pelinnaíon
        summon me
and the sons of Aleúas
    who want to bring Hippokléas
a parade of voices
    men to glorify him

  he savors competition   Antistrophe A (Lines 7–12)
      before a crowd
  of its neighbors, the valley of Parnassós declared
      him supreme
  among the boys
      who ran the díaulos
         Apóllōn
  the human end
      and human beginning
        sweetly

grow when god drives them
        onward
                he doubtless achieved this
through your visionary invention
        and walked
the path of his family line
        in his father's foottracks

twotime victor at Olympía in Árēs'   Epode A (Lines 13–18)
armor that bears war's brunt
        the ordeal in plush
meadows below Kírrha's rocks
        made Phrikías prevail
with his feet
        I hope good fortune attends them
                in days
to come
        so their almighty abundance
                blooms

now that they have gained   Strophe B (Lines 19–24)
        the unmeager gift
of delight in Hellás as their lot
        I hope they do not
stumble onto setbacks
        because the gods
are jealous
        may the heart of god be unhurt
whoever earns the greatest prizes
        through boldness
and muscle
        because he won
                with armstrength or footspeed
becomes the favored subject
        of poets' praisesongs—

and whoever   Antistrophe B (Lines 25–30)
        while yet alive
                sees his young son gather
garlands at Pythó
        according to god's
decree
        the bronzeclad sky
                will never be his

to climb
>   as much splendor
>   as we mortalkind
attain
>   he journeys to the farthest destination
neither by ship nor by foot would you discover
the dazzling route
>   to the company of Hyperbóreoi

once upon a time   Epode B (Lines 31–36)
>   the people's leader
Perseús
>   attended their public feast
>   he entered
their homes
>   and found them lavishly
>   offering one hundred
slaughtered donkeys
>   in honor of the god
their neverending festivity
>   and words of worship
make Apóllōn overjoyed
>   and he laughs
when he sees those creatures arrogantly bray

the Moúsa does not wander   Strophe C (Lines 37–42)
>   far from their ways
khoroí of girls
>   lyre voices
>   and boisterous
auloí thrum everywhere
>   hair bound with goldlit
bayleaf
>   the Hyperbóreoi gather
>   in joyful revelry
neither disease
>   nor grim old age
>   dilutes
that holy people
>   with no toil
>   no conflict

  they make their home there   Antistrophe C (Lines 43–48)
    and evade the rigid justice
of Némesis
    breathing in life with bold heart
      the son
of Danáē one time visited—
    Athēná his escort—
that crowd of fortunate men
    he slew the Gorgó
and brought back her head
    which rippled with snaky curls
a stone death for the islanders
    nothing ever

appears to be   Epode C (Lines 49–54)
    so beyond belief
      that I
am stunned if gods perform it
    stay the oar
and lower from the prow
    quick! the anchor
      sink it
in earth
    defense against the bristly-backed reef
the greatest praisesongs for victory processions flit
like a honeybee
    from one thought
      to another

because of his victory crowns   Strophe D (Lines 55–60)
    I hope with song's power
to render Hippokléas still more a work of wonder
in the eyes of his agemates and elders
    to make him lovely
to unwedded girls
    when Ephyraíoi sweetly
pour my voice out along the banks of Pēneiós
yes different desires
    nettle human hearts

whoever reaches   Antistrophe D (Lines 61–66)
    what they strive for
      should greedily

attend what lies at their feet
      for what may happen
one year hence
      foresight has no map
           I trust
in the warmth of Thórax's welcome
      with his breathless
haste on my behalf
      he yokes this fourhorse
chariot of the Pierídes
      shows affection
toward his friend
      and gladly guides his guide

when put to the test   Epode D (Lines 67–72)
      gold makes its conspicuous mark
on the touchstone
      likewise: an upright mind
           we will praise
his outstanding brothers too
      because they sustain
and amplify
      the ways of the Thessaloí
           worthy men
belong at the prized inherited helm of cities

PYTHIAN 11

Thrasydaíos of Thébai | Boys' Stádion | 474 BCE

In addition to celebrating the success of Thrasydaíos, whose victory appears to have been his family's third (P.11.14), *Pythian 11* recalls that the athlete's father Pythónikos was victorious at Pythó (P.11.14 and 43–50), as his very name—"winner at Pythó"—declares. Apóllōn christened his temple at Thébai, a "storehouse for golden tripods" (P.11.4–5), as the Isménion in honor of Ismēnós, his son with Melía. Oréstēs' nurse Arsinóē rescued him from imminent murder at the hands of his mother Klytaimnéstra, who avenged the death of her daughter Iphigéneia by killing her husband Agamémnōn and the Trojan prophetess Kassándra, Agamémnōn's war prize, upon his return home after the Trojan War (P.11.17–25). Klytaimnéstra plotted to kill her son Oréstēs to ensure that he could not avenge his father's murder. Píndaros gives Amýklai (P.11.31–4) as Agamémnōn's home (in other accounts, his home was Mykḗnai or Árgos). The father of Pyládēs, Stróphios (P.11.35–6), was king of Phōkís, the region where Delphoí is located. When he reached adulthood, Oréstēs exacted retribution for Agamémnōn's murder by killing Klytaimnéstra and her lover Aígisthos (P.11.36–7). Where he interrupts the flow of storytelling (P.11.38–40), the "straight route" from which Píndaros wandered is the song's celebratory occasion and function. Mythology sidetracked him.

    daughters of Kádmos   Strophe A (Lines 1–5)
        Semélē
                neighbor to goddesses
of Ólympos
        and Inó Leukothéa
                you who share
the corridors of sea with Nērēídes
        go
alongside Hēraklés' bestborn mother to Melía
to the storehouse for goldsmithed tripods
        the inner
sanctum that Loxías honored
        beyond all others

    that he consecrated to Ismēnós   Antistrophe A (Lines 6–10)
        truthtelling seat
of soothsayers
        you daughters of Harmonía
                where Loxías
now invites the country's
        assembly of heroines

to join together
> so that at the brink
>> of evening
you may sing out
> in celebration of sacred
Thémis Pythó and the omphalós
> earth's upright judge

a song to grace both sevengated Thébai   Epode A (Lines 11–16)
and Kírrha's contest
> where Thrasydaíos made
his fathers' hearth
> worthy to remember
>> when he
wreathed it a third time
> by winning
>> in the wealthladen
fields of Pyládēs
> friend of Lakōniké's Oréstēs

whom Arsinóē his nurse   Strophe B (Lines 17–21)
> delivered from deathknell
treachery
> at the mighty hands
>> of Klytaimnéstra
after his father's murder
> when with her knifeblade
the woman ruthlessly shipped
> Dárdanos' descendant
>> daughter
of Príamos
> Kassándra
>> to Akhérōn's gloomthick shore

together with Agamémnōn's soul   Antistrophe B (Lines 22–26)
> was Iphigéneia's
cut throat at Eúripos
> far from her homeland
>> the wound
that stirred Klytaimnéstra's unbearable rage?
> Or did
lovemaking at night delude her into wearing
the bridle of another man's bed?

                such a fault
in young wives is loathsome
                and no machinery conceals it:

the tongues of others fly   Epode B (Lines 27–32)
                and townspeople gossip
viciously
                good fortune finds
                                no meager envy
but someone with earthy aspirations roars
unseen
                when he at long last
                                reached renowned
Amýklai
                that hero Atrëídēs perished
                                and wrought

ruin for the soothsayer girl   Strophe C (Lines 33–37)
                after he
unburdened the Tróes' torched halls of their opulence
because of Helénē
                his child Oréstēs journeyed
to Stróphios
                a welcoming elder
                                who lived at the foot
of Parnassós
                but with the help
                                of eventual Árēs
he murdered his mother
                and plunged Aígisthos
                                into bloodshed

I reeled   Antistrophe C (Lines 38–42)
                my friends
                                where three paths cross
                though at first
I followed the straight route
                did some windgust pitch
me off course
                like a rowboat at sea?
                                if you
agreed Moúsa to sell
                your silverminted voice

your task is to spur
        it on from verse
                to verse

whether at this moment   Epode C (Lines 43–48)
        for his father
Pythónikos
        or for Thrasydaíos—
                their happiness and glory
burn bright
        the beautiful champions
                of chariot racing
long ago earned
        through their horses' power
                a bolt
of radiance at Olympía's illustrious games—

and at Pythó   Strophe D (Lines 49–53)
        when they ventured
                the naked footprint
they humbled the people of Hellás
        with their speed
                may I yearn
for the beauty that comes from gods
        seeking what is
possible for my stage in life
        because I
find that a city's middle ranks
        flourish with more
abiding abundance
        I condemn the curse
                of tyranny

I strain every nerve for virtues a city shares   Antistrophe D (Lines 54–58)
this fends off spiteful men
        but if anyone who
attains the height
        and lives in peace
                escapes
from dreadful outrage
        he would reach a frontier
                more beautiful
than death's gloom

>   by leaving his beloved children
> the aura of honor as their greatest possession

this spreads Iólaos' fame   Epode D (Lines 59–64)
            that son of Iphiklés
worthy of praisesong
            and Kástōr's might
                        and you royal
Polydeúkēs
            you sons of gods
                        who dwell one day
at Therápnē
            your resting place
                        the next on Ólympos

PYTHIAN 12

Mídas of Akrágas | Aulós Competition | 490 BCE

Pythian 12 is Píndaros' only *epiníkion* that celebrates achievement in a musical contest, Mídas' 490 BCE victory at Delphoí in the performance of the ancient Hellenic wind instrument called the aulós (plural, auloí), a kind of double flute, with two reeds joined at a bronze mouthpiece. Akrágas, Mídas' hometown, is the second-person addressee in the hymnic opening to *Pythian 12*. The song's mythological narrative to the victory it celebrates. Píndaros describes how Athēná invented the aulós in order to imitate the shrill lament of the Gorgónes Euryálē and Sthenó (Píndaros does not name the latter) over the death of their sister Médousa at the hands of Perseús. Phórkys (P.12.13) is the father of the Gorgónes and the Graíai, the three sisters who shared one eye, which Perseús stole in order to then barter it for information about how to find the Gorgónes. In response to an oracle that a son of his daughter Danáē would kill him, Akrísios locked Danáē away. Zeus appeared as a shower of gold and in that form had sex with Danáē. When he discovered the birth of the child resulting from this, Akrísios confined Danáē and her infant son Perseús in a chest, which he then cast into the sea. The pair came ashore at Sériphos, where Danáē sought refuge and Polydéktēs contracted a ruthless infatuation for her. To remove any potential obstacle to his designs, Polydéktēs sent the Perseús in quest of Médousa's head. With the help of Athēná, Perseús accomplished this task and returned to Sériphos, where he turned people to stone (P.12.6–12) and punished Polydéktēs (P.12.14–17). "The Khárites' city" (P.12.26) is Orkhomenós and "the daughter of Kēphisós" (P.12.27) is Kōpäís.

    splendorloving city   Strophe A (Lines 1–8)
        I pray to you
    most beautiful city among mortals
        Persephónē's home
    you inhabit
        the firmbuilt hilltop
            along the banks
of Akrágas
        where sheepflocks graze
            O Queen
    you who
are ardently kind to deathless gods and men
accept this garland from Pythó
        with Mídas decked
in glory
        and welcome him home
            the man who vanquished

Hellás with music
>   once upon a time
Pallás Athēná invented his art
>   she wove
together the deadly dirge of reckless Gorgónes

Athēná listened   Strophe B (Lines 9–16)
>   as two unwedded creatures
with menacing snakehaired heads
>   poured out their lament
toiling with grief
>   when Perseús battlecried
ruin for a third
>   their sister
>   bringing doom
to seabathed Sériphos
>   and its people
>   Perseús
blotted out
>   the awekindling children
>   of Phórkys
then turned his mother's
>   longlasting slavery
>   and forced bed
into Polydéktēs' mournful meal
>   the son
of Danáē plundered Médousa's gladcheeked head

we know the story   Strophe C (Lines 17–24)
>   flowing gold fathered him
but after the unwed goddess delivered the man
she cherished from these labors
>   she invented
the allvoiced melody of auloí
>   when she replicated
with tools of music
>   the clanging wail
>   that spilled
from Euryálē's strained cheeks
>   goddess invents the aulós
Athēná created it
>   for mortal men
>   to own

she named it the musical mode
      of multiple heads
celebrated summons for people
      to gather at games

this music again and again   Strophe D (Lines 25–32)
      escapes
            through leafthin
bronze
      and reeds that live
            in the Khárites' city
of beautiful dancing
      in the sacred grounds
of the daughter of Kēphisós
      faithful witnesses to dancers
if any happiness exists for humans
      without toil
it does not come into view
      a numinous power
achieves it this very day—
      a fated thing
is unavoidable—
      but there will be a time
that unexpectedly strikes someone
      then grants
one gift beyond understanding
      but another
            not yet

NEMEANS

NEMEAN 1

Khromíos of Syrákousai and Aítna | Chariot Race | 476 (?) BCE

Nemean 1 and *Nemean 9* commemorate chariot race victories of Khromíos, the powerful general of Hiérōn, tyrant of Syrákousai. Píndaros presents a clever and mutually complementary analogy (N.1.25-8), according to Bury: Khromíos is to Hēraklés as Píndaros is to Teiresías. In that case, *phué* "nature" (N.1.25) points to Khromíos' strength and to Píndaros' mind. An elaboration follows: "strength acts in the sphere of deeds" (N.1.26) applies to Khromíos and "the mind [acts] in the sphere of advice" (N.1.27) to Píndaros, who ultimately credits Khromíos with both physical strength and mental gifts (N.1.29-30). The mythology of *Nemean 1* is a résumé of Hēraklés' career. Píndaros situates Teiresías, the blind seer of Thébai, in the episode when two snakes sent by Héra infiltrate the bed of the newborn hero and his brother Iphiklés. After the infant Hēraklés overcomes this lethal threat by strangling the snakes with his bare hands, Teiresías is there to prophesy Hēraklés' future greatness and apotheosis. The phrase "the gods / undying rendered messengers' tales falsehoods for him" (N.1.58-9) implies that Amphitrýōn had heard (incorrect) news of his son's demise. The unnamed villain whom Hēraklés would slay may be Antaíos (N.1.64-6).

    sacred outflow of Alpheiós' waters   Strophe A (Lines 1–7)
        Ortygía
    treebranch of famous Syrákousai
        bed of Ártemis
Délos' sister
        sweetversed praisesong gushes
forth from you
        to lavishly portray the story
of stormswift horsehooves
        a tribute for Zeus of Aítna
Khromíos' chariot and Neméa move me to yoke
this display of song to feats
        that result
                in victory

we have laid down the foundation for our song   Antistrophe A (Lines 8–14)
in honor of gods
    in honor of that man's
godgifted courage
    the height of immaculate glory
exists in fortune's realm
    the Moúsa enjoys
the memory of outstanding competitions
sow now some splendor
    for this island that Ólympos'
lord granted Persephónē
    he shook the hair of his head
as a yes to her
    that he would make Sikelía cropfat

supreme upon fruitbearing earth   Epode A (Lines 15–18)
    the wealth
of its cities unmatched
    and Krónos' son bestowed
upon the island
    a horseriding people
        that courts
bronzeclad war
    a people he often garlanded
with goldlit leaves of Olympía's olivetrees
with no shock of falsehood I have fallen
into step with this moment for so much poetry

I stood at the courtyard threshold of a man   Strophe B (Lines 19–25)
who is good to guests
    I sang in celebration
of beautiful things there
    where he arranged for me
a lavish feast
    where the rooms are never empty
of guests from other lands
    he has enjoyed the lot
in life of friends ready to bring water's answer to smoke
when others slander him
    every person owns
their own skills
    but it is right for anyone
        who plies
straight paths to strive according to their nature

         strength acts in the sphere of deeds   Antistrophe B (Lines 26–32)
                   the mind in the sphere
of advice from those whom the birthgift foresight
              of what
will be attends
                   Hagēsídamos' son
                             the sweep
of your ways embraces both domains
              I have no
desire to bury a pile of wealth in a palace
and keep it there
                   but to be happy with what
I have and to hear something kind because I help
my friends
                   they come to everyone, the hopes

of men who toil long hours   Epode B (Lines 33–36)
              I cling to Hēraklés
among the headiest heights of prowess
              and waken
that old story:
              as soon as the son of Zeus fled
from birthpains
              then appeared with his twin brother
                        out from
his mother's womb
              into the wonderous daylight radiance—

the story that he did not escape   Strophe C (Lines 37–43)
              goldenthroned Héra's
notice
              while he was still wrapped
                        in saffron layers
but in the heat of her anger
              the queen of the gods
dispatched two serpents
              with no delay they slid through
the opened doorway
              into the bedroom's innermost
nook on the hunt to wrap their snapping jaws
around the newborn boys
              but Hēraklés raised his head
alert

           and dared to do battle
                for the first time

he seized the two snakes' necks   Antistrophe C (Lines 44–50)
     with two inescapable
hands
         time forced the strangled beasts
              to breathe out
last life from their dreadful bodycoils
unbearable fear shocked the women
         who were at Alkménē's
bedside to help her give birth
         but her—she rushed
to her feet
         up from her bed
             still unrobed and in spite
of that
         fended off
             the monstrous creatures' violence

the leaders of Kádmos' people sped to the scene   Epode C (Lines 51–54)
altogether
         ready in bronze armor
              and Amphitrýōn arrived
wielding in his hand
     a sword stripped of its sheath
barbwired torment stunned him
         one's own worries
weigh on everyone the same
         but the heart is soon
freed from burdens over another's troubles

Amphitrýōn stood there   Strophe D (Lines 55–61)
     a welter of parental
pride and painful shock
         he witnessed his son's
such extraordinary resolve and power
         the gods
undying rendered messengers' tales
         falsehoods
for him
         Amphitrýōn summoned his neighbor
             the highest

prophet of mosthigh Zeus
        the unerring soothsayer
Teiresías
        and he told Amphitrýōn
                told the people
gathered there
        what great fortunes Hēraklés
                would meet

how many creatures he would slay on land   Antistrophe D (Lines 62–68)
        how many
lawless creatures killed on open sea
        Teiresías
said that Hēraklés would inflict death upon a worse
than malevolent man
        who walks with wayward greed
for always more
        when the gods confront the Gígantes
in battle on Phlégra's plain
        the crush of his arrows
would grime the enemy's shining hair with dirt

he said   Epode D (Lines 69–72)
        Teiresías said that in peace
                for the entire
unbroken span of time
        after Hēraklés earns
his most singular reward
        for grueling labors
                a tranquil
destiny in a palace of happiness
        after he
greets blooming Hébē as his wife and honors
that marriage with a feast at the house of Zeus
Kronídēs
        he would praise the law of reverence

NEMEAN 2

Timódēmos of Akharnaí | Pankrátion | 485 (?) BCE

Timódēmos was a member of the Timodēmídai family from Akharnaí that enjoyed success in athletic competitions (N.16–24). Just as the performance of a short work of verbal art preceded the performance of a longer narrative poem, Timódēmos' victory at Neméa is a prelude for future successes (N.2.1–5). Píndaros elaborates on Timódēmos' promise by creating a poetic figure based on astronomy: just as the rise of the constellation Ōríōn follows that of the Pleiádes, after Timódēmos' current victory at Neméa and his projected victories at the Isthmós and Pythó (the Pleiádes represent these actual and hypothetical victories), a victory at Olympía (Ōríōn represents a future culminating victory) will follow (N.2.10–12). The poem celebrates Salamís as the land that fostered both the hero Aías and the fighter Timódēmos (N.2.13–15). Ancient commentators explain that the athlete grew up on the island. "The people of Kórinthos" and "the slender valleys of worthy Pélops" (N.2.20–1) refer to games at Isthmós, which is located near Kórinthos in the Pelopónnēsos, a placename that means "the Island of Pélops." The "games that honor Zeus" (N.2.24) were local contests at Athénai.

just as the Homērídai   Strophe A (Lines 1–5)
    singers of verses sewn
together
    many times begin with a short song
for Zeus
    this man too
        has laid his cornerstone
for victory in holy games
    in Nemean Zeus'
sacred grove
    so much celebrated in song

the son of Timónoos should—   Strophe B (Lines 6–10)
    if a lifetime that leads
him straight along his ancestors' path has gifted
him as a trophy to great Athénai—
    should often
harvest the most beautiful bloom
    of games at Isthmós
should win in games at Pythó too
    it goes like this:

Ōríōn does not follow far behind   Strophe C (Lines 11–15)
the mountain-dwelling Pleiádes
        yes Salamís
is able to raise a warrior
        at Troía Héktōr
knew the renown of Aías
        and you Timódēmos
unfaltering strength in the pankrátion exalts you

Akharnaí is anciently famous for bravery   Strophe D (Lines 16–20)
        people
herald the Timodēmídai as unmatched in all
that matters in athletic contests
        they carried
home four victories in games on the lofty slopes
of imperious Parnassós
        the people of Kórinthos have

already decorated them   Strophe E (Lines 21–25)
        with eight victory garlands
in the slender valleys of worthy Pélops
seven at Neméa's games that honor Zeus
and those wins at home: more than number reckons
parade in celebration of Zeus
        people
of Akharnaí
        and the glorious homeward return
for Timódēmos
        begin your song
                with sweetversed voice

NEMEAN 3

Aristokleídas of Aígina | Pankrátion | 475 (?) BCE

Nemean 3 opens with a prayer addressed to the Moúsa (N.3.1–17). The khorós are waiting for her to convey to them a song (N.3.1–5). "Those singers' voices" (N.3.11) belong to young men (N.3.5 and 66) who are presumably the choral performers of *Nemean 3*. The Moúsa is the "daughter" (N.3.10) whom the speaker addresses. Hēraklés' journey to the western boundary of the Mediterranean Sea (N.3.24–6) serves as an object lesson in human limitations, but even if the hero is a relevant mythological topic for a victory in games at Neméa, his story veers from the topic of Aígina, as Píndaros acknowledges when he writes, "nor should a man have stronger desire for what / belongs elsewhere" (N.3.30). The poem's attention turns to Aígina's heroes, the Aiakídai Pēleús, Telamón, and, especially, Akhilleús. In order to marry Thétis, "Nēreús' alluring daughter" (N.3.56–7), who possessed shapeshifting power, Pēleús had to cling to her tightly, no matter what shape she assumed (N.3.35–6). Píndaros alludes (N.3.36–7) to the story that Laomédōn, the father of Príamos, reneged on his promise to reward Hēraklés for his help. In retaliation Hēraklés, Telamón, and Iólaos killed Laomédōn and sacked Troía. The poem lists hero-apprentices of Kheírōn, the shamanic kéntauros, culminating with Akhilleús, whose grandfather Aiakós is Aígina's greatest hero. Kheírōn's "chamber" is "rocky" (N.3.53–4) because he lived in a cave on Mount Pélion. It is tempting to associate Píndaros' "four virtues" (N.3.74) with the cardinal virtues, *sophía* (wisdom), *andreía* (courage), *sōphrosýnē* (restraint), and *dikaiosýnē* (justice), but what he means is unclear. The second-person addressee in the passage beginning "You lack none of these qualities" (N.3.76–80) is Aristokleídas. The "drink of song" (N.3.77–80) is Píndaros' metaphorical tag for this *epiníkion*. The song refers to its lateness (N.80) but offers no explanation for the delay. The poem concludes by listing Aristokleídas' victories at Neméa, Epídauros, and Mégara.

      majestic Moúsa   Strophe A (Lines 1–8)
            our mother
                  I call for you
come to Aígina
            Dorian island that welcomes
many guests during Neméa's sacred month
for beside Asōpós' waters await young men
who build this honeyvoiced parade
            who search for
the sound of you
            each deed thirsts for its own reward
athletic victory loves more than anything
            song
the nimblest companion to victory wreaths and mastery

grant ungrudginglyAntistrophe A (Lines 9–16)
    such music from my artistry
begin a worthy praisesong
    daughter
        for ruler
of cloudthick sky
    I will make it known to all
with lyre and those singers' voices
    this land's adornment
requires delightful toil
    the Myrmidónes first made
their homes here
    through the destiny you decree
for him
    Aristokleídas did not defile
        their longstoried
public square with disgrace
    because he faltered

in the pankrátion's campaign of strengthEpode A (Lines 17–21)
    victory
song supplies invigorating cure
    for exhausting
body punches in Neméa's sunken plain
if Aristophánēs' son is beautiful
    if he
performs feats that match his looks
    if he strides ahead
with imposing courage
    it is no more easy to traverse
the untraveled sea
    beyond the Pillars of Hēraklés

that the hero-god established as renownedStrophe B (Lines 22–29)
witnesses of the outer limits of voyage
he tamed the monstrous creatures on open sea
and all alone explored the tidal flows
of shallows
    where he reached the frontier that starts
the journey homeward
    he made the uncharted earth
more known
    to what foreign headland

                my heart
                        do you
divert this voyage?
        I tell you to usher the Moúsa
toward Aiakós and his family line
        the height
of justice attends this saying:
        "praise the worthy"

nor should a man have stronger desire for what   Antistrophe B (Lines 30–37)
belongs elsewhere
        search near home
                and you would stumble
upon a model ready for singing some
sweet song
        among the ancient examples of virtue
Lord Pēleús took pleasure in working the wood
of his one-of-a kind spear
        he conquered Iōlkós alone
without an army
        and struggled to cling to regal
Thétis
        Telamón of unbounded might
                stood side
by side with Iólaos
        and destroyed Laomédōn

then one time followed   Epode B (Lines 38–42)
        Iólaos in pursuit
of the Amazónes' bronzebowed strength
        mantaming fear
never dulled his bravery's sharpened blade
someone endowed with inborn glory bears
their weight well
        but a gloomfast man
                who claims
acquired knowledge
        his purpose wavering moment
to moment
        never walks with a determined step
and samples ten thousand skills
        with aimless intention

Akhilleús with chestnut hair   Strophe C (Lines 43–50)
    remained in Philýra's
household
        and while still a boy
            he played at performing
great feats
    javelin with boysized iron point
windsped
    he wrought bloodshed
        in combat with wild lions
and slaughtered boars
    he carried his kill
        still grunting
out their last breaths to Kheírōn Kronídēs—
    the first time
as a six-year-old boy
    but afterwards ceaselessly
Akhilleús astounded Ártemis and daring Athēná

because he killed red deer without hunting dogs   Antistrophe C (Lines 51–58)
or treacherous nets
    his footspeed overpowered them
this story I tell is one
    that older poets
told
    Kheírōn
        whose art was depth of insight
            raised
Iásōn inside his rocky chamber
    then raised
Asklēpiós
    whom he taught
        the gentlehanded practice
of herbal medicine
    Kheírōn even planned
the marriage of Nēreús' alluring daughter
and educated her child
    that bravest hero
strengthening his spirit in every essential thing

so that he might withstand the spearclash warcry   Epode C (Lines 59–63)
of soldiers from Lykía and Phrygía
    of Dárdanoi

when opensea windgusts carry him to Troía
and when he enters the hand-to-hand fray with Aithíopes
armed with spears
    might cling to his conviction
that their leader
    strongwilled Mémnōn
        cousin
of Hélenos
    may never again go back
        to his home

the farshining light of the Aiakídai radiates from there   Strophe D (Lines 64–71)
the bloodline is yours Zeus
    yours the contest, target
of praisesong that shouts this land's joy
    with young men's voices
this surge of song is where victorious Aristokleídas
belongs
    he yoked this island to gloryrich story
he added the holy Thearíōn of Pythó's god
to his bright endeavors
    put to the test
        the proof
of the ways in which someone excels
    shows clearly forth

boy among young boys   Antistrophe D (Lines 72–79)
    man among men
the third age among elders
    each lifestage we mortalkind
possess
    a lifespan for us
        who are bound to die
drives four virtues onward
    and tells us to be
wise in what lies ready to hand
    you lack none
of these qualities
    khaíre my friend
        I send you this honey
blended with gleaming milk
    a frothcoated concoction
this drink of song with Aiolic breaths of auloí

HoneyVoiced

    even if it is late   Epode D (Lines 80–84)
        swiftest among birds
is eagle
        it hunts from a distance
            then suddenly sets
its talons into bloodstreaked prey
        but grackles
cawingly haunt lowlying zones
        yet for you—
if Kleió on her throne agrees—
        because of your will
to win the prize in games
        from Neméa
            from Epídauros
from Mégara
        daylight shines its look on you

NEMEAN 4

Timásarkhos of Aígina | Boys' Wrestling | 473 (?) BCE

Timásarkhos, a member of the Theandrídai family of Aígina, was the victor in boys' wrestling at Neméa, Athénai, and Thébai. The wrestler's musician father Timókritos has died (N.4.13–24), and *Nemean 4* recalls his deceased uncle Kalliklés (N.4.80), who was an athletic victor at the Isthmós. In mythology, the nýmphai Thébē and Aígina are sisters. The relationship symbolizes the affiliation between Píndaros' home, Thébai, and Timásarkhos' home, Aígina, and explains why Thébai would reward Timásarkhos "in honor of Aígina" (N.4.22). "Hēraklés' wealthy courtyard" (N.4.24) possibly refers to a sanctuary dedicated to the hero near the Élektrai Gates at Thébai; Pausanias reports that a gymnasium and racetrack were located near this sanctuary (9.11.4, 7). Hēraklés' encounter with the giant Alkyoneús (N.4.27) represents adversity's role in success, as "this saying" (N.4.31)—"it is right / that whoever performs some feat suffer from it too" (N.4.31–2)—suggests. The "luminous island" (N.4.49–50) is Leuké in the Eúxeinos Sea (modern Black Sea) near the mouth of the Ístros River (modern Danube). Leuké, the site of a temple for Akhilleús, was sacred to the hero (Paus. 3.19.11). The territory that Neoptólemos rules (N.4.51–3) is Épeiros. As in *Nemean 3*, we again encounter the story that, in order to marry Thétis, who possessed shapeshifting power, Pēleús had to cling to her tightly, however menacing each shape she assumed (N.4.62–5). Timásarkhos' uncle Kalliklés is "that man who dwells alongside Akhérōn's / riverbanks" (N.4.85). "The shorepounding tridentlauncher" (N.4.86–7) is Poseidón. *Nemean 4* concludes with Píndaros imagining Euphánēs, Timásarkhos' musician grandfather, singing in praise of Melēsías (N.4.93), the boy-athlete's wrestling trainer.

joy heals best the toil whose crisis has passed   Strophe A (Lines 1–8)
songs
    the gifted daughters of Moúsai
        soothe drudgery
with their touch
    not even warm water
        as gently
rests the body
    as words of praise
        married with lyre's
music
    more enduringly than deeds do
the spoken word lives—
    whatever language the tongue
frees from wellsprings within
    when the Khárites grant it

```
            I hope to lay down                                    Strophe B (Lines 9–16)
                    a praisesong
                            that launches celebration
for Zeus Kronídēs
            for Neméa
                    for Timásarkhos' skill
at wrestling
            may this fortress
                    where Aiakídai dwell
this daylight for justice
            that guards Aígina's
                    every guest
welcome my song
            if sun's strength still bathed, Timókritos,
your father with its warmth
            he would strum his lyre's
multicolored notes
            would lean on these lyrics
and perform his music in praise of a victorious son

who carted home a string of victory crowns                       Strophe C (Lines 17–24)
from contests at Kleōnaí
            from fatsleek
                    and famous Athénai
in sevengated Thébai
            because near Amphitrýōn's
splendid gravesite
            the people of Kádmos
                    were not
unwilling to load him
            with garlands
                    in honor of Aígina
when he came
            to Hēraklés' wealthy courtyard
                    a friend
among friends
            he beheld a town
                    that welcomes guests

with that hero by his side                                       Strophe D (Lines 25–32)
            mighty Telamón
one time laid waste to Troía
            the Méropes
```

     and giant
violent warrior Alkyoneús
    but not before
he crushed twelve fourhorse chariots with a boulder
and twice as many horsebreaking heroes aboard them
whoever fails to understand this saying
would look untried in combat
    since it seems right
that whoever performs some feat
    suffer from it too

song's law   Strophe E (Lines 33–40)
    and onward urging
        hours stop me
from telling
    the whole long tale
        magic binds
my heart to touch upon the newmoon festival
even if seadeep saltwater locks its arms
around your waist
    fight treachery in spite of its force
we will bring to light
    how we rout our attackers
by reaching shore
    but another man with the look
of envy wallows darkly in empty thought

that crumples to the ground   Strophe F (Lines 41–48)
    whatever genius
Lord Pótmos gave me
    I know well
        that time creeps
ahead
    and will fulfill its fated purpose
        right now
sweet lyre
    finish weaving
        with Lydía's melody
the fabric
    of this beloved song
        for Oinóna
for Kýpros
    where Teúkros

                        son of Telamón
                                rules far
from home
            while Aías keeps his ancestral Salamís

Akhilleús, the luminous island in Eúxeinos Sea   Strophe G (Lines 49–56)
and Thétis prevails at Phthía
            Neoptólemos rules
sprawling Épeiros
            where steep cowherding forelands
arc from Dōdónē to the Ionian Sea
in the foothills
            of Mount Pélion
                        after Pēleús
reduced Iōlkós to servitude with warrior
strength
            he conferred the city
                        upon the Haímones

the time he suffered the devious guile of Hippolýtē   Strophe H (Lines 57–64)
Ákastos' wife
            the son of Pelías sowed
death for Pēleús
            the sword of Daídalos
                        an ambush
Kheírōn defended him
            he carried through
the lot in life
            that Zeus
                        decreed for Pēleús
the hero foiled
            overpowering fire
razorsharp claws
            of ruthlessly tactical lions
the spearpoints of their terrifying teeth

then married one of the highthroned Nērēídes   Strophe I (Lines 65–72)
            Pēleús
beheld a perfect circle of seats
            where rulers
of sky and sea assembled
            they displayed their gifts
for him and his family's inborn might

              we must not
cross the gloomy regions of Gádeira
              turn
the ship's rigging
              back to Európē's
                            solid ground
I cannot travel
              the entire tale
                            of Aiakós' sons

I made my pact with Olympía   Strophe J (Lines 73–80)
              the Isthmós
                            Neméa
and marched ahead
              for the Theandrídai
                            as a ready
herald of games that make the body strong
Neméa
              where those who endure
                            the trial do not
make their homeward return
              without garlands
                            that harvest
renown
              where we hear that your homeland
                            Timásarkhos
                                          is
devoted to songs sung in celebration of victory
but if you still ask that I build a memorial brighter

than Páros' stone for your mother's brother Kalliklés   Strophe K (Lines 81–88)
smelted gold shows its every shimmer
              and praisesong
for worthy feats makes a mortal's destiny equal
kings'
              let that man
                            who dwells alongside Akhérōn's
riverbanks find my poetry singing loudly
where he bloomed with a wreath of wild celery
at Kórinthos in games
              for the shorepounding tridentlauncher

in his old age   Strophe L (Lines 89–96)

　　　　　　your grandfather Euphánēs
　　　　　　　　one time
happily celebrated your uncle in song
young man
　　　　　each generation has its own peers
and every single anyone hopes to tell
the most outstanding story they encounter
firsthand
　　　　　if he should praise Melēsías
　　　　　　　　how he
would rout his rivals
　　　　　the clinchholds of his phrasing
a wrestler in words
　　　　　who cannot be
　　　　　　　　brought down
kind to blameless people
　　　　but:
　　　　　　　　toward those who
injure others
　　　　　a merciless next-up opponent

NEMEAN 5

Pythéas of Aígina | Pankrátion | 483 (?) BCE

Nemean 5 is the first of three *epiníkia* composed for Pythéas and Phylakídas, the sons of Lámpōn (see *Isthmian 5* and *Isthmian 6*). *Nemean 5* commemorates the family's intergenerational successes, the victories at Neméa, Aígina, and Mégara (N.5.41–6) that Euthyménēs, uncle of Pythéas and Phylakídas, gained and their grandfather Themístios' victories at Epídauros in boxing and pankrátion (N.5.50–3). This song's mythology features Aígina's line of heroes, the Aiakídai. Píndaros declines to tell the story that Pēleús and Telamón killed Phókos, their half-brother (N.5.14–16); this tale risks undermining the heroic stature of Pēleús and Telamón and, by extension, the praise of Pythéas. Pēleús and Telamón were exiled from Aígina as a consequence of their fratricide. Where Píndaros tells how "the Moúsai's / stunning khorós sang gladly on Mount Pélion / for those heroes" (N.5.22–3), the heroes are Pēleús and Telamón and the occasion for the Moúsai's performance is the wedding of Pēleús and Thétis. Zeus is "the Father and lord / of guests" (N.5.33) because he oversees *xenía* (ritualized guest-friendship). "That hero" (N.5.43) is Pēleús. In the words "Aígina's native month that Apóllōn loves" (N.5.44), the month in question was named *Delphínios*. During this month Aígina held local games, Hydrophória or Delphínia, in honor of Apóllōn. The word *Delphínios* furthermore recalls *Delphoí*, the name of the site sacred to Apóllōn. Where Píndaros writes, "I enjoy how the entire city strives / for greatness" (N.5.46–7), the city meant is the urban center of Aígina. Ménandros of Athénai (N.5.48) was Pythéas' trainer.

Strophe A (Lines 1–6)

I am no portrait sculptor
    who chisels statues
that stand motionless on pedestals
    by every cargo
ship
    by boat
        travel instead sweet song
           from Aígina
spreading the news
    that Lámpōn's
        more than mighty
son Pythéas won the pankrátion crown
in Neméa's games
    though his cheeks do not yet show
summer's end
    the mother of delicate grapeblossoms

Pythéas honored heroes   Antistrophe A (Lines 7–12)
         spearmen
                  the Aiakídai
sown from Krónos and Zeus
         from the golden Nērēídes
and honored his mothercity
         a land that cherishes
guests
         a land they prayed
                  once upon a time
would be full of good men
         and renowned for ships
when they stood at the altar
         for Father of Hellás
                  and stretched
their hands toward the ether
         the unmistakable
sons of Endēís
         and the mighty ruler
                  Phókos

the goddess's son to whom Psamáthē gave birth   Epode A (Lines 13–18)
beside the sea's breakers
         I am too reverent to tell
of an exploit ventured heedless of justice
         how
they left the celebrated island
         which god
banished the rugged brothers from Oinóna
I hold my ground
         the truth gains nothing more
by completely baring
         its unvarnished face
silence is often
         the wisest human insight

if reckoned right to praise   Strophe B (Lines 19–24)
         wealth
                  or armstrength
                           or ironclad
war
         I hope someone readies the longjump pit
for my leap from there

                I have agile airborne knees
and eagles swoop beyond the sea
                the Moúsai's
stunning khorós sang gladly on Mount Pélion
for those heroes
                and in their midst
                                Apóllōn
strummed the seventongued lyre with golden plectrum

he led them in every sort of melody   Antistrophe B (Lines 25–30)
                they opened
with Zeus
                then sang first
                                in praise of holy Thétis
and Pēleús
                sang how the elegant daughter
                                of Krētheús
Hippolýtē
                wanted to shackle Pēleús
                                with treachery
how her elaborate schemes
                convinced her husband
guardian of Magnēsía's people
                to conspire with her
she alloyed falsehood
                and art in her story
                                that Pēleús
attempted to seduce her
                in Ákastos' bed

the opposite happened   Epode B (Lines 31–36)
                with lying words she pleaded
and pleaded longingly
                her precipitous appeals
provoked his anger
                he abruptly spurned
                                the bride
because he feared
                the wrath of the Father and lord
of guests
                Zeus, king of undying gods
                                took note
and from his skyward seat

           the cloudmover nodded
yes that he would soon make Pēleús' wife one
of Nēreús' majestic daughters
           with distaff of gold

after he sought consent   Strophe C (Lines 37–42)
           from their brother-in-law
Poseidón
           who often journeys
                     from Aigaí
                               to the famous
Dorian Isthmós
           where joyful crowds
                     welcome him
as their god
           with the reedpipe's voice
                     where they compete
with unbridled bodystrength
           inborn Pótmos
judges every feat
           and you Euthyménēs
twice at Aígina
           you landed in victory's embrace
and laid your hands
           on richly colored praisesongs

even now   Antistrophe C (Lines 43–48)
           your mother's brother
                     glorifies
the people
           who share that hero's rootstock
                     by following
close behind you
           Pythéas
                     dovetailed with Neméa
with Aígina's native month
           that Apóllōn loves
he dominated his peers
           who came to compete
at home
           and at Nísos' hill
                     rippling with glens
I enjoy how the entire city strives

for greatness
>	know that you reaped
>>		a delightful reward
for exhausting effort
>	thanks to Ménandros' gifts

a builder of athletes should be from Athénai   Epode C (Lines 49–54)
>	but if you
come to sing of Themístios
>	let the cold linger
no longer
>	lend your voice
>>		and hoist your sails
to the mastheights
>	sing how he earned
>>		twofold distinction
at Epídauros:
>	he won as boxer
>>		and in the pankrátion
together with auburn-haired Khárites
>	bring greenleafed flower
garlands to the portico of Aiakós' shrine

NEMEAN 6

Alkimídas of Aígina | Boys' Wrestling | 465 (?) BCE

Nemean 6 celebrates the multigenerational athletic achievements of the Bassídai, who seem to have earned their victories in boxing (N.6.25). Hagēsímakhos, the great-great-grandfather of Alkimídas, appears to have been a victor, and Alkimídas' grandfather Praxidámas was especially prolific (N.6.17–20). Praxidámas "ended Sōkleídas' oblivion / who became Hagēsímakhos' greatest son" (N.6.20–2) in the sense that Sōkleídas, father of Praxidámas, shared the glory of his sons. Possibly the brothers of Praxidámas, Kallías won in games at Delphoí, Kreontídas at the Isthmós and Neméa (N.6.34–44). Alkimídas achieved his family's twenty-fifth victory at Neméa (N.6.57–61). Píndaros develops a metaphor based upon the victories by members of Alkimídas' family in alternating generations: just as one must leave a field fallow every other year in order to ensure its productivity in crop-growing years, the family line has fallow generations without athletic success and productive generations with victory-yields, the whole family line enjoying the prosperity (N.6.8–11). Píndaros elaborates this metaphor by aligning the cropfield of athletic achievement with poets as "the Pierídes' [=Moúsai] plowmen" (N.6.32). For other details, the "single mother" (N.6.1–2) is Gaía "Earth" and the "bridge of unquitting sea" (N.6.39) is the Isthmós. The "treeshoots of Lētó" (N.6.37) are her children, Ártemis and Apóllōn. Those who host games "at Poseidón's sacred grounds" (N.6.39–41) are "neighbors" because the people living near the Isthmós oversaw the games there. The "lion's pasture" (N.6.42) is Neméa, where victory crowns were made of wild celery. Mémnōn of Aithiopía, son of Ēós (Dawn) and commander of Aithíopes who fought in the Trojan War, died on the battlefield at the hands of Akhilleús and for this reason did not return home (N.6.49–53). Píndaros' "double burden" (N.6.57) is to praise both Alkimídas and his family line for their victories. To schedule bouts for the wrestling match, officials used a lot-casting process, which, it seems, somehow disadvantaged Alkimídas and Polytimídas in games at Olympía (N.6.61–3). The song namechecks the trainer Melēsías (N.6.65), whom we encounter elsewhere in Píndaros' *epiníkia* (O.8.54 and N.4.93).

   mankind   Strophe A (Lines 1–7)
       godkind
              from a single mother
we both kinds
       breathe life
              each ordained ability
widens the gap between the two
       humankind
is a nothing
              but copperplated sky remains
an eternally lasting realm
       even so
              our kind is

something like deathless gods
        a great thought
                the body
although we do not know
        in daylight
                at midnight
toward which finish
        destiny marks out
                our racecourse

Alkimídas already reveals   Antistrophe A (Lines 8–14)
        the hallmarks of inborn
talent that looks like grainrich cropfields in
rotation
        one season they gift men
                with yearly sustenance
from the land
        next season
                they catch their breath
and gather strength
        the boy competitor
                yes
he came from desire-quickening games of Neméa
he followed the tracks
        of this decree from Zeus
and in wrestling bouts
        showed himself
                no luckless hunter

because he steers   Epode A (Lines 15–22)
        his steps
                in the bloodline footprints
of Praxidámas
        his father's father
                the first to win
at Olympía
        he hauled garlands home
                from Alpheiós for the Aiakídai
after they crowned him
        five times at the Isthmós
three crowns at Neméa
        he ended Sōkleídas' oblivion
who became Hagēsímakhos' greatest son

because three athletic victors   Strophe B (Lines 23–29)
    who had their taste
of toil
    scaled the peak of prowess
        thanks
to fortune granted by god
    fistfighting reveals
no other house
    in the heart of Hellás
        that stewards
more garlands
    with these bold words
        as if shooting them
from my bow
    I hope I hit
        the target before me
yes Moúsa
    aim this glorious gust
        of verse straight
toward that house
    when men depart
        from sight

songs and stories   Antistrophe B (Lines 30–36)
    tend for them
        their feats
of beauty
    lack of which
        the Bassídai do
not know
    that family line spoken of
        from long
ago
    shipping their cargo
        of celebration
they are able to furnish
    the Pierídes' plowmen
a hoard of praisesong for worthy achievements
    his hands
wrapped in leather straps
    Kallías
        bloodkin
from this homeland

                was once upon a time dominant
at holy Pythó
                and delighted the treeshoots of Lētó

who works a golden distaff   Epode B (Lines 37–44)
                and beside Kastalía's
spring
                at sunset he shimmered
                                in the light
of the Khárites' crowd
                the bridge of unquitting sea
                                honored
Kreontídas in his neighbors'
                bullkilling biennial
games at Poseidón's sacred grounds
                the lion's
pasture one time crowned him
                when he was
                                victorious
below the shadethick
                primeval hills of Phleioús

on every horizon   Strophe C (Lines 45–51)
                wordsmiths have wide approachways
for adorning this glorious island
                since the Aiakídai
bestowed upon poets their singular destiny
by displaying outstanding greatness
                the sound of their name
wings over land and sea
                to faraway places—
soared even to the Aithíopes
                when Mémnōn failed
to journey home
                the bitter clash of Akhilleús
crashed upon them
                when he dismounted
                                his chariot

his spearpoint full of rage   Antistrophe C (Lines 52–58)
                Akhilleús stripped
his enemy's body
                the son of radiant Ēós

elder singers found these stories a broad roadway
I too attend such valor
    and follow after
they say the wave that batters the ship's rudder always
distresses the spirit most deeply
    I took upon
my willing back
    this double burden
        and came
as herald
    shouting
        that this is the twenty-fifth

acclaim in contests people call sacred   Epode C (Lines 59–66)
    that you
Alkimídas
    furnished your celebrated family
with that glory
    a reckless lot robbed you
        boy
and Polytimídas
    of two garlands
        at Olympía's games
at the sacred grounds
    of Krónos' son
        I would say
Melēsías
    chariot driver of your hands
and strength
    is equal in speed
        to dolphin at sea

NEMEAN 7

Sōgénēs of Aígina | Boys' Péntathlon | 485 (?) BCE

Embodying as it perhaps does Victor Hugo's allusion to Píndaros as a vehicle for parodying the awkward thematic mélange—"precisely the rare and pindaric combinations that demonstrate enthusiasm"—of the mystery play depicted in the second chapter of *Notre-Dame de Paris*, *Nemean 7* invites a litany of elucidations. It is only thanks to Eileíthyia, the goddess of childbirth (N.7.1–4), that we enter into existence, to say nothing of reaching youth, figured as the goddess Hébē (Youth). In the axiom "wise people learn the wind that will rise the third day / nor does the lure of profit harm them" (N.7.17–18), the "the wind that will rise the third day" represents the future. To provide mythological context for Píndaros' treatment of Trojan War events (N.7.20–31), when Akhilleús died on the battlefield at Troía, Odysseús and Aías defended his body against plunder by the Tróes. The Hellenic troops agreed to a contest between Odysseús and Aías to determine who would inherit his armor, which the god Héphaistos had crafted. Odysseús won the contest. Aías committed suicide. Píndaros challenges the Homeric tradition that privileges Odysseús, whose signature virtues are debatably virtuous: Odysseús is skilled at lies and deceitful strategy. The persuasion of Hómēros' poetry must therefore account for the fame of Odysseús, because he was not a greater warrior than Aías (N.7.20–1). Píndaros opposes art that contradicts truth. Neoptólemos' questionably heroic moments in the Trojan War include throwing Héktōr's baby son Astyánax to the ground from the heights of Troía's walls, killing Príamos after he had sought sanctuary at an altar, and sacrificing Príamos' daughter Polyxénē at his father's tomb. But Molossía claims Neoptólemos as its founder (N.7.36–40), and Neoptólemos' visit to Delphoí, where he was warmly welcomed and finally buried in the manner suggestive of a hero cult (N.7.40–7), is complimentary to Akhilleús' son and, by extension, to the Aiakídai of Aígina. "The god's temple" (N.7.40) is Apóllōn's. I have translated Píndaros' "three words" (N.7.48) as "no falsifying witness" (N.7.49). When Píndaros imagines that someone from Akhaía—by which he means Molossía, which traces its origins to Neoptólemos—may hear the performance of *Nemean 7* at Aígina (N.7.64–5), he rhetorically ponders their reactions to his mythography. The javelin "frees the neck / and unsweaty strength from wrestling" (N.7.70–3) in the sense that an athlete could win the péntathlon with successes in earlier events, including the javelin throw, without contesting the last, sweat-inducing event, wrestling. The second-person addressee of the verbs "begin your song" (N.7.77) and "kindle" (N.7.81) is the poet-performer of *Nemean 7* or its chorus leader. The "lily blossom" that the Moúsa "gathers from beneath the sea's foam" (N.7.79) is coral. "This holy ground" (N.7.83) is Aígina. The nýmphē Aígina is the "hero's mother" (N.7.84). There is confusion over the possessive adjective "my" in the phrase "my venerated homeland" (N.7.85): is the text correct?; does the first person voice imply that a chorus from Aígina performed the poem (where "my" means "our")?; does the first person form refer to the poet-performer Píndaros and invoke his homeland of Thḗbai? This one word, "my," exemplifies the many challenges to understanding *Nemean 7*. Hēraklḗs is the second-person addressee of several lines (N.7.90–101) in the last triad of *Nemean 7*. When Píndaros likens the location of Sōgénēs' home to a chariot (N.7.93–4), the idea seems to be that, just as the pole of the chariot runs between each yoked pair of horses, Hēraklés has two sacred sites at Aígina between which Sōgénēs dwells. Zeus' "virgin daughter with gleaming eyes" (N.7.96) is Athēná. The referents of "their" and "them" in Píndaros' wish (N.7.98–101) are Sōgénēs and his father Thearíōn. The aphorism "Kórinthos belongs to Zeus" (N.7.105) exemplifies tedious repetition and may refer to children's wordplay.

    Eileíthyia seated beside the deepthought Moírai   Strophe A (Lines 1–8)
    daughter of Héra
        whose power is vast
                hear us
    midwife of children
        without you
                we look upon
    no light
        upon no gloomy night
                without you
    we do not share
        the lot
                of your brightlimbed sister
    Hébē
        we do not all live and breathe
                for identical
    callings
        onliness isolates
                each
                        of us
    harnessed to a destiny
        by the power
    of your divinity
        we sing Thearíōn's son,
    Sōgénēs, into his fame because he is
    distinguished for strength and skill among pentathletes

    he dwells in the songloving city   Antistrophe A (Lines 9–16)
        of spearclang Aiakídai
    they are eager
        to shelter a spirit
                that knows
    adversity

                if someone enjoys
                            achievement's
fortune
            they send a honeywise spring
                            for the Moúsai's
songflow
            displays of might
                        behold prolific
darkness when they lack praisesongs
            we know how
to mirror
            feats of beauty
                        in only one way:
if someone attains the reward for toils with illustrious
songverse thanks to Mnēmosýnē
            her headband sleek

wise people learn   Epode A (Lines 17–21)
            the wind that will rise
                        the third day
nor does the lure of profit harm them
            wealthy
and poor alike come home to death's tomb
            I have
a feeling that Odysseús' story
            became greater
than his trials
            because of sweetversed Hómēros

because something haunts his lies   Strophe B (Lines 22–29)
            and birdflight invention
wisdom steals
            when it leads astray
                        with speech
the mob of men has a sightless heart
            if they
could see the truth
                then mighty Aías would not
have plunged his polished sword into his organs
because he became enraged about some weapons
the march of Zéphyros' unbending windgusts carried
Aías
            best in battle after Akhilleús

on swift ships to Ílos' city
> to bring a wife back

to Menélaos with chestnut hair   Antistrophe B (Lines 30–37)
> but Háïdēs' seawave
surges everywhere
> and crashes upon
both unrenowned and renowned
> though honor arrives
for those whose luxuriant story
> a god enriches
after they die
> Neoptólemos came
>> as helper
to broadlapped earth's great omphalós
> he lies in Pythó's
holy land
> after he wasted Príamos' city
where the Danaoí also toiled
> as he sailed
away
> Neoptólemos lost
>> the route to Skýros
they wandered
> but his crew came ashore
>> at Ephýra

Neoptólemos ruled in Molossía only a short time   Epode B (Lines 38–42)
but his heirs retain this honor ever after
bringing the best war prizes
> he took from Troía
Neoptólemos visited the god's temple
> where a man shoved
his swordblade into him
> when the hero stumbled
into a clash over sacrificial meat

grief's weight overwhelmed   Strophe C (Lines 43–50)
> Delphoí's people
who welcome visitors
> but Neoptólemos repaid
>> the debt
for his allotted life

it was right for one
of the powerful Aiakídai
    to abide
        for the rest of time
within that very oldest of sacred groves
beside Apóllōn's soundwalled house
    right for one
of them to dwell there as sanctioned overseer
of processions
    for heroes
        that abound in animal offerings
three words
    will suffice
        for making justice
justly named:
    no falsifying witness
judges the feats of your descendants and Zeus'
Aígina
    I have something bold to declare:

there is a road   Antistrophe C (Lines 51–58)
    running from your island
        that governs
words for the radiant achievements of the Aiakídai
but in the midst
    of every undertaking
a moment of repose is sweet
    there can be
too much honey
    too much
        of Aphrodítē's delightful
flowers
    each human is
        by nature
            unique
because we find
    our singular destinies
        in life
each of us, a different lot
    it is
impossible
    for one person

                        to gain the windfall
of untroubled happiness
            I cannot say
that Moíra extended
            such a firmly grounded
finish to any human
            Thearíōn
                        Moíra
gives you a proper measure of good fortune

you who won the boldness for beautiful endeavors   Epode C (Lines 59–63)
Moíra does not injure
            your knowing insight
I am your guestfriend
            fending off
                        gloomy reproach
channeling
            like waterstreams
                        authentic renown
to my cherished friend
            I will sing in praise
of him
            these wages pay tribute
                        to worthy people

if a man from Akhaía is nearby   Strophe D (Lines 64–71)
            a man
who lives beyond the Ionian Sea
            he will find
no fault with me
            I trust my role
                        as ambassador
among the people of my town
            I see
brightsightedly
            because I do not
                        shoot
too far
            because I have driven
                        every act
of violence from my footstep
            I hope the time
that remains approaches graciously

                    anyone who
has learned my ways
            will declare it
                        if I have come
unlyrically
            performing contorted poetry
                        Sōgénēs—
Eúxenos is your forefather—
            I swear
                        I did not
step across the line
            and launch
                        my swift tongue

like a bronzebladed javelin   Antistrophe D (Lines 72–79)
            that frees the neck
and unsweaty strength
            from wrestling
                        before the body
falls beneath sun's blaze
            if there was toil
something more delightful follows
            pardon
me
            if I shouted overeagerly
                        I am not
too rough to render kindness
            especially to
a victor
            it is an easy task
                        to weave
these garlands
            begin your song
                        the Moúsa fuses
gold and brightshining ivory
            with the lily
blossom she gathers
            from beneath
                        the sea's foam

after you remember Zeus   Epode D (Lines 80–84)
            serenely
kindle the famemaking noise

        of hymns
                for Neméa
it is proper
        to sing in praise
                of the king of gods
with peaceful voices
        on this holy ground
for they tell the story
        that when the hero's mother
welcomed his conception
        Zeus sowed
                Aiakós

as cityruler   Strophe E (Lines 85–92)
        in my venerated homeland
as your magnanimous guestfriend and brother
        Hēraklés
if one man tastes
        another man's friendship
                then we
would say
        a steadfastly affectionate neighbor
                is
his neighbor's joy
        worthy
                of every good thing
but if a god should also
        uphold this claim
then Sōgénēs might wish
        through your goodwill
                you who tamed
the Gígantes—
        might wish
                prosperously to dwell
along his ancestors'
        wealthy godtended
                street
while fostering warm affection for his father

since he keeps his home   Antistrophe E (Lines 93–100)
        between your sacred
precincts
        like the yokepole

                        between the chariot's
two horsepairs
            on either hand as he comes
                        and goes
you are right
            blessed hero
                        to sway Héra's husband
and his virgin daughter
            with gleaming eyes
                        you have power
to so often give mortals
            strength in the face
of insurmountable hardships
            I hope that you
                        harmonize
an unshakable life
            with their youth
                        and contented old age
hope that you weave
            for them
                        a fortunate existence
that their children's children
            may always own

this day's prize of honor   Epode E (Lines 101–105)
            as well as greater
honor hereafter
            my heart will never say
that it snapped at Neoptólemos
            with insulting words
to plow again
            the very same soil
                        three times
four times—
            this leaves you no way forward
                        like someone
yelping at children
            "Kórinthos belongs to Zeus"

NEMEAN 8

Deínis of Aígina | Díaulos | 459 (?) BCE

Although there is cautious consensus that this song commemorates Deínis' victory in the *díaulos*, the textual evidence is ambiguous. It is unclear if Píndaros means "double *stádion*" (N.8.16) in the sense of two *stádia* races or in the sense of one *díaulos* race, which is two *stádia* in length. Mégas, father of Deínis, who has died, was once victor at Neméa in the same event (*stádion* or *díaulos*?) as his son. "Oinóna's son" (N.8.7) is the son of Aígina and Zeus (N.8.6), Aiakós. As in *Nemean 7* and *Isthmian 4*, Píndaros explores the story of the contest between Odysseús and Aías for the divinely created arms of Akhilleús after the latter died in battle at Troía (N.8.23–34). In *Nemean 8*, Píndaros stresses that Odysseús wins this contest by speech, though the laconic Aías is a superior warrior, and examines the power of speech to deceive and to tell truth. Where Píndaros compares their battlefield actions, "these heroes" and "them" (N.8.28–32) refer to Aías and Odysseús. The "Moúsa's stone" (N.8.46) metaphorically presents the song as a *stélē*, a commemorative monument often used in funerary contexts, an association that is apposite in *Nemean 8*, which celebrates the victory of Deínis' deceased father Mégas. The "two men" (N.8.48) are Deínis and Mégas. Ádrastos (N.8.51) was one of the heroes recruited by Polyneíkēs to attack Thébai, so that Píndaros concludes this poem by alluding to the Seven Against Thébai story in order to illustrate the great antiquity of celebratory praisesong.

majestic Hóra   Strophe A (Lines 1–5)
    herald of Aphrodítē's
ambrosial loves
    you who descend
        upon innocent
eyes of girls and boys
    you clutch one person
with compulsion's gentle hands
    someone else
with other hands
    if what we embrace
        does not stray
from balance in each act
    it can exert
its power over desires more sublime

such shepherds of Kypría's gifts   Antistrophe A (Lines 6–10)
    tended the bed
of Zeus and Aígina
    Oinóna's son sprouted

                    as king
supreme in strength and judgment
            so many people
petitioned again and again to see him
            with no
summons
            the leading heroes
                        who lived nearby
were eagerly willing
            to follow his commands

both those who ordered soldiers in their ranks   Epode A (Lines 11–17)
at rocky Athénai
            and those in Spárta
                        Pélops's
descendants
            as suppliant of Aiakós
                        I grasp
his holy knees
            on behalf of his cherished city
of its citizens here
            I wear my headband
of Lydía
            intricately embroidered
                        with unbridled
music
            Neméa's adornment
                        for the double
stádion footraces
            of Deínis
                        and his father
Mégas
            people possess
                        more lastingly
a prosperity
            that has taken root
                        with god's blessing

such prosperity   Strophe B (Lines 18–22)
            once upon a time
loaded Kinýras
            with wealth
                        on Kýpros surrounded

by sea
>   I stand on agile feet
>   and pause
to breathe before I speak
>   many words said
in many ways
>   but whoever discovers
>   something
new to say
>   to submit their words
>   to touchstone
interrogation
>   as a test
>   of their truth
risks every danger
>   the spoken word
>   is a delicacy
for the envious
>   and envy always
>   clings
to good men
>   but does not clash
>   with common people

envy even gnawed   Antistrophe B (Lines 23–27)
>   the son of Telamón
folded him over
>   his swordblade
>   oblivion subjects
anyone
>   wordless but bravehearted
>   to mournful
spite
>   while the most outstanding prize
>   of honor
has gone to a slippery lie
>   in a hidden vote
the Danaoí indulged Odysseús
>   but when they robbed him
of golden armor
>   Aías grappled with bloodshed

these heroes inflicted   Epode B (Lines 28–34)
>   such unequal wounds

into their foes' warm flesh
> as the spear
>> that guards
mortals bore down on them in defense of just-killed
Akhilleús
> and in deadly days of further toils
deceit was also inimical long ago
the company of cloying stories
> treacherous
>> a disgraceful
wrongdoer
> deceit violates the bright
>> but buttresses
the decaying aura
> of undistinguished people

I hope such ways of being   Strophe C (Lines 35–39)
> may never be
>> mine
Father Zeus
> but that I lay claim
>> to life's
straightforward roads
> so that I do not impose
a notorious reputation
> upon my children
when I die
> some pray for gold
>> others, an unhedged
field
> but I pray they cover my limbs
>> with earth
after I delight
> my town's people
>> by praising
what ought to be praised
> by sowing reproach for the wicked

virtue is rampant   Antistrophe C (Lines 40–44)
> like a tree that surges
with greenfresh dewdrops—
> virtue among wise and just
men elevated to heights of liquid ether

beloved men are the source of every kind
of kindness
      above all in times of adversity
but even enjoyment
      seeks to set fidelity
in eyesight
      Mégas, to carry back your soul

is beyond my power   Epode C (Lines 45–51)
      the outcome of destitute hopes
            falters
but it is easy work
      to bolster
           the Moúsa's
stone
      for your homeland
           for the Khariádai
                in honor
of the doubly auspicious feet of two men
I am overjoyed to launch a loud boast
that matches the deed
      but any man renders drudgery
painless with healing song
      there was long ago
parade and praisesong
      even before the conflict
between Ádrastos and Kádmos' people arose

NEMEAN 9

Khromíos of Aítna | Chariot Race | 474 (?) BCE

Nemean 9 celebrates the victory of Khromíos, the general of Hiérōn, tyrant of Syrákousai and founder of the city Aítna, in local games at Sikyón in the northeastern Pelopónnēsos. The "twin children / who share the same destiny as guardians of sheer Pythó" (N.9.4–5) are Apóllōn and Ártemis, children of the goddess Lētó (N.9.53). Píndaros locates the origin of Sikyón's games in the mythological past: Ádrastos established equestrian games while in exile there (N.9.9–10) prior to his expedition against Thébai. Ádrastos and his allies did not follow the divine advice, communicated through a form of divination that involves interpreting birdflight and through Zeus' lightning, against waging their campaign against Thébai (N.9.18–20). Píndaros describes funerals for war dead, who were cremated, in florid language—"fattened whitely blooming smoke with bodies" (N.9.23)—and expresses concern about possible conflict with "Phoiníke's soldiers," or the Carthaginians (N.9.28–9). *Nemean 9* records Khromíos' victory in battle at Hélōros River in Sikelía (N.9.34–43). "That goddess" (N.9.36) is Aidós, which I translate as "reverence" (N.9.33). The "wargod" (N.9.37) is Árēs.

we will parade from Apóllōn's temple at Sikyón   Strophe A (Lines 1–5)
   Moúsai
       to newly founded Aítna
           where
the number of guests defeats outspread doorways
       together
to the wealthy home of Khromíos
       make
our praisesong sweet with verses
       when he climbs
aboard his chariot with winning horses
       he conjures
forth a songvoice for mother and twin children
who share the same destiny
       as guardians of sheer Pythó

people have a saying: Strophe B (Lines 6–10)
       do not bury
underground
       the achievement
           of a worthy
feat with silence
       godinfused song

                        agrees
with lyric exultation
            we will launch
the lyre's sound
            the sound of aulós
                        for this ultimate
of equestrian games
            that Ádrastos founded
                        for Phoíbos
beside the streams of Asōpós
            in memory of them
I will adorn the hero
            with echoing acclaim

he was king there at that time   Strophe C (Lines 11–15)
            and by glorifying
the city with new religious festivals
            men
competing in strength
            and well-planed chariots
                        he brightened
its light
            he one time fled
                        the ambitious schemes
of Amphiáraos and terrible crisis
            fled his ancestral
home and Árgos
            victims of sedition's
violence, Talaós' sons no longer ruled
            the stronger
man brings a former justice to an end

those who gave Oiklés' son   Strophe D (Lines 16–20)
            mantaming Eriphýlē
as wife
            to affirm their pledge
                        became the mightiest
chestnut-haired Danaoí
            once upon a time
they led an army of men to sevengated
Thébai
            along a road
                        not sanctioned by birdflight
the son of Krónos

       shook
               his lightningbolt
and ordered those angerblind men
       not to march away
from their homeland
       but to abandon their campaign

they nevertheless rushed   Strophe E (Lines 21–25)
       as a mob
               with bronze weapons and horsetack
to reach a clearbright ruin
       beside the banks
of Ismēnós
       they wagered the sweetness
               of homeward return
and fattened whitely blooming smoke
       with bodies
seven funeral pyres feasted
       on younglimbed
mortal remains
       but for Amphiáraos
               Zeus
clove
       the barrelchested earth
               with his powerful
thunderbolt and hid them
       both hero and horses

before he inflicted shame   Strophe F (Lines 26–30)
       upon his swordsman's
courage
       by being hit in the back
               with Periklýmenos'
spear
       in the face of supernatural fear
even gods' children flee
       if it can be done
son of Krónos
       I delay
               as long as
possible
       this obdurate ordeal over
death and life

                with warspears hurled
                        by Phoiníke's
soldiers
                and ask you to grant
                        a destiny long-governed
by custom
                to the children
                        of Aítna's citizens

and to meld   Strophe G (Lines 31–35)
        its people
                with communal splendor
Father Zeus
        you already know the men here
cherish horses
        and possess spirits
                stronger than
possessions
        I said something
                beyond belief
the reverence that delivers glory
        is secretly
stolen under the influence of greed
        if you
had carried Khromíos' shield
        among warcry footsoldiers
among horses
        or in shipbattle
                in the perilous
thick of earsplitting warcry
        you would have judged

how that goddess equipped   Strophe H (Lines 36–40)
        his warrior energy
                to fend off
the wargod's havoc in combat
        few have power
of strength
        of spirit
                to resolve to drive the cloud
of impending bloodshed
        toward enemy frontlines
                they say
that fame flowered for Héktōr

                nearby Skámandros' streams
that near the steep rockface
                above the Hélōros River

where there is a ford   Strophe I (Lines 41–45)
                people call Areía's
this brightness
                threw its look
                                upon the son
of Hagēsídamos in his youthful stage of life
I will tell
                many feats
                        of other days
on dustcovered land
                and feats on neighboring sea
from toils that accompany youth
                that accompany justice
in oldage
                a tranquil time of life
                                emerges
let him who gained
                the lot
                        of awe-inspiring
happiness
                know it comes
                        as a gift from gods

if someone should attain   Strophe J (Lines 46–50)
                the aura
                        of glory
in addition to many possessions
                it is
impossible for a mortal
                to plant two feet
upon another more distant
                mountain height
tranquility loves the symposium
                victory's new blossoms
grow with the tending of mild song
                the voice
becomes adventurous
                beside the winebowl
                        have someone

         mix this drink
                 the victory parade's sweet prophet

have someone share   Strophe K (Lines 51–55)
         around the grapevine's
                 mighty
child
         in silver drinking cups
                 that his mares
once won for Khromíos
         and sent home
                 from holy Sikyón
along with the son of Lētó's garlands
         woven
according to tradition
         Father Zeus
I pray to sing
         in praise of this prowess
                 accompanied
by the Khárites
         pray to honor his victory
with words
         beyond the power
                 of many poets
throwing my javelin nearest the Moúsai's target

NEMEAN 10

Theaíos of Árgos | Wrestling | 444 (?) BCE

Nemean 10 celebrates Theaíos' victory in local games at Árgos during the *Heraía* (or *Hekatómbaia*), a festival in honor of Héra. *Nemean 10* catalogs mythological figures of Árgos (N.10.1–18). According to ancient sources, the prize offered in these games was a bronze shield (cf. N.10.22). The "seagates" (N.10.27) refer to the Isthmós, the strip of land between the Gulf of Kórinthos and the Saronic Gulf. "Ádrastos' rite" (N.10.27) alludes to the story that the hero founded games at Neméa. Theaíos was prolifically victorious at Pythó, the Isthmós, and Neméa (N.10.24–8). Where he writes that Theaíos' "mouth silences what he desires within" (N.10.29), Píndaros portrays Theaíos as too temperate to express his desire for victory at Olympía, which would have made him a *periodoníkēs*. Theaíos' athletic career resembles the performance of song: just as a preliminary short performance, "an overture" (N.10.33), precedes a longer performance, Theaíos' victories at Athénai precede his hoped-for future victory at Olympía. The Panathenaic Festival at Athénai included athletic competitions, whose victory prize was a large amphora of olive oil, a valuable commodity (N.10. 35–6). "Héra's courageous people" (N.10.36) are citizens of Árgos, Theaíos' homeland. We learn of the achievements of Theaíos' relatives in games at Isthmós and Neméa, as well as in local Peloponnesian games (N.10.37–44). The "valleys of Kórinthos" (N.10.42) are the venue for games held at the Isthmós. The citizens of Kleōnaí oversaw games at Neméa (N.10.42). Pampháēs, an ancestor of Theaíos, practices *theoxénia* (N.10.49–50) for the Tyndarídai, Kástōr and Polydeúkēs, a ritual in which humans host a god or gods at a meal. The ensuing mythological narrative (N.10.55–90) attends to Kástōr's death and the arrangement struck between Polydeúkēs and Zeus that the brothers would share immortality and death, each dwelling in the underworld one day, on Ólympos the next. The "monument offered to Háïdēs" (N.10.67) is the funerary monument of Aphareús, father of Lynkeús and Ídas.

  city of Danaós and his fifty daughters   Strophe A (Lines 1–6)
    with thrones
  of splendor
      Árgos
        a proper home for such
  a god as Héra—
      Khárites
        sing in praise
  of Árgos
     which glows with fire
       of endless valor
  in courageous feats
     long to tell
       the story

of Perseús and Médousa the Gorgó
        how Árgos founded
many towns in Aígyptos through Épaphos' shrewd ways
Hyperméstra did not wander astray
        she kept
her sword in its sheath and cast its lonely vote

Athēná   Antistrophe A (Lines 7–12)
        with chestnut hair
                with eyes that catch
the light
        one time made Diomédēs
                a deathless
god
        in Thébai the earth
                when struck by Zeus'
weaponry
        the thunderbolt
                embraced the son
of Oiklés
        the prophet
                war's stormcloud
                        since long ago
Árgos surpasses other cities for women
with beautiful hair
        Zeus made the clearest case
for this because he came to Alkménē and Danáē
Árgos harmonized
        for Ádrastos' father
                for Lynkeús
the harvest of insight
        with plainspoken justice

Árgos fostered Amphitrýōn's spearpoint   Epode A (Lines 13–18)
        unrivalled
in good fortune
        he joined that great god's lineage
when equipped with bronze armor
        he slew the Tēlebóai
taking on the look of Amphitrýōn
        the king
of undying gods
        entered the hero's home
                delivering

the fearless seed of Hēraklés
> and Hébē
>> who walks
Ólympos alongside the mother
> Héra Teleía
is wife of Hēraklés
> most beautiful
>> among all goddesses

my mouth is too brief   Strophe B (Lines 19–24)
> to catalog all
>> the abundant
goodness whose destiny
> the sacred ground of Árgos
enjoys
> the ravenous greed of humans is
a burden to confront
> wake nevertheless
the lyre's musical strings
> and weigh the meaning
of wrestling
> the contest for bronze prizes
>> stirs
the crowd to sacrifice
> oxen to Héra
>> to judge
the games
> where son of Oulías
>> Theaíos
>>> forgot
the toils he bore with poise
> by winning twice

another time   Antistrophe B (Lines 25–30)
> he overpowered ranks
of Héllēnes at Pythó
> and setting out with fortune's
company
> attained the victory crown
>> at Isthmós
and Neméa
> he gave the Moúsai
>> soil to plow

by three times
	taking the garland
		at the seagates
three times too
	in the holy plain
		in Ádrastos'
rite
	his mouth silences
		what he desires within
Father Zeus
	the achievement of every feat
depends on you
	summoning his resolve
with a not untoiling heart
	he prays
		for your favor

I sing what god knows—   Epode B (Lines 31–36)
	and anyone
		who pours out
effort to summit
	the heights of competition
Písa is home to Hēraklés' most skyward festival
like an overture
	to future victories
		on two
occasions heavenly voices
	sweetly paraded
in celebration of him
	during solemn rituals
of Athénai's people
	olivetree's fruit travelled
in fire-kilned earth
	in the lavishly decorated
bastions of amphoras
	to Héra's courageous people

hardwon honor   Strophe C (Lines 37–42)
	often follows
		the famous
bloodline of your mother's ancestors
	Theaíos

Nemeans

thanks to Khárites and Tyndarídai
    if I were kinsman
to Thrásyklos and Antías
    I would be expected
not to hide away
    my eyes' light in Árgos
with such wagonloads of victory
    the horsebreeding
town of Proítos
    abounded
        in the valleys
of Kórinthos
    four times before
        the men of Kleōnaí

and awarded silver   Antistrophe C (Lines 43–48)
    they departed from Sikyón
with winebowls
    departed from Pellḗnē cloaked
in fine wool
    it is impossible to reckon
        the quantities
of bronze—
    that arithmetic needs
        a leisure more
longlasting—
    that Kleítōr and Tegéa and Akhaía's uphill
cities and Lykaíon
    furnished for Zeus' racecourse
for anyone
    who wins with strength
        of feet and arms

if Kástōr   Epode C (Lines 49–54)
    and his brother Polydeúkēs
        visited
Pampháēs
    to renew their friendship
        it is nothing
marvelous
    that this family shares
        the inborn
talent of victorious athletes

          since those stewards
of broadspaced Spárta
          oversee the teeming
fate of contests
          with Hermés and Hēraklés
beside them
          and they deeply care
               for just men
the community of gods
          is certainly worthy
               of trust

the Dióskouroi   Strophe D (Lines 55–60)
          exchange their states of being
               and abide
one day with their cherished father Zeus
the next day below the innermost chambers of Earth
in Therápnē's valleys
          fulfilling their mutual destiny
when Kástōr perished in war
          Polydeúkēs chose
this existence rather than to be
          unconditionally
divine and dwell in heaven
          Ídas boiled
over—
          who knows why?—
               over cattle and wounded
Kástōr with his spearhead's sharpened bronze

Lynkeús scanned the horizon from Mount Täýgetos   Antistrophe D (Lines 61–66)
and saw
          the Dióskouroi hunkered down
               inside
an oak tree's trunk
          Lynkeús had the sharpest
eyesight of every earthbound human
          with rapid
feet they arrived at once
          the sons of Aphareús
and quickly improvised their exploit
          then felt
the dreaded power of Zeus' schemes:

        Léda's son
Polydeúkēs strode immediately forth
    to stalk them
they stopped and faced him
        near their father's tomb

from where they tore up   Epode D (Lines 67–72)
        a monument offered to Háïdēs
stone worked smooth
    and hurled it into Polydeúkēs'
chest
    but they did not crush him
        or even knock
him back
    he attacked—
        his javelin sped—
            and shoved bronze
through Lynkeús' ribcage
    Zeus' firebearing thunderbolt
smoldered for Ídas
    a direct blow
        fires consumed
the sons of Aphareús
    together in being alone
conflict with stronger forces is bitter company

Tyndarídēs rushed back   Strophe E (Lines 73–78)
    to his mighty brother
        he found
him not yet dead
    but shaking violently
        with labored
breathing
    his face hot with tears
        a heartsick groan
Polydeúkēs cried out at the top of his voice
    "Father, son
of Krónos
    what will deliver me
        from such grief?
decree my death here
    with my brother
        ruler of sky

when you lose the people you love
>	honor ghosts
>>	away
in the throes of hardship
>	few mortals are loyal enough

to share its weight"   Antistrophe E (Lines 79–84)
>	he prayed
>>	then Zeus came face
to face with him
>	and voiced these words:
>>	"you are
my son
>	but in Kástōr's case
>>	the hero, her husband
Tyndáreōs
>	side by side with your mother
>>	he spilled
his mortal seed
>	but hear me
>>	I grant you these choices
if you wish to dwell—
>	you alone—
>>	on Ólympos
with me
>	with Athénai's goddess
>>	with Árēs
>>>	whose spear
is gloom
>	escaping death and detested old age

that allotted destiny is yours   Epode E (Lines 85–90)
>	but if you persist
on behalf of your brother
>	if you intend to divide
everything equally
>	then you would breath life below
earth half your time
>	and half your time
>>	among heaven's
goldwashed homes"
>	after Zeus spoke
>>	Polydeúkēs harbored no

twofold purpose in his thoughts
        but set free
first the eye
        then the voice
                of bronzebelted Kástōr

NEMEAN 11

Aristagóras of Ténedos | Attainment of Office of *Prýtanis* | 446 (?) BCE

Prytáneis (officials) served on the *prytaneía* (city council). Citizens held this public office in rotation for a defined period of time, twelve months in the case of Aristagóras (N.11.10). They met at the *prytaneíon* (city hall) (N.11.1), which was a public building sacred to Hestía, the goddess of the hearth, where cities maintained a communal fire. When Hellenic *póleis* (cities) established colonies, colonists transported fire from the *prytaneíon* of the *metrópolis* (mothercity) to the new settlement. Aristagóras' family enjoyed the distinction of sixteen victories in wrestling and the pankrátion in local games (N.11.19–21). Kastalía, the sacred spring at Delphoí, and the "pinecovered Hill of Krónos" at Olympía (N.11.24–6)—Píndaros asserts that Aristagóras would have won in games at these sites. "That festival Hēraklés / sanctions every four years" (N.11.27) is the festival at Olympía. The "here" in the phrase "led here" (N.11.35) is Ténedos, home of Aristagóras.

Rheía's daughter	Strophe A (Lines 1–5)

    Rheía's daughter   Strophe A (Lines 1–5)
        you who earned
    the destiny of city halls
        Hestía
    sister of loftiest Zeus and Héra
    who shares his ruling seat
        welcome
    Aristagóras into your sanctuary
        and beside
    your splendid staff of power
        welcome
    his companions
        who guard the stability
    of Ténedos by revering you

    by often worshipping you   Antistrophe A (Lines 6–10)
        first among gods
    with offerings of wine
        often with fatrich
    smoke of sacrifice—
        the lyre chimes
    for them
        and so does song
            they honor
    the customs of Zeus

        god of hospitality
at their everflowing tables
may he traverse his twelvemonth term
with glory
        with uninjured heart

the man—   Epode A (Lines 11–16)
        I see his father Arkesílas
happy
        his son a stunning presence
endowed with inborn bravery
        if someone
who enjoys abundance
        outruns
others in beauty
        if someone who
excels in games
        displays their strength
then let them remember they clothe mortal limbs
and wear at the end a garment of earth

it is right to see him   Strophe B (Lines 17–21)
        praised with words
of admiration from townspeople
        to make
melodies for him
        decorated with songs
that sound like honey
        from the hands
of his neighbors
        sixteen bright victories
garlanded Aristagóras and his famous
homeland for wrestling
        for swaggering pankrátion

overtimid hopes of parents   Antistrophe B (Lines 22–26)
held their son's strength back
        from daring
to compete
        at Pythó and Olympía
on oath I contend
        that if he had journeyed
to Kastalía or pinecovered Hill of Krónos

Aristagóras would have returned home more
distinguished than his fierce wrestling opponents

after he celebrated victory   Epode B (Lines 27–32)
pageantry at that festival Hēraklés
sanctions every four years
    after he
wrapped his hair with purple garlands
emptyheaded boasting banishes
one mortal from good fortune's realms
while someone else
    who too much faults
their strength
    an uncourageous spirit
drags them backward
    by the arms
and spoils the dignity of their household

it is easy   Strophe C (Lines 33–37)
    to piece together Peísandros'
long-ago bloodline
    from Spárta—from Amýklai
with Oréstēs
    he travelled and led here a bronzeclad
army of Aiolian soldiers—
a bloodline from the streams of Ismēnós
blended with the hero Melánippos
his mother's ancestor
    primordial virtues

though they vary from generation   Antistrophe C (Lines 38–42)
to generation of men
    offer up
their strength again
    so it is that cropfields
with crumbling soil do not grant
a harvest in every season
    nor do
trees wish to bring forth fragrant blossoms
equal in their wealth
    each yearly
cycle

>   but they fluctuate
> >   destiny
> also guides we mortal fauna

like this   Epode C (Lines 43–48)
>   an unmistakable sign
from Zeus does not visit humans
>   but we
nevertheless embark upon
outstanding feats of courage—
>   we yearn
for such achievement
>   our limbs submit
to irreverent hope
>   and foresight's waters
lie far away
>   it is right to hunt
for restraint to personal gain
>   the madness
of desires beyond reach is a knifeblade

ISTHMIANS

ISTHMIAN 1

Hēródotos of Thébai | Chariot Race | 458 (?) BCE

With the stylized apology for the composer's busyness and an appeal to Délos for understanding (I.1.1–4), the song begins by declaring the necessity to defer another song's completion—a paián (I.1.7–9)—in order to compose this *epiníkion*. Hēródotos drove his own chariot (I.1.15). This is remarkable because those who entered chariot race competitions typically contracted a chariot driver. The shipwreck metaphor (I.1.36–8) alludes to some misfortune experienced by Asōpódōros, Hēródotos' father. The son of Krónos to whom Píndaros refers (I.1.52–3) is Poseidón, who is "our neighbor" (I.1.53) in the sense that there was a religious site sacred to the god at Onkhēstós, which is near Thébai. *Isthmian 1* lists local games (I.1.55–9) in which Hēródotos found success.

  my mother   Strophe A (Lines 1–6)
    goldshield Thébē
      I will make
  your feats overcome my lack of leeway
    I hope
  rockcovered Délos
    for whom I have poured out my poetry
  seeks no vengeance
    what do good people hold
  more dear than cherished parents?
    Apóllōn's land
  allow me this song
    with help from gods
      you know
  I will hitch one poem's completion to another's

  by dancing among seafaring men in honor   Antistrophe A (Lines 7–12)
  of Phoíbos with uncut hair
    at seabathed Kéōs
  and the seaflanked ridge of Isthmós
    because that country

granted Kádmos' people crowns from six games
their homeland's beautiful emblem of victory glory
the land where Alkménē mothered her fearless child

once upon a time Gēryón's brash hounds　　　　　　　Epode A (Lines 13–17)
quaked before him
       but I
            by crafting song's honor
for fourhorse chariot
       honor for Hēródotos—
he controlled the reins with no other man's hands—
I intend to harmonize him with a praisesong
for Kástōr—or song for Iólaos
       one in Lakedaímōn
one in Thébai
       they were born the strongest
chariot drivers among all the ancient heroes

as athletes they tried their hands in more contests than anyone　　Strophe B (Lines 18–23)
else and adorned their homes with tripods
       cauldrons
cups of gold
       enjoying the taste of victory's
crowns
       in naked footraces
            in armorclad races
when shields clatter
       their prowess shines brightly forth—

brightly　　　　　　　　　　　　　　　　　　Antistrophe B (Lines 24–29)
       when with armstrength they hurled javelins
launched the discus made of stone
       the péntathlon
did not exist
       but for each event there were
established prizes
       hair so often bound
with thickly woven victory wreaths
       nearby Dírkē's
streams
       beside Eurótas
            they were revelations

both son of Iphiklés   Epode B (Lines 30–34)
    belonging to the same people
as Spartoí kin
    and Tyndarídēs
        who dwells among Akhaioí
in his hometown Therápnē
    high above the plain
khaírete
    as I cloak Poseidón and godtended Isthmós
and riverbanks of Onkhēstós with song
    along
with this man's honors
    I will sing the greatfamed
lot in life his father Asōpódōros enjoys

sing Orkhomenós   Strophe C (Lines 35–40)
    their homeland soil that welcomed
him back
    after shipwreck upon unbounded sea
crushed him with bonechill misfortune
    but now his family's
destiny has embarked him once again
upon his old good weather days
    whoever
toils furnishes the mind with forethought as well

if someone devotes their whole passion to upright ways   Antistrophe C (Lines 41–46)
paying the cost and struggling through
    then others
must roar with pride and check their jealous thoughts
for those who find such goodness:
    it is a gift
easy to give
    for a man of wisdom
        to say
the proper words
    to offer up a shared beautiful
something in answer to every kind of hard work

the wages people enjoy for different trades   Epode C (Lines 47–51)
differ
    for shepherd plower fowler
        and the worker

for whom the sea provides
>   every person
strives to keep relentless hunger away
from their belly
>   but those who inherit a graceful aura
by competing in games
>   or facing combat
>   >   receive
the loftiest yield when praised in public:
>   the blossom
of what fellow citizens and foreigners say of them

it is right for us to repay Krónos' earthshaking son   Strophe D (Lines 52–57)
our neighbor
>   for his good works on behalf of chariots
by singing in praise of him
>   as horserace god
right to call on your sons
>   Amphitrýōn
>   >   on Minýas'
valley
>   on Eleusís
>   >   Dēmétēr's holy ground—
so glorious—
>   to call on Eúboia
>   >   its arcing racecourse

I include your precinct   Antistrophe D (Lines 58–63)
>   Prōtesílaos
>   >   in Phyláke
land of Akhaioí
>   every single victory
that Hermés
>   the god of games
>   >   bestowed upon
Hēródotos and his horses
>   praisesong's short reach
removes occasion to tell
>   and yet a story
silenced oftentimes brings
>   still greater joy

Epode D (Lines 64–68)

I pray that
    lifted up on splendid wings
of the sweet-toned Pierídes
    Hēródotos might yet build
a bulwark for his strength at Pythó
    in games
at Olympía with finest wreaths of Alpheiós
    as he builds
honor for sevengated Thébai
    whoever
hoards hidden wealth at home
    and amuses himself
by attacking others
    fails to reckon the debt
of his soul to Háïdēs
    without a shred of glory

ISTHMIAN 2

Xenokrátēs of Akrágas | Chariot Race | 470 (?) BCE

This song is addressed to Thrasýboulos, son of Xenokrátēs, who seems to have died prior to its composition. *Pythian 6* commemorates Xenokrátēs' chariot victory at Delphoí (490?), *Olympian 2* and *Olympian 3* the chariot victory (476) of Xenokrátēs' brother Thérōn. *Isthmian 2*, the fourth of Píndaros' *epiníkia* for the Emmenídai, appears to lament the practice of commissioned works of art like *epiníkia* (I.2.6–11). Ancient sources identify "The man from Árgos" (I.2.9) as Aristódēmos of Spárta, who had an original connection with Árgos, according to Bury. The second-person addressee (I.2.12) is Thrasýboulos. The Panathenaic festival at Athénai (I.2.20) included athletic competitions. The chariot driver Nikómakhos was also the chariot driver for Thérōn (I.2.22–9). The "heralds of Hórai" (I.2.23) declared the truce that attended the festival at Olympía. Nikásippos (I.2.47) may have been the leader of the khorós that performed this song, the person responsible for conveying the composition to Akrágas for Thrasýboulos, or both. Sailing and seasons (I.2.39–42) depict the lavish extent of Xenokrátēs' practice of *xenía* (ritualized guest-friendship). "He" (I.2.44) is Thrasýboulos.

    the mortals of former times   Strophe A (Lines 1–5)
        Thrasýboulos
            who stepped
    aboard the chariot of Moúsai
        garlanded in gold
    confronted the lyre's acclaim
        and deftly shot
    their arrows of honeyvoiced praisesongs for boys—
        whichever
    beautiful of them possessed the sweetest latesummer
    beckon of Aphrodítē
        (her throne is marvelous)

    the Moúsa was not at all profitloving back then   Antistrophe A (Lines 6–10)
    no hired worker
        honeysound Terpsikhórē
    did not cart her silverclad softvoiced songs
    to market
        but now she insists
            we obey the proverb
    coined by the man from Árgos
        that strides nearest the truth:

"money, money: this is a man" Epode A (Lines 11–16)
    he said
when deprived of property and friends alike
    but you
you are wise
    I sing of things not unknown:
at Isthmós the fourhorse chariot victory that Poseidón
bestowed upon Xenokrátēs
    the god sent a wreath
of wild Dorian celery to crown his hair

gifting with honor the man Strophe B (Lines 17–21)
    whose chariot sails
the man
    who is light for the people of Akrágas
        at Krísa
the impossibly mighty Apóllōn witnessed him
and decked him in splendor there
    and when Xenokrátēs
reaped the celebrated acclaim of Erekhtheídai
at fat and bright Athénai
    he had no reproach
at all
    for the hand that kept his chariot safe
the hand of the man
    who drove the horses on

the hand that Nikómakhos plied with expert timing Antistrophe B (Lines 22–26)
four sets of reins at once
    the heralds of Hórai
read out his name
    men of Élis
        who tend the truce
of Zeus Kronídēs
    probably because they enjoyed
a generous welcome
    and with sweetbreeze voices they greeted
him when he fell upon golden Níkē's knees

in their land that people call the holy grove Epode B (Lines 27–32)
of Olympian Zeus
    where Ainēsídamos' sons are water
for the wine of undying honors

   your household is far
from unfamiliar
    Thrasýboulos
     with seductive
victory pageants
   or honeybold triumphant songs

no hill, and the road does not steeply climb   Strophe C (Lines 33–37)
   if someone
conveys the honor of Helikón's Moúsai
   to homes
of famous men
    I launched my discus
     and hope
to hurl my javelin as far
   as Xenokrátēs distances
others in gentle manners
   in the company
of his city's people
   he was esteemed

he followed horsetending customs common   Antistrophe C (Lines 38–42)
   to all Héllēnes
he warmly welcomed every feast for gods
never did wind swirling around his table make him
furl his sail
   but he voyaged to Phásis in summer
weather
   sailing to Neílos' shore in winter

since envious hopes haunt mortal minds   Epode C (Lines 43–48)
   he should never
be silent about his father's greatness—
   nor
these praisesongs
   because I did not perfect them only
so they laze away
   share these thoughts with him
Nikásippos
   when you see my respected friend

ISTHMIAN 3

Mélissos of Thébai | Chariot Race | 474/3 (?) BCE

Isthmian 3 and *Isthmian 4*, both for Mélissos of Thébai, are the only two songs among Píndaros' *epiníkia* that share the same metrical design. This correspondence has led some editors and commentators to regard the individual songs as a single composition, but others treat them as separate poems. *Isthmian 3* seems to reach an end, *Isthmian 4* to begin a separate song. *Isthmian 3* commemorates Mélissos' chariot victory at Neméa, *Isthmian 4* his *pankrátion* victory at Isthmós. *Isthmian 3* happens to refer to this *pankrátion* victory. This detail and the metrical equivalence of the two songs justify including *Isthmian 3* among Pindar's Isthmian *epiníkia* instead of among his Nemean *epiníkia*. The "the barrelchested lion's hollow" (I.3.11–12) is Píndaros' allusive manner of referring to the site of Neméa which recalls Hēraklés' feat of killing the Nemean lion. Mélissos "heralded the name of Thébē" (I.3.12) in the sense that the formal announcement of his victory named the athlete's home city, Thébai, for which the nýmphē Thébē is the eponym.

    if anyone whom fortune favors   Strophe A (Lines 1–6)
        in glorious games
  or with wealth's strength
        tempers the galling gluttony for more
  that lurks in the mind
        he earns accolades from his city's
  people
        great talent attends mortals through your power
  Zeus
        the prosperity of those who practice
  reverence thrives more abundantly
        but does not
  as abidingly
        as bloomingly
            gather with wayward minds

  to reward his illustrious feats   Antistrophe A (Lines 7–12)
        we must sing in praise
  of a good man—must
        with pageantry
            with poetry's gentle
  touch
        exalt him
            Mélissos has the good fate

of double prizes to aim his heart toward joyful
celebration
      he greeted victory crowns
in the glens of the Isthmós
      and then in the barrelchested
lion's hollow
      he heralded the name of Thébē

when he won the chariot race   Epode A (Lines 13–18)
      Mélissos does not
indict the ability he inherits from forebears
you doubtless know
      of Kleónymos' ageold glory
for chariots
      kin to Labdakídai in his mother's
family line
      they journeyed the ways of wealth
toiling for fourhorse chariots
      in the eddies
of day-to-day
      life renders everything otherwise
only children of gods remain unscathed

ISTHMIAN 4

Mélissos of Thébai | Pankrátion | 474/3 (?) BCE

Although widely known for their virtues and their successes in athletic competition (I.7–15), four members of Mélissos' family, the Kleōnymídai, lost their lives in battle (I.4.16–17b). Mélissos' achievement recalls victories by members of his family in games at Athénai and Sikyón (I.4.25–30); Píndaros' song thus enacts the principle (I.4.19–24) that intentional recollection reanimates the significance of past achievements. "The earthquake- / maker who inhabits Onkhēstós and the seabridge / before the walls of Kórinthos" is Poseidón (I.4.19–20). Hellenic warriors at Troía did not shower upon Aías, son of Telamón, the honor he earned, but Hómēros ensured his fame by celebrating the hero (I.4.33–9). Although Mélissos' physical stature was small for a pankratist (I.4.49–51), the struggle between Hēraklés and Antaíos (I.4.52–5) illustrates how a smaller combatant might overcome a bigger adversary. We learn of rituals and games in honor of Hēraklés and his sons at Thébai (I.4.61–8), then Píndaros records Mélissos' success in these local athletic competitions (I.4.69–71). "This man" is Mélissos (I.4.70). The "helmsman" Orséas (I.4.71–2) was Mélissos' trainer.

    because gods so will it   Strophe A (Lines 1–6)
        Mélissos
                ten-thousand pathways
    open for me in every direction
        in games
    at Isthmós
        you revealed the machinery
                to render a praisesong
    portrait of your family's virtues
        the Kleōnymídai
    thanks to a god
        they everbloomingly reach
    life's finish: death
        from moment to moment
                winds shift
    chase down every mortal
        and drive them off

    they are said to be honored   Antistrophe A (Lines 7–12)
        from the beginning
    at Thébai
        said to welcome neighbors
                to lack

boisterous insult
      the witness of this family's
unbounded renown
      whether they have withered
away or live—
      whatever this witness whispers
into human ears
      they have attained it
according to every verdict
      venturing out
from home
      they touch the hinterland Pillars of Hēraklés

strive no more for vaster   Epode A (Lines 13–18)
      prowess than theirs
they bred horses and delighted bronzeclad Árēs
      yet war's
ruthless winter emptied their home's blessed hearth—
four men gone in one single day
      but now
after gloomwashed months of stormracked darkness
inventive earth now blooms with reddening roses

in accord with the gods' designs   Strophe B (Lines 19–24)
      the earthquake-
maker who inhabits Onkhēstós and the seabridge
before the walls of Kórinthos
      who endows
this family with our wondrous praisesong
      rekindles
their ageold
      but slumbering
            fame for celebrated
feats
      it drifted off to sleep
            but a fame
reawakened brightens its look
      like the splendor
of Ēōsphóros
      brightest among the other stars—

a fame that heralded   Antistrophe B (Lines 25–30)
      the chariot victorious on hilltops

of Athénai
        in games at Sikyón for Ádrastos
                fame
that bestowed such leaves of song
        as these
                upon those
who lived then
        they did not keep their curved chariotdeck
away from holy days the whole land shares
in competition with all of Hellás
        they took
such joy in what they spent on horses
                unreckoned
silences belong to those untried in trials

to remain unseen: Epode B (Lines 31–36)
        the fortune even of those
who fight
        until they have reached achievement's height
chance deals out
        some this some that
                the skill
of inferior rivals throws down and overwhelms
a stronger man
        you know well the bloodshed strength
of Aías
        through which he drove a blade
                midnight hour
by slumping over his own sword
        Aías earned blame
from every son of Héllēnes who sailed to Troía

but Hómēros has of course brought Aías honor   Strophe C (Lines 37–42)
in people's eyes—
        Hómēros
                who exalted all
of Aías' valor and displayed it with his staff
of otherworldly verse for future poets
to perform
        this deathless echo marches on
if anyone tells any story well
        the unquenchable
radiance of worthy feats has everlastingly

swept across allfruitful earth
    over sea

I hope we find the Moúsai eager to fire   Antistrophe C (Lines 43–48)
the torchlight of praisesongs for Mélissos
    a well-earned crown
for pankrátion
    praisesong for Telesiádas' vineshoot
midfight his bravery has the fierce look of wild
lionroar
    his cleverness the look of a fox
        that counters
the eagle's swoop by flopping onto her back
one ought to use every ploy to dim an adversary

Ōríōn's colossal height was not his lot   Epode C (Lines 49–54)
in life
    while Mélissos is a sight to scorn
his strength is a burly mass to face in a fight
he one time came from Kádmos' Thébai to Antaíos'
home
    someone humble in height
        but with soul unflinching
came to wheatrich Libýē
    to wrestle
        and to bar him
from roofing Poseidón's temple with visitors' skulls:

Alkménē's son   Strophe D (Lines 55–60)
    who strode to Olympía after he
explored all earth's places and pewter sea's sheercliffed bottom
after he tamed the seaways for sailing
    now he
lives in Zeus' palace enjoying a happiness
beyond beautiful:
    deathless gods have honored him
as one of their own
    he is Hébē's husband
        he rules
a goldwashed home
    he is Hēra's son-in-law

outside the Élektrai Gates   Antistrophe D (Lines 61–66)
        we people of Thébai
ready for him a feast and newly built garland
of altars
        where we will heap burnt offerings for eight bronzearmed
men who died
        sons whom Megára
              Kréōn's daughter
mothered with him
        in honor of them
              as sun's radiance
sets
        a dawnbright flame keeps an all-night vigil
and shocks the sky with meaty smoke of sacrifice

and the second day sees the culmination of yearly   Epode D (Lines 67–72)
games
        a test of strength
              here this man
                      his head bright
with myrtle garland
        displayed his double victory
in addition to a previous win
in contests for boys
        by putting his trust in the clever
strategy of his helmsman who steers the tiller
I will celebrate him
        along with Orséas
the delight of poetry's spell trickling over them

ISTHMIAN 5

Phylakídas of Aígina | Pankrátion | 478 (?) BCE

Isthmian 5 and *Isthmian 6* celebrate victories of Phylakídas in games at the Isthmós. Phylakídas is the second, younger son of Lámpōn. The other is Pythéas, whose victory in the pankrátion *Nemean 5* celebrates. *Isthmian 5* addresses Theía (I.5.1–6), whom Hēsíodos identifies as the mother of Ēós, Hélios, and Selénē (*Theog.* 371–4). An ancient commentator on the passage offers this allegorical interpretation: "Hélios comes from Theía and Hyperíōn, and gold from Hélios. To each heavenly body, some natural material refers: gold to Hélios, silver to Selénē, iron to Árēs, lead to Krónos, amber to Zeus, tin to Hermés, bronze to Aphrodítē." In this song celebrating an athlete from Aígina, Píndaros fittingly includes mythography about the hero Aiakós and his descendants, Akhilleús in particular (I.5.19–45). When Píndaros turns to the subject of the Trojan War, the addressee of the imperative verb (I.5.39) is unspecified, but the language resembles an invocation of the Moúsai at the beginning of a catalog of characters or events in narrative poetry. The exploits of Akhilleús segue to praise for the bravery of Aígina's sailors during the Battle of Salamís in 480 BCE (I.5.46–50). Pythéas seems to have been Phylakídas' trainer (I.5.59–61).

    mother of Hélios   Strophe A (Lines 1–6)
        manynamed Theía
            people
    worship gold for the sake of your divinity
    as a strength far greater than any other
    when ships clash at sea
        or horses yoked to chariots
    through the esteem you give, our queen,
        they become
    something wondrous in competition's flurry

    and in the ordeals of athletes' contests he   Antistrophe A (Lines 7–12)
    achieves the renown he craves
        if luxuriant garlands
    of wild celery crown the hair of any
    man who prevails with armstrength
        with footspeed
            divinity
    discerns men's strength
        two things alone tend life's
    most joyful harvest in times of fullflower prosperity:

                if someone basks in good luck   Epode A (Lines 13–21)
                        if someone hears
                another speak well of them
                        do not strive to become
                a Zeus
                        you claim every good fortune if the divinely
                allotted share of those two gifts should find you
                mortal aspirations are proper for mortals
                for you at the Isthmós
                        a double boldbloom pankrátion
                achievement
                        Phylakídas
                                endures
                                        at Neméa for both—
                you and Pythéas
                        my heart does not enjoy
                the taste of praisesong without the Aiakídai
                        I
                have come for Lámpōn's sons in the company of Khárites

                to this city with honored traditions   Strophe B (Lines 22–27)
                        if Aígina
                has taken the purified path of godgifted feats
                let no envy limit the drink of clamor
                and song we make to reward the island's toil
                among the ancient heroes
                        outstanding warriors
                also earned their tale
                        they have their fame
                because of lyres and allvoiced harmonies of auloí

                for as long as time is time   Antistrophe B (Lines 28–33)
                        the will of Zeus:
                reverence for heroes confers upon poets their purpose
                in Aitōlía's remarkable sacrifices
                the dominant Oinëídai
                        in Thébai
                                horsedriving Iólaos
                takes honor's prize
                        Perseús in Árgos
                                the weaponry
                of Kástōr and Polydeúkēs alongside Eurótas' currents

but in Oinóna the greathearted intensity　　　　　　　　　Epode B (Lines 34–42)
of Aiakós and his sons
　　　in combat they twice attacked
the Tróes' city
　　　the first time when they followed
Hēraklés
　　　then as allies of the Atrëídai
　　　　　now launch
me from the flatlands
　　　tell who slayed Kýknos
　　　　　who slayed
Héktōr
　　　slayed the fearless bronzarmed commander
of the Aithíopes' army
　　　who wounded proud Télephos
with his spearthrust along the banks of Káïkos

voices declare Aígina their homeland　　　　　　　　　　Strophe C (Lines 43–48)
　　　the unmatched island
long ago its people founded Aígina
as a tower to climb with lofty valor
my tongue's deft words have rafts of arrows to fire off
songs of praise for those heroes
　　　even today
the city of Aías
　　　Salamís
　　　　　would witness that Aígina's
sailors rescued it in the havoc of Árēs

during Zeus' lethal storm with its haildown　　　　　　Antistrophe C (Lines 49–54)
bloodshed for countless men
　　　and yet drench this boast
with silence
　　　Zeus deals both good and bad
　　　　　the Zeus
who rules over everything
　　　under the charms
of honey's allure
　　　even such honors as these
welcome with affection the joy of beautiful
victory
　　　let someone battle to succeed

275

in athletes' contests after he has studied   Epode C (Lines 55–63)
the family line of Kleónikos
    the endless drudgery
of men does not hide from sight
    nor have heavy costs
rankled their reverence for aspiration
    I praise
as well Pythéas
    another limbtaming pankrátion
fighter
    righting the speed and aim of Phylakídas'
fists—
    Pythéas
        skilled at tests of armstrength
clever at wrestling maneuvers
    take for him
a garland
    bring him a headband of felted wool
and send along with them this new wingborne praisesong

ISTHMIAN 6

Phylakídas of Aígina | Boys' Pankrátion | 480 BCE

Since *Isthmian 6* mentions only one of Phylakídas' Isthmian victories and *Isthmian 5* records two, it appears that Píndaros composed *Isthmian 6* prior to *Isthmian 5*. Ancient commentators explain the conventional procedure for the ritual of libation as follows: the first libation is for Zeus as the chief god of Ólympos; the second, for Gaía and heroes; the third, for Zeus *sōtér* "Zeus the savior" (cf. I.6.8). Bury suggests that the first and third libations are relatively fixed by custom, but the occasion determined the second libation's dedicatee. Píndaros metaphorically adapts this ritual (I.6.1–9) to the poetic offering of *epiníkion*: the first libation is for Pythéas' victory at Neméa (I.6.3), celebrated in *Nemean 5*; the second libation, for Phylakídas' first victory at the Isthmós (I.6.5–7), celebrated here in *Isthmian 6*; and the third libation, for a hoped-for third victory at Olympía (I.6.7–9). The theme of libation recurs in the mythological narrative and the song's conclusion. The "lord of Isthmós" (I.6.5) is Poseidón. The sisters of Klōthó (I.6.17) are Lákhesis and Átropos. As in other *epiníkia* for athletes from Aígina, *Isthmian 6* features the mythology of the island's hero Aiakós and his descendants. Hēraklés' prayer that Telamón may have a virtuous son (I.6.42–9) touches on a familial theme relevant to this song: the good fortune of a father, such as Lámpōn, whose sons are distinguished. In order to appreciate the wordplay of Hēraklés' proposal to name Telamón's son Aías (I.6.53–4), it is necessary to know that the Hellenic word *aietós* means "eagle": Hēraklés enjoins Telamón to name his son Aías after the *aietós*, the providentially appearing bird associated with Zeus. The last twenty lines of the poem celebrate the achievements of the Psalykhiádai, both the sons of Lámpōn, Phylakídas and Pythéas, and their maternal uncle Euthyménēs (I.6.57–62). Hēsíodos' saying, to which Píndaros alludes (I.6.66–8), is "deliberate effort helps work's cause" (*Op.* 412).

    like wine and water mixed   Strophe A (Lines 1–9)
        when the men's symposium
flowers
        we mix a second bowl of lyrics
gifts of the Moúsai
        for the victorious family
of Lámpōn
        the first bowl we mixed for you Zeus
            at Neméa
where we welcomed the bloom of victory garlands
but now a second bowl for lord of Isthmós
and the fifty Nērēídes
        because Phylakídas
            Lámpōn's

youngest son
    has won
        I pray we ready
a third bowl for Zeus the savior
    Zeus of Olympía
and pour out an offering of honeyvoiced songs for Aígina

if any human attains godgifted greatness   Antistrophe A (Lines 10–18)
because he enjoys paying the price and toil's strain
if a god plants for him an alluring garden of glory
then as a godhonored man
    he casts his anchor
at good fortune's farthest shores
    the son of Kleónikos
prays that he may meet Háïdēs
    and gray old age
after he has known such sheer joy
    I invoke
highthroned Klōthó
    and her sister Moírai
        attend
the worthy petitions of the man
    my friend

and you   Epode A (Lines 19–25)
    Aiakídai with goldclad chariots
        I
declare that this decree is most clear to me:
to rain down on you words of praise when I visit
this island
    ten-thousand roadways for your majestic
feats have been cut
    each one
        one hundred feet wide
beyond Neílos' sources
    through northlands of Hyperbóreoi
there is no city so foreign
    so destitute
of language
    that it does not hear of Pēleús renown
the hero blessed to be brother of gods by marriage—

  Isthmians

hear of Aías   Strophe B (Lines 26–34)
     son of Telamón
          or his father
Alkménē's son brought Telamón aboard to sail
as a ready ally
     along with soldiers of Tíryns
for war that delights in armor
     war against Troía,
the bane of heroes, to answer Laomédōn's crimes
with Telamón Hēraklés overtook Pérgamos
     murdered
the Méropes' people
     and in Phlégra
          when he tracked down
Alkyoneús
     the cowherd big as a mountain
          he did not
keep his hands away from baritone bowstring

but when Hēraklés arrived to invite Aiakídas   Antistrophe B (Lines 35–43)
on that voyage
     he happened to find them enjoying
a feast
     Telamón then urged the mighty spearman
son of Amphitrýōn
     who stood there cloaked in lion
skin
     to pour the first offering of nectarlike drink
Telamón
     that bravest of men
          lifted up to him
the wine-embracing cup that bristled with goldbright
and Hēraklés then stretched his indomitable hands skyward and spoke
aloud a speech like this one
     "if ever
          my father
Zeus
     you hear my prayers with open heart

now   Epode B (Lines 44–50)
     with this reverent prayer
          I now entreat you
to grant this man and Eríboia an intrepid son

a son fated to be my friend
         with unbreakable build
   like the hide of the beast that now roams around
   my shoulders—
         I one time killed it at Neméa
   the first of my many trials
         and may the child's
   spirit match his stature"
         the god sent in reply
   to him that said these words a great eagle
         commander
   of birds
         a wave of gratitude surged within

   and again he spoke   Strophe C (Lines 51–59)
         a voice just like a soothsayer's:
   "he will be a child whom you praise
         Telamón
   and because this bird appeared
         name him mighty
   Aías in memory of it
         a dreaded portent
   in the peoples' wartime toils"
         when he had spoken
   Hēraklés abruptly took his seat
         long would be
   the time for me to inventory their every
   achievement
         and yet I have come
               my Moúsa
   to dole out
   unbridled celebration for Phylakídas
         for Pythéas
   for Euthyménēs
         in the style of Árgos' people
   I will tell the story as briefly as I can

   they clinched three pankrátion victories   Antistrophe C (Lines 60–68)
         one at the Isthmós
   two at treeleaf Neméa
         the splendid sons
   of Lámpōn and their mother's brother
         what

a destiny of praisesongs they led up into the light
they water the homeland of Psalykhiádai with loveliest
dewdrops of the Khárites
    they have exalted
the house of Themístios
    they dwell in this city dear
to gods
    by investing his actions with diligence
Lámpōn certainly honors that saying of Hēsíodos
and by telling it to his sons
    he teaches them

and thus adorns his town with a communal crown   Epode C (Lines 69–75)
he garners affection for his kindness to guests
he intends moderation
    he adheres to moderation
his speech does not veer away from his thoughts
    you might say
that among competitors
    he is the bronzetaming whetstone
of Náxos among other stones
    I will have him drink
Dírkē's sacred water
    which the deepbelted
daughters of Mnēmosýnē
    who wears a robe of gold
made flow beside the bulwark gates of Kádmos

ISTHMIAN 7

Strepsiádas of Thébai | Pankrátion | 454 (?) BCE

Isthmian 7 attends more to the victor's uncle, also named Strepsiádas, who died in war (I.7.24–36), than to the athlete's victory in the pankrátion. By saying that Thébē, the eponymous Nýmphē of Thébai, "welcomed / the mightiest of gods" (I.7.5), Zeus, Píndaros alludes to the conception of Hēraklés, son of Zeus and Alkménē, who emigrated with her mortal companion, Amphitrýōn, from the Pelopónnēsos to Thébai. Píndaros adapts the story of Zeus visiting Danáē in Árgos as a rain of gold to Zeus' liaison with Alkménē. By enjoining Thébē, "and so sing Strepsiádas too" (I.7.20–1), Píndaros means that Strepsiádas' achievements, in addition to the ancient splendor of Thébai, cataloged in the poem's opening (I.7.1–15), also merit praise. The "Earthembracer" (I.7.38) is Poseidón, whom games at the Isthmós honored, so that Strepsiádas' victory at the Isthmós contributes to the consolation of "clearsky weather." This song contains some of Píndaros' most profound reflections on mortality (I.7.42–8).

    which of all your land's outstanding feats brightened   Strophe A (Lines 1–5)
    your spirit most
        blessed Thébē?
            was it when you
    brought forth plushtressed Diónysos as companion
    to bronzeringing Dēmétēr?
        or when you welcomed
    the mightiest of gods as a midnight snowfall of gold

    that time he stood in Amphitrýōn's doorway and sought   Antistrophe A (Lines 6–10)
    the hero's wife to father Hēraklés?
        or Teiresías
    his enigmatic counsel?
        or Iólaos
            skilled horseman?
    or those tireless spearmen
        the Spartoí?
            or when you sent
    Ádrastos away from the overwhelming warcry

    bereft of ten thousand friends—   Epode A (Lines 11–17)
        Ádrastos
            back
    to horsetending Árgos?
        or were you happiest when you
    founded your Dorian colony of Lakedaímōn's people

on the steep foothill
>and the Aigeídai
>>your posterity
overtook Amýklai
>in obedience
to Pythó's oracular counsel?
>but your ancient
splendor slumbers
>mortal memories falter

if anything fails to reach the flowering heights   Strophe B (Lines 18–22)
of poetry yoked to a triumphant flow of lyrics
and so sing Strepsiádas too
>with sweetversed praisesong
he brings you a pankrátion victory at the Isthmós
astonishing strength
>a build to behold
>>he acts
with a rectitude no less worthy than his body

the Moúsai   Antistrophe B (Lines 23–27)
>wreathed in violets
>>make him gleam
and he shared his wild celery crown with the uncle
whose name he shares
>true:
>>bronzeshield Árēs mixed
for him the drink of death's doom
>but honor rewards
good men
>whoever stands beneath war's cloud
and drives back bloodshed's hailstorm in defense
of his beloved homeland
>unleashing ruin

for a hostile army   Epode B (Lines 28–34)
>let him clearly know
that he is the man who makes glory grow most greatly
for his fellow townsmen's kin while he lives
and when he dies
>and you, son of Diódotos
>>rivaled
the heroism of warrior Meléagros

                    rivaled Héktōr
and Amphiáraos
               when you breathed forth fullbloom youth

fighting among the frontline warriors   Strophe C (Lines 35–39)
               where soldiers
bravely fended off war's clash with the desperate
hopes one has before ceasing to hope
               they suffered
unspeakable sorrow
               but now the Earthembracer
has sent me clearsky weather after that storm
I adorn my hair with garlands
               I will sing
let no envy among undying gods trouble

whatever everyday delight I pursue   Antistrophe C (Lines 40–44)
as I journey unburdened toward old age and life's
allotted end
               we are all alike
                         we die—
but our fortunes differ
               if someone stares off after
faraway things
               they are unworthy to reach
the gods' bronzepaved home
               and so winged Pégasos threw

his rider off   Epode C (Lines 45–51)
               Bellerophóntēs
                         because he aspired
to ride to the palace of sky and join Zeus' gathering
the bitterest end attends a sweetness that clashes
with what is right
               but Loxías
                         you who bloom
with goldstreaked hair
               grant our wish for a laurel-leaf
victory garland in your contests at Pythó

ISTHMIAN 8

Kléandros of Aígina | Boys' Pankrátion | 478 BCE

Píndaros expresses his grief (I.8.5) over events that afflicted Hellás during the Persian Wars and portrays the troubled times as the Hellenic people's stone of Tántalos (I.8.9–11), a metaphor for adversity. In the injunction "do not worship your misery" (I.8.7), the speaker appears to address himself. The mythological genealogy of the Asōpídes, Thébē and Aígina, twin daughters of Metópē and Asōpós, supplies Píndaros with a vehicle (I.8.16–18) for characterizing the relationship between his homeland of Thébai and the homeland of Kléandros, Aígina, as a traditional one. This alignment accounts for why a poet from Thébai, which allied with Persia at the Battle of Plátaia in 479 BCE, would celebrate an athlete from Aígina, which fought with the Hellenic alliance against the Persians. When Zeus and Poseidón squabbled over Thétis (I.8.27–9), Thémis informed them of the prophecy that the daughter of Dōrís and Nēreús would give birth to a son more powerful than his father (I.8.31–5). The two gods then agreed to endorse a marriage between Thétis and Pēleús, a son of Aiakós, the celebrated hero of Aígina (I.8.38–45). The son to whom Thémis refers in her speech (I.8.35–45) is Akhilleús. Kheírōn (I.8.41) oversaw the marriage of Thétis and Pēleús. The mythological narrative catalogs Akhilleús' major exploits and the honor the gods conferred upon him (I.8.47–60). The poem's last strophe (I.8.61–70) juxtaposes the Moúsai's funerary praisesong for Akhilleús with the celebration of Nikokléēs, a cousin of Kléandros, who is "the son of his father's / distinguished brother" (I.8.65). Nikokléēs had won a boxing contest at the Isthmós, then died during the conflict with Persia.

    one of you young men   Strophe A (Lines 1–10)
        go to the splendid doorway
of his father Telésarkhos
        then for Kléandros—
and for his youth—
        wake up a song parade
to repay his hard work with glory
        to reward his victory
at the Isthmós—
        and because he found such strength
in games at Neméa
        I too
                although my heart mourns
they ask me to call on golden Moúsa
        freed
from overwhelming sorrows
        let's not plummet
into deprivation of victory crowns

and do not worship your misery
      now that we
enjoy respite from devastating woe
we will perform some sweet song before the people
even in the wake of our adversity
because some god has turned away from us
the boulder suspended over Tántalos' head

an unbearable burden for Hellás   Strophe B (Lines 11–20)
      but fear's
passing away has ended my stubborn worry
in every circumstance
      to look to what lies
at our feet
      is always better
            a treacherous time looms
above the heads of men and crumples life's
trajectory
      freedom
            this can heal even
such ordeals that mortals face
      a man
needs to think about worthy hope
      a man cared for
at sevengated Thébai needs to dedicate
the Khárites' first fruits at Aígina
      because their father's
twin daughters were born the youngest of the Asōpídes
and they delighted Zeus the king
      he settled
Thébē alongside Dírkē's lovely streams
as ruler of the chariot-loving city

And you   Strophe C (Lines 21–30)
      Aígina
            after Zeus brought you to Oinopía
island
      he used to bed down beside you
            and there
you mothered divine Aiakós
      whom his thunderboom
father most adored of all earthbound mortals
he even rendered judgment in disputes

among the gods
        his godlike sons and their children
who earned Árēs' favor
        excelled all other warriors
in courage
        when faced with bronzeclad battlegroans
they practiced moderation
        they practiced prudence
the gatherings of even the blessed gods recalled
their character
        when Zeus and brightshining Poseidón quarreled
over marriage to Thétis
        because each one wanted her
to be his lovely wife
        Érōs held them
in its grasp
        but the gods' undying knowledge
did not bring about for them that marriage

when they heard the prophetic decree   Strophe D (Lines 31–40)
        insightful
Thémis spoke among the gods
        it was fated:
this sea goddess would mother a son whose reign
would be mightier than his father's
        a son who would wield
with all his might another weapon stronger
than thunderbolt or intractable trident
        if she
stirs her limbs together with Zeus or Zeus'
brothers
        "check your yearning
                but let her look
upon a son killed in battle
        after she finds
a mortal's bed—
        a son who looks like Árēs
in armstrength
        who looks like a lightning flash in footspeed
my advice:
        bestow the godgifted prize
of honor to marry her upon Pēleús
Aiakídas who
        so they say

                    tends the open
spaces of Iōlkós with unmatched reverence

this report must go forth at once   Strophe E (Lines 41–50)
          straight to Kheírōn's
unwithering cave
          and do not let the daughter
of Nēreús put leafkindling for conflict in the hollow
of our hands a second time
          and on fullmoon
evenings she might unfasten her virginity's
lovely bridle for the hero"
          the goddess
spoke explaining everything to the Kronídai
they lowered their deathless heads in agreement
          the fruit
of her words did not waste away
          they say that lord Zeus
heeded the shared approval for Thétis' marriage
and the voices of poets displayed the youth
          the valor
of Akhilleús
          for those who do not know it—
                    Akhilleús
who bloodied the vineyard-laden plain of Mysía
spattering that land with Télephos' gruesome death

who built the bridge to homeward return for the Atreïdai   Strophe F (Lines 51–60)
who helped free Helénē
          cutting down Troía's muscle
with his spear—
          Troía's muscle that one time tried
to block his path as he waged his mortalslaying
battlefield work
          Mémnōn's overbold strength
                    Héktōr
and other bravest warriors
          by showing them
the way to Persephónē's house
          Akhilleús
                    bastion
of Aiakídai
          shined fame's light on Aígina

and their rootstock
> not even when he died
did songs abandon him
> but Helikón's maidens stood
beside his pyre and tomb
> and poured their manyvoiced
mourning over him
> and so the undying gods deemed
it good to gift a brave mortal with the goddesses'
praisesongs after he has withered away

and even now   Strophe G (Lines 61–70)
> this judgement proves right
>> the Moúsai's
chariot speeds along to build a song
memorial for Nikokléēs
> the boxer
>> honor him
who had the fortune to win a leafy crown
of Dorian celery in the valley of Isthmós
and because he also one time defeated the men
who lived nearby when he sent them scattering off
with his inescapable fist
> the son of his father's
distinguished brother
> does not discredit him
therefore have one of his agemates weave around
Kléandros' head
> a luxurious myrtle crown
for the pankrátion
> and because Alkáthoos' contest
and youth of Epídauros welcomed him before
when he found success
> a good man is allowed
to praise him
> he did not bury his youth in a hole
so that it had no taste of something beautiful

ISTHMIAN 9

Unknown Victor from Aígina | Event Unknown | Date Unknown

Like other songs by Píndaros for athletes from the island, the eight lines of this fragment mention Aiakós and Aígina.

   famous the story of Aiakós
        famous too
   Aígina
        celebrated for its ships
   the Dorian troops of Hýllos and Aigimiós
   came and established it in obedience to destiny
   the people of Aígina govern their land on the basis
   of their blueprint
        transgressing neither custom
   nor what is right in treatment of guests
        they are like
   dolphins in their seafaring prowess
        they wisely
   oversee the Moúsai and athletes' trials

GLOSSARY

This glossary includes all proper nouns that occur in Píndaros' *epiníkia*, select Hellenic terms for athletics and poetics, and a few domesticated English entries (for example, "Hyperian Fountain" and "Trojan War"). I adapt this glossary from William J. Slater's *Lexicon to Pindar*. The "Pronunciation Guide" explains the orthographic conventions I adopt. Glossary entries with lower-case first letters are common nouns. Where it may be useful, I provide in parentheses very commonly occurring domesticated English equivalents for glossary items. Conventional abbreviations refer to Píndaros' *epiníkia*: O refers to Olympian *epiníkia*, P to Pythian *epiníkia*, N to Nemean *epiníkia*, and *I* to Isthmian *epiníkia*. Thus O.1.1 refers abbreviatedly to "*Olympian 1*, line 1." I cite passages of Píndaros' poetry only when doing so may mitigate ambiguity and selectively cross-reference glossary entries with **bold type**.

Ábas	Mythological figure. Son of Hyperméstra and Lynkeús (1). Grandfather of Ádrastos.
Ádmētos	Mythological figure. Son of Phérēs, cousin of Iásōn and Melámpous.
Adrastídai	Mythological figures. The word means "descendants of Ádrastos."
Ádrastos	Mythological figure. Son of Talaós. King of Árgos and Sikyón. Central figure in the **Seven Against Thébai** story. Led **Epígonoi** in a second attack of Thébai. Father of Argeía and Aigialeús. Grandfather of Thérsandros.
Agamémnōn	Mythological figure. Married Klytaimnéstra. Brother of Menélaos. Son of Atreús. King of Árgos. Leader of the Héllēnes in their campaign against Troía. See **Trojan War**.
Agläïa	Deity. Her name means "splendor" or "celebration." One of the Khárites.
agorá	Generally, a gathering of people or the place of such a gathering. More specifically, the city center, site of a marketplace.
Aiakídas (plural: Aiakídai)	Mythological and historical figures. The word means "descendant of Aiakós." Refers to sons of Aiakós—Pēleús (P.3.87 and I.8.39) and Telamón (I.6.35)—or to his descendents (Aías, Neoptólemos at N.7.45, Akhilleús at I.8.55) or to people of Aígina (O.13.109, P.8.23, N.3.64, N.4.11, N.5.8, N.6.17, N.6.46, N.7.10, I.5.20, and I.6.19).
Aiakós	Mythological figure. Son of Aígina and Zeus. Father of Pēleús, Telamón, and Phókos. Married Endēís. Had an affair with Psamáthē, daughter of Nēreús. Original king of Aígina and worshipped historically there.
Aías (Ajax) (1)	Mythological figure. From Salamís. Son of Telamón. See N.2.14, N.4.48, N.7.26, N.8.27, I.4.35, I.5.48, I.6.26, and I.6.53.
Aías (Ajax) (2)	Mythological figure. Son of Oïleús. Fought in **Trojan War**. Games were held at Opoús (3) in honor of him (O.9.112).
Aiétēs	Mythological figure. Son of Hélios. Father of Médeia. King of Kolkhís.
Aigaí	The name of two cities, one on Eúboia, one in Akhaía, both sacred to Poseidón.

Glossary

Aigeídai
Mythological and historical figures. The word means "descendants of Aigeús," one of the Spartoí of Thébai. Refers to a family linked to Thébai and Spárta. Píndaros claims to belong to this family (P.5.75–6).

Aigialeús
Mythological figure. Son of Ádrastos.

Aigimiós
Mythological figure. Father of Dýmas and Pámphylos. A founder of Dorian people.

Aígina
Mythological figure. A *nýmphē*. Daughter of Metópē and Asōpós. Sister of Thēbē. Mother of Aiakós (father: Zeus) and Menoítios (father: Áktōr). Eponym of the island Aígina in the Saronic Gulf.

Aigíokhos
The word means "Aigísbearer." Epithet of Zeus.

aigís
Divine weapon of Athēná or Zeus. A shield or animal hide with power to defend or to terrify.

Aígisthos
Mythological figure. Lover of Klytaimnéstra. Killed Agamémnōn when he returned to Árgos from Troía. Oréstēs killed him to avenge his father.

Aígyptos (Egypt)
Region of northern Africa that neighbors Libýē. As mythological figure and eponym of the African region, brother of Danaós and father of Lynkeús (1).

Ainéas
Historical figure. According to ancient commentators, the trainer of the *khorós* that performed O.6.

Ainēsídamos
Historical figure. Father of Thērōn and Xenokrátēs. Grandfather of Thrasýboulos.

Aiolic/Aiolian
Refers to a variety of ancient Hellenic language that is often associated with the region that includes the island Lésbos, home of the lyric poets Sápphō and Alkaíos, who lived during the late seventh and early sixth centuries BCE. Píndaros associated particular poetic rhythms and musical melodies with Aiolic Hellenic.

Aíolos
Mythological figure. Husband of Enarétē. Father of Sísyphos and Krētheús. The patrilineal genealogy for major figures in the mythology of Kórinthos is: Aíolos father of Sísyphos; Sísyphos father of Glaúkos; Glaúkos father of Bellerophóntēs; Bellerophóntēs father of Hippolókhos; Hippolókhos father of Glaúkos. Píndaros, however, depicts Bellerophóntēs as the father of the younger Glaúkos (O.13.61–4). Krētheús is an ancestor of Aísōn, his son Iásōn, and Pelías.

Aípytos
Mythological figure. Son of Élatos. Brother of Ískhys. King of Phaisána, a city in Arkadía.

Aísōn
Mythological figure. Son of Krētheús. Grandson of Aíolos. Father of Iásōn.

Aithíopes
The people of Aithiopía.

Aithiopía (Ethiopia)
Hellenic exonym for the region of the upper (i.e. inland, in the direction of its source) Neílos River.

Aítna (1) (Aetna)
Volcanic mountain of Sikelía. Zeus buried the monster Typhós under it.

Aítna (2) (Aetna)
Town of Sikelía, founded by Hiérōn in 476 (?) BCE on the site of Katánē, near Mount Aítna.

Aitōlía
Region on the northern coast of the Gulf of Kórinthos.

Ákastos
Mythological figure. Son of Pelías. Husband of Hippolýtē. King of Iōlkós. Hippolýtē attempted to seduce Pēleús, who rejected her. Claiming that he attempted to rape her, she persuaded her husband Ákastos to kill Pēleús. Ákastos stole Pēleús' sword, made by Daídalos, and conspired with the Kéntauroi to attack the unarmed hero, but Kheírōn intervened and restored to Pēleús his special weapon. Pēleús then defeated Ákastos and the Kéntauroi and overtook Iōlkós.

Glossary

Akhaía	Either the region of northeastern Pelopónnēsos along the southern coast of the Gulf of Kórinthos (N.10.47) or a region of southeastern Thessalía (N.7.64 and I.1.58).
Akhaioí	Mythological figures. The word means "people of Akhaía." The poetry of Hómēros often identifies Héllēnes who fought at Troía as Akhaioí. Píndaros occasionally adopts this convention, referring to Héllēnes as Akhaioí.
Akharnaí	A deme of Athénai.
Akhérōn	Underworld river.
Akhilleús	Mythological figure. Son of Thétis and Pēleús. Greatest warrior among the Héllēnes who fought at Troía in the **Trojan War**.
Akrágas (1)	City of Sikelía (modern Agrigento).
Akrágas (2)	River that flowed through city of same name. Also the *nýmphē* associated with the river.
Ákrōn	Historical figure. From Kamárina. Father of Psaúmis.
Áktōr	Mythological figure. Father of Menoítios.
Alétēs	Mythological figure. Descendant of Hēraklés. Dorian who became king of Kórinthos by defeating descendents of Sísyphos.
alétheia	The noun means "truth" or more radically "unforgetting." Píndaros personifies Alétheia as a divine figure and daughter of Zeus (O.10.4).
Aleuádai	Historical figures. The word means "descendents of Aleúas." Prominent family of Lárisa, a city in Thessalía.
Aleúas	Mythological figure. Son of Hēraklés. King of Thessalía. Namesake ancestor of the Aleuádai.
Alexibiádas	Historical figure. The word means "son of Alexibías." Refers to Kárrhōtos.
Alexídamos	Legendary figure. An ancestor of Telesikrátēs.
Alkäídas (plural: Alkäídai)	Mythological figure. The word means "descendant of Alkaíos." Refers to Amphitrýōn's family line, which includes Hēraklés (O.6.68).
Alkáthoos	Mythological figure. Son of Hippodámeia and Pélops. Local games at Mégara were held in his honor.
Alkimédōn	Historical figure. From Aígina. Son of Iphíōn. Brother of Timosthénēs. Victor in boys' wrestling at Olympía.
Alkimídas	Historical figure. From Aígina. Son of Théōn. Member of Bassídai family. Victor in boys' wrestling at Neméa.
Alkmaíōn	Mythological figure. Son of Eriphýlē and Amphiáraos. Killed his mother to avenge the death of his father. One of the Epígonoi.
Alkmaiōnídai	Mythological and historical figures. The word means "descendents of Alkmaíōn." Refers to a prominent family of Athénai.
Alkménē	Mythological figure. Married Amphitrýōn. Mother of Hēraklés and Iphiklés. Half-sister of Likýmnios.
Alkyoneús	Mythological figure. Son of Gaía and Ouranós. A giant killed by Hēraklés and Telamón.
Alpheiós	River in the Pelopónnēsos that flows along the southern perimeter of Olympía. See **Aréthousa**.
Áltis	Placename for the sacred grove at Olympía, the area dedicated to religious structures and practices.
Amazón (plural: Amazónes)	Mythological figures. Name for tribe of women warriors from the northern reaches of world known to ancient Héllēnes. Bellerophóntēs and Telamón fought against them.
Aménas	River in Sikelía near Aítna.

Glossary

Ámmōn	Deity. Hellenic name for Amun. Main deity of Thébai in Aígyptos and part of the pantheon in the religion of Aígyptos. Hellenic sources identify Amun with Zeus. The oracle of Zeus Ámmōn was a significant feature of religious practice in **Kyrénē**.
Amphiáraos	Mythological figure. Son of Oiklés. Husband of Eriphýlē. Father of Alkmaíōn. A prophet. King of Árgos. One of the band of seven that attacked Thébai (see **Seven Against Thébai**).
Amphitrítē	Deity. Daughter of either Dōrís and Nēreús or of Tēthýs and Ōkeanós. Married Poseidón.
Amphitrýōn	Mythological figure. Grandson of Perseús. Originally from Árgos, then from Thébai. Husband of Alkménē. Natural father of Iphiklés and adoptive, mortal father of Hēraklés.
Amýklai	City located near Spárta. Hērakleídai and Aigeídai captured it.
Amyntorídai	Mythological figures. The word means "descendents of Amýntōr." Refers to descendents of Tlēpólemos, the grandson of Amýntōr. Tlēpólemos led the colonization of Rhódos.
Amytháōn	Mythological figure. Son of Krētheús. Brother of Aísōn. Father of Melámpous.
angelía	The word generally means "public announcement" or "message." Angelía understood as a poetic version of a formal victory announcement is a simple speech genre that regularly occurs in *epiníkia*. The personified Angelía is the daughter of the messenger god Hermés (O.8.81–2).
Antaíos (1)	Mythological figure. Son of Gaía and Poseidón. A giant. Lived in Libýē. Forced travellers to fight him. He mortally defeated all of them because he was invulnerable as long as he touched his mother (Gaía, the earth). Fatally overcome in a wrestling bout with Hēraklés, who managed to hoist Antaíos up so that the giant's feet made no contact with the earth.
Antaíos (2)	Mythological (?) figure. A king of Libýē. May be same figure as **Antaíos (1)**.
Antēnorídai	Mythological figures. The word means "Descendants of Anténōr." Refers to people of Troía.
Antías	Historical figure. A maternal relative of Theaíos of Árgos who was victorious in games.
Antílokhos	Mythological figure. Son of Néstōr. Mémnōn killed him at Troía.
Aphareús	Mythological figure. Father of Ídas and Lynkeús (2).
Aphrodítē	Deity. Daughter of Diónē and Zeus or born from severed genitals of Ouranós. Goddess of sex and sexual desire.
Apóllōn	Deity. Son of Lētó and Zeus. Brother of Ártemis. God of healing, prophecy, and music. Delphoí was sacred to him. Father of Aristaíos, Asklēpiós, and Íamos. Worshipped as Apóllōn Karnéios at Kyrénē.
Areía	Name of a site on the **Hélōros** River in Sikelía.
Árēs	Deity. Son of Héra and Zeus. God of war. Sometimes the god's name is a metonym for warfare, mortal conflict, or lethal destruction.
Aréthousa	A spring located on **Ortygía**. According to traditional stories, the river-god Alpheiós pursued the *nýmphē* Aréthousa, the eponym of the spring, whose flight took her to Ortygía. The spring Aréthousa is the site where the waters of the Alpheiós River in the Pelopónnēsos were said to resurface after flowing underground from Hellás.
Argó	Ship of Iásōn and Argonaútai.
Argonaútai (singular: Argonaútēs)	Mythological figures. The heroes who sailed with Iásōn on the Argó in his quest for the Golden Fleece.

Glossary

Árgos	City in Pelopónnēsos just inland from Argolic Gulf. Site of local games called Hēraía or Hekatómbaia that celebrated Héra.
Aristagóras	Historical figure. From Ténedos. *Nemean 11* commemorates his election to the office of prýtanis.
Aristaíos	Mythological figure. Son of the *nýmphē* Kyrénē and Apóllōn. Aristaíos is a culture-hero who transmits to humans knowledge of agricultural practices such as apiculture, viticulture, and olive oil production.
Aristokleídas	Historical figure. From Aígina. Son of Aristophánēs. Winner in pankrátion at Neméa.
Aristoménēs	Historical figure. From Aígina. Son of Xenárkēs. Winner in wresting at Pythó in 446 BCE.
Aristophánēs	Historical figure. From Aígina. Father of Aristokleídas.
Aristotélēs	Legendary figure. Also known as Báttos. According to tradition, founded Kyrénē.
Arkadía	Region of central Pelopónnēsos. Píndaros represents Stýmphalos as the mother of Arkadía (O.6.100).
Arkesílas (1)	Historical figure. Son of Báttos IV. King of Kyrénē. Victor at Pythó in chariot race in 462 BCE. See P.4 and P.5.
Arkesílas (2)	Historical figure. From Ténedos. Father of Aristagóras. See N.11.
Arkhéstratos	Historical figure. From Zephyrian Lokrís. Father of Hagēsídamos.
Arkhílokhos	Historical figure. From Páros. Iambic poet of seventh c. BCE.
Arsinóē	Mythological figure. Nurse of Oréstēs.
Ártemis	Deity. Daughter of Lētó and Zeus. Sister of Apóllōn. Goddess associated with wild places and hunting. In capacity as hunter-goddess of woods and mountains, Ártemis also retains divine oversight of rivers.
Asía	For Píndaros designates generally the Anatolian Peninsula.
Asklēpiós	Mythological figure. Son of Korōnís and Apóllōn. Kheírōn the kéntauros raised him. Legendary healer worshipped in historical religious practice.
Asōpídes	Mythological figures. The word means "daughters of Asōpós." Refers to Aígina and Thébē.
Asōpikhos	Historical figure. From Orkhomenós. Son of Kleódamos.
Asōpódōros	Historical figure. From Orkhomenós. Father of Hēródotos.
Asōpós (1)	River in Boiōtía. The eponymous river-god associated with this river is father of Aígina and Thébē (mother: Metópē). Perhaps for this reason, Píndaros can locate "Asōpós' waters" (N.3.3–4) on the island of Aígina.
Asōpós (2)	River in northern Pelopónnēsos. The city Sikyón is located along it (N.9.9).
Astydámeia	Mythological figure. Daughter of Amýntōr. Wife of Tlēpólemos.
Atabýrion	Mountain on Rhódos. Site of a temple of Zeus.
Athēná	Deity. Daughter of Zeus. Goddess of wisdom, crafts, and warcraft. Patron deity of Athénai.
Athénai (Athens)	Hellenic city in the region of Attikḗ.
Átlas	Deity. Son of Klyménē (or Asía) and Iapetós (or Ouranós). One of the Titánes. According to tradition, assigned the labor of supporting Earth on his shoulders.
Atrĕídēs (plural: Atrĕídai)	Mythological figure(s). The word means "son of Atreús." Refers to Agamémnōn or Menélaos or, in plural, both.
Atreús	Mythological figure. Son of Hippodámeia and Pélops. Father of Agamémnōn and Menélaos. King of Mykénai.

Glossary

Augeías	Mythological figure. King of Epeioí, the people of Élis. Hēraklés killed him.
aulós (plural: auloí)	A wind instrument made of two reeds with finger-holes played with each hand simultaneously.
Áxeinos	An adjective meaning "inhospitable." The Áxeinos ("Inhospitable") Sea is known today as the Black Sea.
Bassídai	Historical figures. Prominent family of Aígina.
Battídai	Historical figures. The word means "descendants of Báttos." Refers to the ruling family of Kyrēnē (2).
Báttos	Legendary figure. Also known as Aristotélēs. From Théra. Son of Phronímē and Polýmnēstos. Descended from Minýai. His name means "Stammerer," and stories about him include the detail that he suffered from a speech impediment. According to tradition, founded Kyrēnē (Paus. 10.15.7).
Bellerophóntēs	Mythological figure. Son of Eurymédē (or Eurynómē) and Glaúkos. From Kórinthos. See also **Pégasos**. See **Aíolos** for the patrilineal genealogy of major figures in the mythology of Kórinthos.
Blepsiádai	Historical figures. Prominent family of Aígina.
Boibiás	A lake in Thessalía.
Boiōtía (Boeotia)	Region of Hellás north of Gulf of Kórinthos that bordered Attikḗ. Thḗbai is located there.
Boréas	Deity. The north wind. Son of Ēós and Astraíos. Said to live in Thrákē. Father of Zétēs and Kálaïs (mother: Oreíthyia).
Daídalos (Daedalus)	Mythological figure. From Athénai. Known for consummate ingenuity as artist and engineer. Lived on Krḗtē, where he is said to have designed the labyrinth.
daímōn (plural: daímones)	This word designates a god, a spiritual entity, or a spiritual quality.
Damágētos	Historical figure. Father of Diagóras of Rhódos.
Damóphilos	Historical figure. From Kyrēnē. An exile from that community who seems to have commissioned P.4.
Danáē	Mythological figure. Daughter of Akrísios. Mother of Perseús.
Danaoí	Name applied to Héllēnes who besieged Troía. Píndaros also refers to early, legendary inhabitants of the Pelopónnēsos (P.4.48) and the **Epígonoi** (P.8.52) as Danaoí.
Danaós	Mythological figure. King of Árgos. Father of fifty daughters, the Danáïdai.
Dárdanoi	Mythological figures. Since Dárdanos was an early king of Troía, Dárdanoi "Dardanians" is synonymous with **Tróes** "Trojans."
Dárdanos	Mythological figure. Early King of Troía.
Deínis	Historical figure. From Aígina. Son of Mégas. Member of Khariádai family. Winner in *stádion* at Neméa.
Deinoménēs (1)	Historical figure. From Syrákousai. Father of Hiérōn, Gélōn, Polýzēlos, and Thrasýboulos.
Deinoménēs (2)	Historical figure. Son of Hiérōn. Ruler of Aítna (2). See P.1.58.
Délios	An adjective meaning "having to do with Délos." An epithet of Apóllōn.
Délos	A Cycladic island near Mýkonos said to float according to some stories. The site where Lētó gave birth to Apóllōn and Ártemis.
Delphoí (Delphi)	Site of panhellenic sanctuary sacred to Apóllōn. Hosted the Pythian Games.
Dēmḗtēr	Deity. Daughter of Rheía and Krónos. Goddess of agriculture. Mother of Persephónē (father: Zeus).
Dēmodíkē	Mythological figure. Stepmother of Phríxos.

Glossary

Deukalíōn	Mythological figure. Son of Klyménē (or Kelainó) and Promētheús. From Mount Parnassós. Husband of Pýrrha, with whom he refounded the human race after a destructive flood sent by Zeus destroyed all other mortals.
Diagóras	Historical figure. From Rhódos. Son of Damágētos. Member of Eratídai family. Prolific winner in boxing, including at Olympía in 464 BCE.
díaulos	A footrace whose course was the *stádion* run out and back and thus twice the distance of the *stádion* (about 400 meters).
díkē	The word means "justice" or "sound judgment." One of the cardinal virtues. The word also denotes specific legal procedures.
Díkē	Diety. Divine embodiment of díkē "justice." One of the Hórai. Daughter of Thémis and Zeus.
Diódotos	Historical figure. From Thébai. Father of Strepsiádas (2).
Diomédēs	Mythological figure. Son of Tydeús. Fought in **Trojan War**.
Diónysos	Deity. Son of Semélē and Zeus. God of vital fluids, such as juice of fruit and sap of trees.
Dióskouroi	Mythological figures. The brothers **Kástōr** and **Polydeúkēs**, who were worshipped in connection with horses. Therápnē hosted a cult site dedicated to the Dióskouroi.
Dírkē	Spring and stream in Thébai.
Dōdónē (Dodona)	Religious site in Épeiros sacred to Zeus, whose oracle is located there.
dolikhós	An athletic event. The long footrace.
Dorian/Doric	Refers to a variation of ancient Hellenic language and the Hellenic regions, people, traditions identified as Dorian. Píndaros' poetic language includes features of Doric variety of ancient Hellenic.
Dóryklos	Legendary figure. From Tíryns. Said to be the first winner in boxing at Olympía.
Earthembracer	Deity. Epithet of Poseidón.
Earthshaker	Deity. Epithet of Poseidón.
Eilatídas	Mythological Figure. The word means "son of Élatos" and refers to Aípytos.
Eileíthyia	Deity. Daughter of Héra. Goddess of childbirth.
Eirénē	Deity. Her name means "peace." One of the Hórai. Daughter of Thémis and Zeus.
Ékhemos	Mythological figure. From Tegéa in Arkadía. Said to be the first winner in wrestling at Olympía.
Ekhíōn	Mythological figure. Son of Antiáneira and Hermés. Brother of Érytos. One of the Argonaútai.
Ēkhó (Echo)	Mythological figure. A *nýmphē*.
Élektrai Gates	One of the seven entryways to Thébai. See **Seven Against Thébai**.
Eleusís	Site in Attikḗ sacred to Dēmḗtēr. Hosted local games in honor of Dēmḗtēr and Persephónē.
Élis	Regional name for the part of the Pelopónnēsos where Olympía is located. Hellanodíkai, judges of athletic competitions at Olympía, came from here. The people of Élis oversaw the religious site of Olympía and the games held there in honor of Zeus.
Emmenídai	Historical figures. Prominent family of Akrágas. Includes Ainēsídamos, Thérōn, Xenokrátēs, and Thrasýboulos. Claimed descent from Kádmos.
Endēís	Mythological figure. Daughter of Khariklṓ and Kheírōn the kéntauros. Married Aiakós. Mother of Telamṓn and Pēleús.

Glossary

Ēós	Deity. The name means "Dawn." Daughter of Theía and Hyperíōn. Brother of Hélios. Mother of Mémnōn (father: Tithōnós).
Eōsphóros	The word means "dawnbringer." Refers to the morning star.
Épaphos	Mythological figure. Son of Ió and Zeus. Originally from Árgos, journeyed to northern Africa, where he was father of the *nýmphē* Libýē.
Epeioí	Legendary figures. Very ancient inhabitants of Élis.
Épeiros	Region of northern Hellás that extends between Píndos Mountains and Ionian Sea. Dōdónē is located there.
Ephármostos	Historical figure. From Opoús (2). Winner in wrestling at Olympía in 468 BCE.
Ephiáltēs	Mythological figure. A giant. Son of Iphimédeia and Poseidón. Brother of Ótos. These brothers killed each other at Náxos.
Ephýra	Principal city of Molossía in Épeiros (N.7.37).
Ephyraíoi	Legendary figures. The people of Ephýra, the ancient name of the city Kranón in Thessalía (P.10.55), not the city **Ephýra** in Molossía.
Epídauros	City located in Pelopónnēsos in the Argolid near the Saronic Gulf. Site of religious sanctuary for Asklēpiós. Hosted Asklēpíeia, games held in honor of the healing god.
Epígonoi	Mythological figures. The seven descendents of the seven heroes who banded together to attack Thébai. See **Seven Against Thébai**.
Epimētheús	Mythological figure. His name means "afterthought." Son of Klyménē (or Asía) and Iapetós. Brother of Promētheús.
epiníkion (plural: epiníkia)	Ancient Hellenic name for the victory song.
Eratídai	Historical figures. Prominent family of Rhódos that claimed descent from Astydámeia and Tlēpólemos.
Erekhtheídai	Historical figures. The word means "descendents of Erekhtheús." Refers to people of Athénai, who are said to descend from the legendary king Erekhtheús.
Erekhtheús	Legendary king of Athénai.
Ergínos	Mythological figure. King of Orkhomenós. Son of Klýmenos. Father of Trophónios and Agamédēs, who founded the temple of Apóllōn at Delphoí according to tradition. One of the **Argonaútai**, he competed in a footrace in armor when the Argó landed at Lémnos.
Ergotélēs	Historical figure. Son of Philánōr. Originally from Krétē. Relocated to Himéra in Sikelía. Winner in *dolikhós* at Olympía.
Eríboia	Mythological figure. Mother of Aías. Married Telamón.
Erinýs	Deity. Underworld goddess represented with wings, snaky hair, and whips or torches in hand. Punishes wrongdoers with destructive madness.
Eriphýlē	Mythological figure. Daughter of Talaós. Sister of Ádrastos. Married Amphiáraos.
Erítimos	Historical figure. Son of Terpsías. Nephew of Ptoiódōros.
érōs	The word means "sexual desire" or "intense (potentially reckless) passion."
Érytos	Mythological figure. Son of Antiáneira and Hermés. Twin brother of Ekhíōn. One of the Argonaútai.
Eteoklés	Mythological figure. Son of Iokástē (Jocasta) and Oidípous. Brother of Polyneíkēs.
Euádnē	Mythological figure. Daughter of Pitánē and Poseidón. Mother of Íamos (father: Apóllōn).

Glossary

Eúboia	Large island off the east coast of Boiōtía. Hosted local games.
Eunomía	Deity. Her name means "adherence to custom." The divine embodiment of social order. One of the Hórai. Daughter of Thémis and Zeus.
Euphánēs	Historical figure. From Aígina. Maternal grandfather of Timásarkhos.
Eúphēmos	Mythological figure. Son of Európē and Poseidón. From Taínaros. One of the Argonaútai. Mythological ancestor of Battídai of Kyrénē.
Euphrosýnē	Deity. Her name means "gladness." One of the Khárites.
Eúripos	The straight between Eúboia and the Hellenic mainland.
Európē	Mythological figure. Daughter of Tityós. Mother of Eúphēmos (father: Poseidón).
Eurótas	Main river in southeastern Pelopónnēsos. Spárta was located along its banks.
Euryálē	Mythological figure. Immortal daughter of Phórkys. One of the three **Gorgónes**.
Eurýpylos	Mythological figure. Another name for Trítōn, a seagod and son of Poseidón.
Eurystheús	Mythological figure. King of Tíryns. Son of Sthénelos. Assigned twelve labors to Hēraklés. Iólaos killed him.
Eurytíōn	Mythological figure. One of the Argonaútai. Son of Íros. Grandson of Áktōr. Nephew of Pēleús, who accidentally killed him during a hunt.
Eúrytos	Mythological figure. Son of Moliónē and Poseidón. Brother of Ktéatos. Hēraklés killed him at Kleōnaí.
Euthyménēs	Historical figure. Maternal uncle of Pythéas and Phylakídas, athletes from Aígina.
Eúxeinos	The adjective means "hospitable." Applies to the sea known today as the Black Sea. With this adjective Píndaros riffs on the more common phrase: the "Hospitable Sea" is often referred to as the "Inhospitable Sea" (see **Áxeinos**).
Eúxenos	Historical figure. An ancester of Sōgénēs.
Gádeira	Ancient Hellenic name for modern Cadiz, city and port on southwestern coast of Spain. Represents the western frontier of the known world, near the Pillars of Hēraklés.
Gaía	Deity. Her name means "earth." According to the poet Hēsíodos, the first divinity to emerge from Kháos. Mothered parthenogenetically Ouranós ("Sky"), mountains, and Póntos ("Sea"). Mother of Titánes and Titanídes (father: Ouranós).
Ganymédēs	Mythological figure. Descendant of Dárdanos, founder of Troía. Son of Kallirhóe amd Trós. Ganymédēs' beauty moved Zeus to metamorphose into an eagle and to abduct the young man to Ólympos. Zeus installed him as cupbearer to the gods. Ganymédēs was also Zeus' beloved, and it is this "same duty" that Pélops fulfilled for Poseidón (O.1.31-3).
Gélōn	Historical figure. Ruler of Syrákousai (485–478 BCE). Son of Deinoménēs. Brother of Hiérōn.
Gēryón	Mythological figure. Son of Kallirrhóē and Khrysáōr. A triple-headed, triple-bodied giant. Known for keeping a dog (or dogs). Hēraklés killed him.
Gígantes	Mythological figures. Offspring of Gaía and Ouranós.
Glaúkos	Mythological figure. Son of Bellerophóntēs. King of Lykía. See **Aíolos** for the patrilineal genealogy of major figures in the mythology of Kórinthos.
Gorgó (plural: Gorgónes)	Mythological figure. A powerful woman with wings and snakes for hair. Daughter(s) of Kētó and Phórkys. Médousa (mortal) and her (immortal) sisters Euryálē and Sthenó are Gorgónes.
Hagēsías	Historical figure. Member of Iamídai family, with homes in Syrákousai and Stýmphalos. Son of Sóstratos. Winner at Olympía in 468 BCE.

Glossary

Hagēsídamos (1)	Historical figure. From Epizephyrian **Lokroí**. Victor at Olympía 476 BCE. Son of Arkhéstratos. See O.10 and O.11.
Hagēsídamos (2)	Historical figure. From Akrágas. Father of Khromíos. See N.1 and N.9.
Hagēsímakhos	Male ancestor of Alkimídas, possibly his great-great-grandfather.
Háïdēs (Hades) (1)	The underworld.
Háïdēs (Hades) (2)	Deity. God of the dead. Ruler of underworld. Son of Rheía and Krónos. Brother of Zeus. Married Persephónē.
Haímones	A group of people of Thessalía.
Haliróthios	Mythological figure. Father of Sámos. According to tradition the first victor in the four-horse chariot race at Olympía.
Harmonía	Mythological figure. Daughter of Aphrodítē and Árēs. Married Kádmos. Mother of Semélē and Inó.
Hébē	Deity. Daughter of Héra and Zeus. Her name means "youth." Wife of Hēraklés after he became immortal.
Hekábē (Hecuba)	Mythological figure. Queen of Troía. Married Príamos.
Héktōr	Mythological figure. Greatest warrior of Troía (see **Trojan War**). Son of Hekábē and Príamos. Akhilleús killed him.
Helénē	Mythological figure. Daughter of Léda and Zeus (her adoptive mortal father is Tyndáreōs). Wife of Menélaos. See **Trojan War**.
Hélenos	Mythological figure. Son of Hekábē and Príamos. Twin brother of Kassándra. A prophet.
Helikón	Mountain in Boiōtía. Home of Moúsai.
Hélios	Deity. The sun god. Son of Theía and Hyperíōn. Brother of Ēós and Selénē. Father of Aiétēs.
Hellanodíkas (plural: Hellanodíkai)	Historical figure(s). The title of judges in games at Olympía.
Hellás	The regional name that refers collectively to places where the inhabitants of the southern Balkan Peninsula and broader Mediterranean region that share ancient Hellenic cultural traditions and language live.
Héllēnes	The people of Hellás.
Hellótia	Local games held at Kórinthos in honor of Athēná.
Hélōros	River in Sikelía. See **Khromíos**.
Héphaistos (Hephaestus)	Deity. Son of Héra and Zeus. God of fire and metalsmithing. His name may refer by metonymy to fire.
Héra	Deity. Wife and sister of Zeus. Sister of Hestía. Mother of Eileíthyia. The epithet Héra Teleía, "Héra the Fulfiller," captures the goddess's role in affirming marriage. Specially worshipped in Árgos. Héra was worshipped as Héra Parthenía, that is, as Héra of Unwedded Women, at Stýmphalos (Paus. 8.22.2).
Hērakleídai	Mythological figures. The word means "descendents of Hēraklés."
Hēraklés	Mythological figure. Son of Alkménē and Zeus (adoptive mortal father: Amphitrýōn). Father of Tlēpólemos. Eurystheús assigned him twelve labors. Founded games at Olympía. The Pillars of Hēraklés are the opposite shores of the Strait of Gibraltar and designate the western perimeter of the known world.
Hermés	Deity. Son of Maía and Zeus. Herald of gods. Conducts souls of the dead to Háïdēs.

Hēródotos	Historical figure. From Thḗbai. Son of Asōpódōros. Victor in chariot race at Isthmós.
Hēsíodos (Hesiod)	Poet from Boiōtía. According to tradition, composed *Theogony* and *Works and Days*, poems conventionally dated to 750 BCE.
Hestía	Deity. Daughter of Rheía and Krónos. Goddess of the hearth.
hēsykhía	The noun means "peace, tranquility, imperturbability." As a proper noun, the divine personification of such qualities.
Hiérōn	Historical figure. Ruler of Syrákousai (478–466 BCE). Founder of the city Aítna on the site of Katánē. Son of Deinoménēs. Brother of Gélōn.
Himéra (1)	City in Sikelía located on Himéra River.
Himéra (2)	River in Sikelía. In 480 BCE Hiérōn and Hiérōn's older brother Gélōn allied with Thḗrōn, tyrant of Akrágas, against a large Carthaginian force, which they defeated, in a battle at Himéra.
Hípparis	River in Sikelía that flows past Kamárina to the sea.
Hippodámeia	Mythological figure. Daughter of Oinómaos, King of Písa. Married Pélops. Her name means "Horsetamer."
Hippokléas	Historical figure. From Pelinnaíon. Winner in boys' race in games at Pythó in 498 BCE.
Hippokrátēs	Historical figure. From Athḗnai. Member of Alkmaiōnídai family. Father of Megaklḗs.
Hippolýtē	Mythological figure. Daughter of Krētheús. Married Ákastos. See **Ákastos**.
Homērídai	Historical figures. The word means "descendants of Hómēros" and refers to performers of Homeric poetry.
Hómēros (Homer)	The name is commonly taken to refer to the author of the *Iliad*, *Odyssey*, and *Homeric Hymns*. Although even Píndaros appears to use the name in this way, it more properly identifies a tradition of poetic composition and performance.
Hṓrai (singular: **Hṓra**)	Deities. The word means "the Seasons." Daughters of Thémis and Zeus. The Hṓrai are Díkē, Eirḗnē, and Eunomía. Considered as goddesses of nature, they oversee cycles of generation, growth, and fruiting. Considered as goddesses of culture, they oversee virtues that foster communal integrity and vitality. Píndaros invokes Hṓra as the personification of youthfulness (N.8.1).
Hýllos	Mythological figure. Son of Hēraklḗs. With Dýmas and Pámphylos, the sons of Aigimiós, led incursion of Dorians into Hellás.
Hyperbóreoi	Mythological figures. The word means "the people beyond the north" and refers accordingly to people said to live in remotely northern lands. They especially revered Apóllōn, who in return favored them.
Hyperian Spring	A water spring at Pheraí in Thessalía.
Hyperíōn	Deity. Son of Gaía and Ouranós. One of the Titánes. Married Theía. Father of Ḗos, Selḗnē, and Hḗlios.
Hyperméstra	Mythological figure. Daughter of Danaós. Married Lynkeús (1). Only one of Danaós' fifty daughters who did not murder her husband (N.10.6). Mother of Ábas.
Hypseús	Mythological figure. King of Lapíthai. Son of Pēneiós. Grandson of Ōkeanós. Father of Kyrḗnē.
Hypsipýlē	Mythological figure. From Lḗmnos. Daughter of Mýrina and Thóas. To answer for Aphrodítē's curse, the women of Lḗmnos were to kill all males on the island. Hypsipýlē hid Thóas, who was the only male to survive. After the Argonaútai landed at Lḗmnos, Hypsipýlē and Iásōn had two sons.

Glossary

Iálysos — Mythological figure. Grandson of Hélios. Legendary founder of the city Iálysos in Rhódos.

Iamídai — Historical figures. The word means "descendants of Íamos." Prominent family with traditional responsibility to tend the altar of Zeus at Olympía.

Íamos — Mythological figure. Son of Euádnē and Apóllōn. A prophet.

Iapetós — Deity. Son of Gaía and Ouranós. One of the Titánes. Married Klyménē. Father of Átlas, Epimētheús, Menoítios, and Promētheús.

Iásōn (Jason) — Mythological figure. Son of Aísōn. From Iōlkós. Kheírōn educated him. Leader of Argonaútai.

Ída — Although perhaps referring to the more well-known Mount Ída (modern Psiloritis) in Krḗtē (O.5.18), ancient sources indicate that a cave at Olympía, where the Hill of Krónos and the Alpheiós River are also located, was called the Cave of Ída.

Ídas — Mythological figure. King of Messḗnē. Son of Aphareús. Brother of Lynkeús (2). Polydeúkēs killed him.

Ílas — Historical figure. Trainer of Hagēsídamos (1) of Lokrís.

Ílios (Ilium or Ilion) — Another name for Troía.

Ílos — Mythological figure. Grandfather of Príamos. Founder of Ílios (=Troía).

Inó — Mythological figure. Daughter of Harmonía and Kádmos. Married Athámas. Mother of Melikértēs and Léarkhos. When a madness afflicted her and her husband Athámas, they murdered their sons. Inó cast herself into the sea and became one of the Nērëídes. As sea goddess, known as Leukothéa.

Iólaos — Mythological figure. Son of Iphiklés. Grandson of Amphitrýōn, whose burial site he shares (P.9.82–3). Friend of his uncle Hēraklés. Thḗbai hosted games in honor of him (O.9.98–9).

Iōlkós — A city in Thessalía. Home of Iásōn. See **Ákastos**.

Ionian Sea — Located south of the Adriatic Sea. Lies between the bottom of Italy's "boot" and the western coast of the Balkan Peninsula.

Iphigéneia — Mythological figure. Daughter of Klytaimnḗstra and Agamémnōn. Her father sacrificed her in order to appease Ártemis, who prevented the Akhaioí from sailing to attack Troía.

Iphiklés — Mythological figure. Son of Alkmḗnē and Amphitrýōn. Brother of Hēraklés. Father of Iólaos.

Iphimédeia — Mythological figure. Mother of Ótos and Ephiáltēs.

Iphíōn — Historical figure. From Aígina. Father of Alkimédōn and Timosthénēs.

Írasa — City in Libýē located on Lake Tritōnís.

Ískhys — Mythological figure. From Arkadía. Son of Élatos. Brother of Aípytos. Lover of Korōnís. Apóllōn killed him.

Ismēnós (1) — River near Thḗbai. As a river-god, the son of Tēthýs and Ōkeanós.

Ismēnós (2) — Mythological figure. Son of Melía and Apóllōn. Apóllōn named his temple at Thḗbai, the Isménion, in honor of his son.

Isthmós — The strip of land that connects the Pelopónnēsos with mainland Hellás. Also refers to site near Kórinthos where Isthmian Games were held in honor of Poseidón.

Ístros — Ancient Hellenic name for Danube River.

Ixíōn — Mythological figure. Zeus punished him for his attempts on Héra.

Glossary

Kádmos	Mythological figure. Son of Agénōr. Brother of Európē. Married Harmonía. Founder of Thébai. In mythology and historically, the people of Kádmos are therefore the people of Thébai. Father of Agaué, Autonóē, Inó, and Semélē. According to tradition, Kádmos was ancestor of Emmenídai family of Akrágas in Sikelía.
Káïkos	River in Mysía.
Kálaïs	Mythological figure. Son of Oreíthyia and Boréas. Brother of Zétēs. One of the Argonaútai.
Kalliánax	Historical figure. Ancestor of Diagóras of Rhódos.
Kallías	Historical figure. Member of the Bassídai family of Aígina. Competed as a boxer.
Kalliklés	Historical figure. Uncle of Timásarkhos.
Kallímakhos	Historical figure. From Aígina. Deceased relative of Alkimédōn.
Kalliópē	Deity. One of the Moúsai.
Kallísta	Original name for the island Théra. The word means "the most beautiful one."
Kamárina	City in Sikelía, located along Hípparis River. The homecity of Psaúmis. The *khorós* represents Kamárina as the eponymous *nýmphē* of the city by addressing her as "daughter of Ōkeanós" (O.5.2) and by singing of her as the "local lake" (O.5.11).
Kámeiros	Mythological figure. Grandson of Hélios. Legendary founder of the city Kámeiros in Rhódos.
Karneiádas	Historical figure. Father of Telesikrátēs of Kyrénē.
Kárrhōtos	Historical figure. Son of Alexibías. Relative of Arkesílas IV of Kyrénē. Chariot-driver for Arkesílas' victory at Pythó in 462 BCE.
Kassándra	Mythological figure. Daughter of Hekábē and Príamos. A prophetess. Agamémnōn claimed her as war prize after the Hellenic alliance won the war at Troía.
Kastalía	A spring at Delphoí.
Kástōr	Mythological figure. Son of **Léda** and Tyndáreōs. Brother of **Polydeúkēs**, with whom he enjoyed reverence and cult worship, particularly in connection with horses. Píndaros once makes Zeus father of both Kástōr and Polydeúkēs (P.4.171). Píndaros refers to a Kástōr-melody, suggesting music associated with Kástōr and, possibly, horseriding (P.2.69 and I.1.16; compare O.1.101). See also **Dióskouroi**.
Kéntauros	Mythological figure. Represented with equine body and legs and human torso, arms, and head. Dwells in mountainous regions such as Arkadía and Thessalía.
Kéōs	Mediterranean island among the Cyclades in the Aegean Sea. Modern Kea.
Kēphisís	Mythological figure. A *nýmphē*. Eponym of Kēphisós River.
Kēphisós	River that rises on Mount Parnassós and empties into Lake Kōpäís, which mythology represents as the daughter of Kēphisós. Orkhomenós in Boiōtía is located along Kēphisós River.
Kérberos	Mythological figure. Multi-headed dog of Háïdēs.
Khaíre (plural: Khaírete)	An imperative verb in ancient Hellenic that means, "Health and happiness to you [singular or plural]!" A salutation.
Khariádai	Historical figures. Prominent family of Aígina.
Kharikló	Mythological figure. A daughter of Apóllōn (or Ōkeanós). Married Kheírōn.

Glossary

kháris — Common meanings of the word are "splendor" and "grace." Designates the splendor of art, physical attractiveness, a beneficial thing for which one is grateful, or a principle of reciprocity according to which one gratifies another (sometimes with sexual connotations) in return for kindness or flattery.

Kháris (Charis, Grace) — Divine embodiment of **kháris**. One of the three **Khárites**.

Khárites (Charites, the Graces) — Plural of **Kháris**. Daughters of Eurynómē and Zeus. Three sisters: Agläía, Euphrosýnē, and Thalía.

Kheírōn — Mythological figure. Son of Philýra and Krónos. A kéntauros. Married Khariklό. Lived in a cave on Mount Pélion in Thessalía. Practiced healing. Famous for wisdom. Teacher of heroes, including Akhilleús, Asklēpiós, and Iásōn. Oversaw the marriage of Thétis and Pēleús (N.3.56–7, I.8.41–2).

Khímaira — Mythological figure. Child of Ékhidna and Typhós. A part-goat, part-lion (and part-snake in some representations) creature. Bellerophóntēs killed the Khímaira.

khorós (chorus) — Performance ensemble of singer-dancers.

Khromíos — Historical figure. From Syrákousai and Aítna. Son of Hagēsídamos. Led forces at the Battle of Hélōros River in Sikelía (492 BCE) against Syrákousai while serving under Hippokrátēs, tyrant of Géla. Gélōn came to power after Hippokrátēs and, in turn, when Gélōn died (478 BCE), his younger brother Hiérōn came to power. Khromíos thus commanded military forces for these powerful Sicilian tyrants. Winner in chariot race at Neméa.

khrónos — Hellenic word for "time." Píndaros personifies Khrónos at O.2.17 and O.10.55.

Kilikía — Southern region of the Anatolian Peninsula north of Kýpros.

Kinýras — Mythological king of Kýpros. A favorite priest of Aphrodítē (P.2.15–17). He is a byword for wealth.

Kírrha — Town on north coast of the Gulf of Kórinthos below Delphoí that served as the port for Delphoí and Krísa. Píndaros refers to Kírrha and Krísa as sites for Pythó's games.

Kithairón — Mountain that serves as boundary between Boiōtía and Attikḗ. Site of the Battle of Plátaia in 479 BCE.

Kléandros — Historical figure. From Aígina. Son of Telésarkhos. Winner in boy's pankrátion in games at Isthmós.

Kleió (Clio) — Deity. One of the Moúsai.

Kleitómakhos — Historical figure. From Aígina. Uncle of Aristoménēs.

Kleítōr — City in Arkadía. Hosted games in honor of Persephónē.

Kleódamos — Historical figure. From Orkhomenós. Father of Asópikhos. He died prior to his son's victory.

Kleōnaí — City near Neméa. Its citizens administered games at Neméa.

Kleónikos — Historical figure. From Aígina. Father of Lámpōn. Grandfather of Phylakídas and Pythéas.

Kleōnymídai — Historical figures. The word means "descendants of Kleónymos." Name of a prominent family in Thḗbai.

Kleónymos — Mythological figure. Hero associated with Thḗbai. The family of Mélissos claimed him as an ancestor.

Klōthó — Mythological figure. The name means "spinner." One of the Moírai.

Klýmenos — Historical figure. From Orkhomenós. Father of Ergínos.

Glossary

Klytaimnéstra	Mythological figure. Daughter of Léda and Tyndáreōs. Sister of Helénē, Kástōr, and Polydeúkēs. Married Agamémnōn. Mother of Iphigéneia, Oréstēs, and Ēléktra.
Knōssós	Historically the largest Bronze Age settlement on Krḗtē. In mythology the city ruled by Mínōs.
Koiranídas	Mythological figure. The word means "son of Koíranos." Refers to Polýeidos, a mythological soothsayer from Kórinthos.
Kólkhoi	People who live in the city of Kolkhís, the home of Aiḗtēs and Médeia, located on the east coast of the Black Sea.
Kórinthos (Corinth)	City located on the isthmus between Attikḗ and the Pelopónnēsos. Oversaw games at Isthmós in honor of Poseidṓn.
Korōnís	Mythological figure. Daughter of Phlegýas. Mother of Asklēpiós (father: Apóllōn). Fell in love with Ískhys.
Kréōn	Mythological figure. King of Thḗbai. Father of Megára.
Kreontídas	Historical figure. From Aígina. Ancestor of Alkimídas. Member of Bassídai family.
Kréousa	Mythological figure. Mother of Hypseús, King of Lapíthai and father of Kyrḗnē.
Krḗtē (Crete)	Large island located south of Pelopónnēsos.
Krētheús	Mythological figure. Son of Enarétē and Aíolos. Father of Hippolýtē, Aísōn, and Phérēs. Founded Iōlkós.
Krísa	City located near Kírrha on north shore of the Gulf of Kórinthos, below Delphoí. Píndaros refers to Kírrha and Krísa as sites for Pythṓ's games.
Kroísos (Croesus)	Historical figure. King of Lydía (560–546 BCE). Famous for his vast wealth.
Kronídēs (plural: **Kronídai**)	Deity. The word means "son of Krónos."
Krónos (Cronus)	Deity. Son of Gaía and Ouranós. Married Rheía. Father of Dēmḗtēr, Háidēs, Hḗra, Hestía, Kheírōn, Poseidṓn, and Zeus. The Hill of Krónos overlooks the site of Olympía.
Ktéatos	Mythological figure. Son of Meliónē and Poseidṓn. Brother of Eúrytos.
Kýknos (1)	Mythological figure. Son of Kalýkē and Poseidṓn. Although gifted with invulnerability, Akhilleús killed him at Troía (O.2.82 and I.5.39). He metamorphosed into a swan; the Hellenic word *kýknos* means "swan."
Kýknos (2)	Mythological figure. Son of Pelópeia and Árēs. Attacked and killed travellers to Delphoí. Hēraklés killed him (O.10.15).
Kyllḗnē	Mountain in Arkadía near Stýmphalos. Site of Hermḗs' birth.
Kýmē (Cumae)	City located in Italy on the coast of the Tyrrhenian Sea north of the Bay of Naples. Hiérōn defeated an alliance of Carthaginian and Etruscan forces in a naval battle off the coast of Kýmē in 474 BCE.
Kypría	Deity. Epithet of Aphrodítē. Recalls the goddess's association with the island of Kýpros.
Kýpros (Cyprus)	Island located in the eastern Mediterranean Sea south of the Anatolian Peninsula. Site of the birth of Aphrodítē.
Kyrḗnē (1)	Deity. A *nýmphē*. Daughter of Hypseús. Mother of Aristaíos (father: Apóllōn). Eponym of Kyrḗnē (2).
Kyrḗnē (2)	Hellenic community located in Libýē. According to tradition, Báttos founded it as colony of Thḗra.

Glossary

Labdakídai	Historical figures. A prominent family of Thébai that claimed descent from Lábdakos, grandson of Kádmos and grandfather of Oidípous.
Láïos	Mythological figure. Son of Lábdakos. Father Oidípous.
Lakedaímōn	Another name for Spárta. City located in south-central Pelopónnēsos. A Dorian community.
Lakéreia	City in Thessalía near Lake Boibiás.
Lákhesis	Deity. The name means "allotter." One of the Moírai.
Lakōniké	The region of southern Pelopónnēsos where Spárta, or Lakedaímōn, is located.
Lámpōn	Historical figure. From Aígina. Member of Psalykhiádai family. Son of Kleónikos. Father of Pythéas and Phylakídas.
Lamprómakhos	Historical figure. From Opountian Lokrís. Victor at Isthmós. Relative of Ephármostos.
Laomédōn	Mythological figure. King of Troía. Son of Ílos. Father of Príamos. Reneged on promise of reward to Hēraklés, who attacked Troía in revenge with Telamón.
Lapíthai (Lapiths)	Mythological figures. A group of people from Thessalía.
Léda	Mythological figure. Married Tyndáreōs. Zeus, disguised as a swan, raped her. Léda's children conceived with Tyndáreōs are mortal and those conceived with Zeus are immortal: Helénē (father: Zeus), **Kástōr** (father: Tyndáreōs), Klytaimnéstra (father: Tyndáreōs), and **Polydeúkēs** (father: Zeus). Léda's twin sons (O.3.34–35) are Kástōr and Polydeúkēs.
Lémnos	Island in northern Aegean Sea.
Lérna	Site south of Árgos near Argolic Gulf.
Lētó	Mythological figure. Daughter of Phoíbē and Koíos. Mother of Apóllōn and Ártemis.
Leukothéa	Mythological figure. The name means "bright goddess." **Inó** assumes the name Leukothéa when she becomes a sea goddess.
Libýē (1) (Libya)	Mythological figure. Daughter of Épaphos. Eponym for Libýē, the geographical region.
Libýē (2) (Libya)	The region of northern Africa that neighbors Aígyptos. Kyrénē (2) is located in Libýē.
Likýmnios	Mythological figure. Son of Midéa and Ēlektrýōn. Half-brother of Alkménē. Tlēpólemos killed him.
Líndos	Mythological figure. Grandson of Rhódos and Hélios. Legendary founder of the city Líndos on Rhódos.
Lokrís	The name refers, first, to a Hellenic region subdivided into three parts, to only one of which Píndaros refers in his *epiníkia*: Opountian Lokrís, according to tradition, founded by **Opoús (2)**, was located north of Boiōtía along the coast of the Gulf of Eúboia. Píndaros once calls Epizephyrian **Lokroí** *Zephyría Lokrís* (Western Lokrís) (P.2.18–19).
Lokroí	The placename of Epizephyrian (or Western) Lokroí, a colony of Opountian Lokrís located in modern Calabria, a region of Italy (P.2.19). The people of Opountian **Lokrís** (O.9.20) or Epizephyrian Lokroí (O.10.13 and 98, O.11.15) are also known as the Lokroí.
Lokrós	Mythological figure (O.9.60). King of **Opoús (3)**. Married an unnamed daughter of **Opoús (1)**; she was pregnant by Zeus. Became adoptive father of her son **Opoús (2)**, grandson of Opoús (1).
Loxías	Deity. Epithet of Apóllōn. The word means "the oblique god," suggestive perhaps of the ambiguity of Apóllōn's oracles.

Glossary

Lydía	An ancient kingdom in western Anatolia. Ruled by Kroísos (560–546 BCE). Píndaros sometimes identifies particular poetic rhythms and musical melody as Lydian.
Lykaíon	Mountain in Arkadía. Site of altar to Zeus and games in his honor. A local festival at Parrhasía commemorated the god's association with Mount Lykaíon.
Lykía	Region of southwest coast of the Anatolian Peninsula.
Lynkeús (1)	Mythological figure. Son of Aípytos. Married Hyperméstra. Became a ruler of Árgos. Father of Ábas. See N.10.12.
Lynkeús (2)	Mythological figure. Son of Aphareús. Brother of Ídas. Polydeúkēs killed him. See N.10.61 and N.10.70.
Magnēsía	Region of Thessalía.
Maínalon	Mountain in Arkadía associated with Zeus and Pan.
Mantíneia	A city in Arkadía.
Marathón	Site in Attiké that hosted games in honor of Hēraklés. The Battle of Marathón between Héllēnes and Persians occurred here in 490 BCE.
Médeia (Medea)	Mythological figure. From Kolkhís. Daughter of Aiétēs. Granddaughter of Hélios. A powerful magician. Píndaros represents her as a prophet in *Pythian 4*. Married Iásōn. Honored historically at Kórinthos (cf. O.13.53–4), where her journeys take her before she emigrates to Athénai.
Mēdía	Kingdom located southwest of the Caspian Sea. Cyrus the Great of Persia conquered Mēdía in 550 BCE, absorbing it into his Persian Empire.
Médoi	Historical figures. Properly the people of Mēdía, but ancient Hellenic sources refer to the Persians as Médoi. Píndaros mentions the Médoi (P.1.78) by way of alluding to the Battle of Plátaia (479 BCE) between Héllēnes and Persians.
Médousa (Medusa)	Mythological figure. Mortal daughter of Phórkys. One of the **Gorgónes**. Perseús killed her.
Megaklés (Megacles)	Historical figure. From Athénai. Member of Alkmaiōnídai family. Son of Hippokrátēs, uncle of Periklés. Winner in four-horse chariot race at Pythó in 486 BCE.
Megára	Mythological figure. Daughter of Kréōn, king of Thébai. Married Hēraklés.
Mégara	City on the Isthmós of Kórinthos, at the western perimeter of Attiké. Hosted games in honor of Alkáthoos and Apóllōn.
Mégas	Historical figure. From Aígina. Father of Deínis.
Meidylídai	Historical figures. Prominent family of Aígina.
Melámpous	Mythological figure. Son of Eidoménē and Amytháōn. Cousin of Iásōn. A soothsayer.
Melánippos	Mythological figure. Hero of Thébai. Defended the city against the attack by the Seven Against Thébai. Wounded Tydeús, who killed him. See **Seven Against Thébai**.
Meléagros	Mythological figure. Son of Althaía and Oineús. Apóllōn killed him.
Melēsías	Historical figure. From Athénai. Trained wrestlers. Victor at Neméa as a boy and then later as a man in the pankrátion (O.8.54–9).
Melía	Mythological figure. A *nýmphē*. Daughter of Tēthýs and Ōkeanós. Mother of Téneros and Ismēnós (father: Apóllōn).
Mélissos	Historical figure. From Thébai. Son of Telesiádas. Member of Kleōnymídai family. Victor in games at Neméa and Isthmós.
Mémnōn	Mythological figure. Son of Ēós and Tithōnós. King of Aithiopía. Fought at Troía. Killed Antílokhos. Akhilleús killed him.
Ménandros	Historical figure. From Athénai. Trained wrestlers.

Glossary

Menélaos	Mythological figure. Married Helénē. Brother of Agamémnōn. Son of Atreús. King of Spárta. Fought at Troía.
Menoítios	Mythological figure. Son of Aígina and Áktōr. Father of Pátroklos.
Méropes	Mythological figures. A group of people said to live in Kós. Hēraklés and Telamón attacked them in the course of their return from Troía.
Messḗnē	Region of southwestern Pelopónnēsos, near Pýlos. Among the lands that the hero Néstōr ruled (P.6.35).
Metópē	Mythological figure. A *nýmphē*. Eponym for a spring at Stýmphalos. She was the mother of Aígina and Thḗbē (father: Asōpós), the eponym for the city Thḗbai, which was Píndaros' hometown—or as he puts it (O.6.84–5), his "mother's mother."
Mídas	Historical figure. From Akrágas. Winner in aulós contest at Pythó.
Midéa (1)	Mythological figure. Mother of Likýmnios (father: Ēlektrýōn). See O.7.29.
Midéa (2)	City in the Argolid. Ēlektrýōn ruled there. See O.10.66.
Minýai (Minyans)	Mythological and historical figures. The word means "people of Minýas." Identifies those living in Boiōtía at Orkhomenós. Píndaros once refers to Argonaútai as Minýai (P.4.69).
Minýas	Mythological figure. King of Orkhomenós.
Minýeia	Region around Orkhomenós where Minýai lived.
Mnēmosýnē	Deity. Her name means "memory." Daughter of Gaía and Ouranós. Mother of Moúsai (father: Zeus).
moíra	The word means "fate, destiny, one's given lot in life."
Moírai (singular: **Moíra**)	Deities. The Fates. Klōthó ("spinner") spins the thread of life, Lákhesis ("allotter") measures it out, and Átropos ("unturning") cuts it. They oversee *moíra*.
Molíones	Mythological figures. The word means "sons of Moliónē" and refers to Eúrytos and Któatos, twin brothers and sons of Poseidón. Hēraklés killed them at Kleōnaí.
Molossía	A region of Ḗpeiros inhabited by Molossoí, descendents of Molossós, son of Andromákhē and Neoptólemos.
Mópsos	Mythological figure. One of the Argonaútai. A prophet.
Moúsai (Singular: **Moúsa**) (Muses)	Deities. Nine daughters of Mnēmosýnē and Zeus. Goddesses of performing arts, especially song and dance. Often depicted as companions of Apóllōn.
Mykḗnai (Mycenae)	City in Argolid region of the Pelopónnēsos.
Myrmidónes	Mythological figures. Early inhabitants of Aígina. Departed for Thessalía with Pēleús, whose son Akhilleús led them in the **Trojan War**.
Mysía	Region of the northwestern Anatolian Peninsula, south of the Sea of Marmara.
Naïás (plural: Naïádes)	*Nýmphē* associated with natural water springs, streams, and ponds.
Náxos	Largest island of the Cyclades in the Aegean Sea.
Neílos (Nile)	River in Aígyptos.
Neméa	Argolid site in the Pelopónnēsos where a sanctuary for Zeus was located. Hosted Nemean games in honor of Zeus.
némesis	The word means "righteous anger toward injustice." Píndaros personifies Némesis (P.10.44).
Neoptólemos	Mythological figure. Son of Dēïdámeia and Akhilleús. Fought at Troía, where he killed Príamos. King of Molossía. Killed at Delphoí.

Glossary

Nērēídes (Nereids)	Mythological figures. The word means "daughters of Nēreús." They are daughters of Dōrís and Nēreús. The Nērëídes include Thétis and Psamáthē.
Nēreús	Deity. A god of the sea known as The Old Man of the Sea. Son of Gaía and Póntos. Father of Thétis, Psamáthē, and other Nērēídes (mother: Dōrís).
Néstōr	Mythological figure. Son of Khlōrís and Nēleús. King of Pýlos. Father of Antílokhos. Hellenic hero who fought in the **Trojan War** against the Tróes.
Nikásippos	Historical figure. Possibly a friend of Píndaros. His name compounds Hellenic roots for the words "win" and "horse." Nikásippos may have been the leader of *khorós* that performed I.2, the person responsible for conveying the composition to Akrágas for Thrasýboulos, or both.
Nikeús	According to tradition, first winner in the discus event in games at Olympía.
Nikokléēs	Historical figure. Cousin of Kléandros of Aígina. Winner in boxing at the Isthmós.
Nikómakhos	Historical figure. Chariot driver for Xenokrátēs.
Nísos	Mythological figure. King of Mégara. The Hill of Nísos is a site at Mégara.
Nótos	Deity. The south wind.
Nýmphē (plural: **Nýmphai**)	Deity. Young, female goddess of uncultivated spaces.
Óanos	River in Sikelía. Kamárina was located along its banks.
Odysseús	Mythological figure. Hero featured in the *Odyssey* of Hómēros, which tells of Odysseús' return from Troía.
Oidípous (Oedipus)	Mythological figure. King of Thébai. Son of Iokástē (Jocasta) and Láïos. Father of Eteoklés and Polyneíkēs, who fought on opposing sides in the battle portrayed in the **Seven Against Thébai** story.
Oiklés	Mythological figure. Father of **Amphiáraos**.
Oinēídai	Mythological figures. The word means "sons of Oineús." Refers to Meléagros and Tydeús.
Oinómaos	Mythological figure. King of Písa in Élis. Son of Árēs. Father of Hippodámeia.
Oinóna	Older name of Aígina. The name means "land of wine."
Oinopía	Older name of Aígina. The name means "winefaced."
Oiōnós	Mythological figure. From Árgos. Son of Likýmnios. According to tradition the first winner in the *stádion* at Olympía.
Ōkeanós	Deity. Son of Gaía and Ouranós. The body of water surrounding the known world and thus its outermost boundary. Considered the father of thousands of rivers.
Oligaithídai	Historical figures. Prominent family of Kórinthos known for success in athletic competitions.
Olympía	Panhellenic sanctuary sacred to Zeus. Located in Élis in the Pelopónnēsos. Site of athletic competitions held every four years in honor of Zeus.
olympiónikos	Either an adjective meaning "victorious at Olympía" or a noun meaning "winner at Olympía."
Ólympos	Highest mountain in Hellás in northern Thessalía. In mythology, it is the home of the gods.
omphalós	The word means, literally "navel," figuratively, "focal point." Ancient Héllēnes regarded Delphoí as the "navel" of the world.
Onkhēstós	A town in Boiōtía. Site of sanctuary and festival in honor of Poseidón.
Opoús (1)	Mythological figure. King of Epeioí of Élis. Father of unnamed daughter who married **Lokrós** after Zeus had sex with her.
Opoús (2)	Mythological figure. Grandson of **Opoús (1)**.

Glossary

Opoús (3)	A city of Opountian **Lokrís**. Located north of Boiōtía along the northern coast of the Gulf of Eúboia.
Oréstēs	Mythological figure. Son of Klytaimnéstra and Agamémnōn. Killed his mother to avenge his father's murder by Klytaimnéstra and her lover Aígisthos.
Ōríōn	Mythological figure. Son of Euryálē and Hyrieús (or Poseidón). Giant, hunter, and constellation. There are multiple tales of his romantic relationships, among them the story that Ēós fell in love with him.
Orkhomenós	City in Boiōtía. Its citizens worshipped especially the Khárites. The Minýai were mythological inhabitants of the city.
Orpheús	Mythological figure. Son of one of the Moúsai (often identified as Kalliópē) and Oíagros (or Apóllōn). From Thrákē. Renowned for singing talent. One of the Argonaútai.
Orséas	Historical figure. Trainer of wrestlers.
Orthōsía	Deity. At Spárta a sacred appellation for Ártemis.
Ortygía	The word means "Quail Island." In the *epiníkia* of Píndaros, it refers to an island off the coast of Sikelía, the original site of Syrákousai. Ortygía was a site sacred to Ártemis. Píndaros identifies Ortygía as the sister of Délos (N.1.4) because Ortygía was another name for the latter. See also **Aréthousa**.
Ótos	Mythological figure. A giant. Son of Iphimédeia and Poseidón. Brother of Ephiáltēs. These brothers accidentally killed each other at Náxos.
Oulías	Historical figure. From Árgos. Father of Theaíos.
Ouranídēs (plural: Ouranídai)	Deity or deities. The word means "descendant of Ouranós." It refers to either an individual god (Zeus at P.3.4) or the Olympian deities collectively (P.4.194).
Ouranós	Deity. The word means "sky." Father of Titanídes and Titánes (mother: Gaía).
Paián (Paean)	Deity. The word means "the healer." In some Hellenic texts, the name of a healer that tended the gods. An epithet of Apóllōn (P.4.270).
pálē	The athletic competition of wrestling.
Pallás	Deity. An epithet of Athēná. Píndaros represents Pallás Athēná as patron deity of Kamárina (O.5.10).
Pampháēs	Historical figure. A maternal ancestor of Theaíos.
Pámphylos	Mythological figure. Son of Aigimiós. Brother of Dýmas. Eponym for the Pámphyloi, a Dorian family line.
Pan	Deity. God of shepherds and flocks, sometimes said to be the son of Hermés. Part-human, part-goat, and master of the most pastoral of musical instruments, the panpipe. Born and abiding in Arkadía.
Panéllēnes	A word that means "all the people of Hellás."
Pangaíon	A mountain range in Thrákē.
pankrátion	An athletic competition that blended *pygmé* "boxing" and *pálē* "wrestling."
Páris	Mythological figure. From Troía. Son of Hekábē and Príamos. Instigated the **Trojan War** by abducting or seducing Helénē.
Parnassós	A mountain that rises from the north shore of the Gulf of Kórinthos. Site of Delphoí.
Páros	An island of the Cyclades in the Aegean Sea west of Náxos. Famous for the quality of the marble quarried there.
Parrhasía	A region of southern Arkadía. A festival here commemorated Zeus' connection to Mount Lykaíon.
Pátroklos	Mythological figure. Son of Menoítios. Fought in **Trojan War**. Píndaros represents him as the beloved of Akhilleús (O.10.19).

Pégasos	Mythological figure. A winged horse. Said to be born from Médousa's severed neck, making the animal her son (father: Poseidón). Embedded in the creature's name is the word *pēgé* "spring." Bellerophóntēs attempted to reach the gods' home by riding Pégasos skyward.
Peirénē	The name of a spring located in Kórinthos.
Peísandros	Mythological figure. From Spárta. With Oréstēs colonized Lésbos and Ténedos.
Peithó	Divine embodiment of "persuasion," the meaning of the name. Often associated with Aphrodítē.
Pēleídēs	Mythological figure. The word means "son of Pēleús" and refers to Akhilleús.
Pēleús	Mythological figure. Son of Endēís and Aiakós. Married Thétis. Father of Akhilleús. See **Ákastos**.
Pelías	Mythological figure. Son of Tyró and Poseidón. A descendant of Aíolos. Brother of Aísōn. Father of Ákastos. King of Iōlkós.
Pelinnaíon	A city in Thessalía. Home of Hippokléas (P.10.4).
Pélion	Mountain in Thessalía. In mythology, the site of Kheírōn's cave.
Pellénē	A city in Akhaía, region of northern Pelopónnēsos along the Gulf of Kórinthos. Hosted games with the prize of a wool cloak.
Pélops	Mythological figure. Son of Tántalos. Emigrated from Lydía to Hellás, where he founded a new settlement, giving rise to the placename *Pelopónnēsos* "Island of Pélops." Pélops was Poseidón's beloved (O.1.31–33). He married Hippodámeia and became King of Písa in Élis.
Pēneiós	River in Thessalía. Also refers to the river-god of the same name.
péntathlon	Athletic competition that included five contests: *stádion* (200-meter footrace), *dískos* (discus throw), *hálma* (long-jump), *ákōn* (javelin throw), and *pálē* (wrestling).
Pérgamos	Placename for the acropolis of Troía.
periodoníkēs	The word means "victor in the circuit of games" and applies to an athlete who was victorious in all four crown games at Olympía, Delphoí (Pythó), Neméa, and Isthmós.
Periklýmenos	Mythological figure. From Pýlos. Son of Khlōrís and Nēleús (or Poseidón). One of the Argonaútai. Defended Thébai against the Seven. See **Seven Against Thébai**.
Persephónē	Deity. Daughter of Dēmétēr and Zeus. Married Háïdēs after he abducted her. Worshipped with Dēmétēr at the religious sanctuary in Eleusís.
Perseús	Mythological figure. Son of Danáē and Zeus. He killed Médousa.
Phaisána	A city in Arkadía located along the Alpheiós River.
Phálaris	Historical figure. Tyrant of Akrágas (*c.* 570–549 BCE). Known for his cruelty. According to storytelling tradition, killed people by cooking them in a bull made of bronze.
Phásis	River in Kolkhís, a region on the east coast of the Black Sea. Modern Rioni River in western Georgia.
Pherénikos	Hiérōn's victorious racehorse. The name means "Victor-Bearer" or "Victory-Bringer."
Phérēs	Mythological figure. Son of Krētheús. Uncle of Iásōn. Eponym of Pheraí in Thessalía.
Philánōr	Historical figure. Father of Ergotélēs.

Glossary

Philoktétēs	Mythological figure. From Thessalía. Son of Dēmónassa and Poías. Inherited the bow and arrows of Hēraklés from his father. Joined Hellenic expedition against Troía but was left behind on the island of Ténedos when his foot became so badly infected after a snakebite that the stench of the wound was intolerable to others.
Philýra	Mythological figure. Mother of Kheírōn (father: Krónos).
Phíntis	Historical figure. Driver of mulecar for Hagēsías.
Phlégra	Ancient name for Pellḗnē in Thrákē.
Phlegýas	Mythological figure. King of Lapíthai. Father of Korōnís.
Phleioús	City in northern Pelopónnēsos along Asōpós River and near Neméa.
Phoíbos	Deity. The word means "radiant." An epithet of Apóllōn.
Phoiníkē (Phoenicia)	Píndaros uses the name to refer to Carthage, a Phoenician colony on Mediterranean shore of modern Tunisia. Hiérōn joined Kýmē to defeat an alliance of Carthaginian and Etruscan forces in a naval battle off the coast of Kýmē in 474 BCE.
Phókos	Mythological figure. Son of Psamáthē and Aiakós. Half-brother of Pēleús and Telamón, who killed him.
Phórkys	Mythological figure. Father of Gorgónes and Graíai (mother: Kētó).
Phrástōr	According to tradition, first winner in javelin contest at Olympía.
Phrikías	Historical figure. The name of either the racehorse of Hippokléas or the father of Hippokléas.
Phríxos	Mythological figure. Son of Nephélē and Athámas. Fled to Kolkhís to escape mortal danger by riding a golden ram that Zeus sent him. Iásōn and the Argonaútai sailed in quest of the fleece of that ram.
Phrygía	A kingdom of central Anatolia. For Píndaros the people of Phrygía fought as allies of the Tróes in the **Trojan War** (N.3.60).
Phthía	City in Thessalía. Homeland of Akhilleús.
Phylákē	City in the region of Phthiótis in Thessalía. Site of a shrine for Prōtesílaos.
Phylakídas	Historical figure. From Aígina. Member of Psalykhiádai family. Son of Lámpōn. Brother of Pythéas.
Pierídes	Mythological figures. The name means "daughters of Píeros." Píeros is the eponym for Piería. The "daughters of Píeros" are the Moúsai, who are associated with Piería, a region north of Mount Ólympos.
Píndos	Mountain range in northwestern Hellás on the border between Thessalía and Ḗpeiros.
Písa	The region where Olympía lies.
Pitánē (1)	One of Spárta's four villages.
Pitánē (2)	Mythological figure. *Nýmphē*. Daughter of Eurótas. Mother of Euádnē (father: Poseidón). Eponym of Pitánē (1).
Pleiádes	Mythological figures. Their name means "daughters of Plēiónē" (father: Átlas). These seven daughters of Plēiónē became the stars of the constellation known as Pleiades.
Plēiónē	Mythological figure. Daughter of Tēthýs and Ōkeanós. Mother of Pleiádes (father: Átlas).
Poías	Mythological figure. Father of Philoktétēs. As he lay dying, Hēraklés gifted Poías with his bow and arrows.
Polydéktēs	Mythological figure. King of Sériphos. Threatened Danáē with sexual violence. Perseús turned him (and others) to stone with the head of Médousa.

Glossary

Polydeúkēs	Mythological figure. Son of **Léda** and Zeus. Brother of **Kástōr**. Polydeúkēs and Kástōr are known as the **Dióskouroi**. When Kástōr was mortally wounded, Polydeúkēs agreed to share the benefits of his divine parentage with his brother, negotiating with his father Zeus that the brothers would exchange existences, each dwelling one day as deceased mortal in the underworld, the next day dwelling as an immortal on Ólympos (N.10.55–90).
Polýmnēstos	Mythological figure. Father of **Báttos**.
Polyneíkēs	Mythological figure. Son of Iokástē (Jocasta) and Oidípous. Father of Thérsandros.
Polytimídas	Historical figure. From Aígina. Relative of Alkimídas. Member of Bassídai family.
Porphyríōn	Mythological figure. King of Gígantes. Apóllōn killed him.
Poseidón	Deity. Son of Rheía and Krónos. Married Amphitrítē. God of sea, earthquakes, and horses, as his epithet Poseidón Hípparkhos (ruler of horses) indicates. His weapon is the trident. Games at the Isthmós honored him.
pótmos	The word means "that which befalls someone, lot, fortune," whether good or bad. Personified as a deity (N.4.42).
Praxidámas	Historical figure. The first of Aígina's athletic victors at Olympía. Member of Bassídai family. Grandfather of Alkimídas.
Príamos (Priam)	Mythological figure. Son of Laomédōn. Married Hekábē. King of Troía. Father of Héktōr, Hélenos, Kassándra, and Páris. Neoptólemos killed him.
Proítos	Mythological figure. Son of Ábas. Brother of Akrísios. King of Árgos.
próphasis	Hellenic word that means "pretext" or "excuse." Píndaros personifies Próphasis as daughter of Epimētheús.
Prōtesílaos	Mythological figure. From Thessalía. King of Phylákē. Fought in the **Trojan War**.
Prōtogéneia	Mythological figure. Daughter of Pýrrha and Deukalíōn. Ancestor of the people of **Opoús (3)**.
Psalykhiádai	Historical figures. A prominent family of Aígina.
Psamáthē	Mythological figure. Daughter of Dōrís and Nēreús. Mother of Phókos (father: Aiakós).
Psaúmis	Historical figure. From Kamárina in Sikelía. Son of Ákrōn. Winner at Olympía in the chariot race (or mule wagon race?) in 452 BCE and the mule wagon race in 448 BCE (?). Played a significant role in the reestablishment of Kamárina after **Gélōn** destroyed the city (c. 485 BCE).
Ptoiódōros	Historical figure. From Kórinthos. Brother of Terpsías. Father of Thessalós. Grandfather of Xenophón.
pygmé	The athletic competition of boxing.
Pyládēs	Mythological figure. Son of Stróphios, king of Phōkís. Friend of Oréstēs.
Pýlos	City in western Pelopónnēsos. According to tradition founded by Nēleús.
Pýrrha	Mythological figure. Daughter of Pandóra and Epimētheús. From Mount Parnassós. Wife of Deukalíōn, with whom she refounded the human race after a destructive flood sent by Zeus.
Pythéas	Historical figure. From Aígina. Son of Lámpōn. Member of Psalykhiádai family. Brother of Phylakídas. Victor in *pankrátion* at Neméa.
Pythó	Another name for **Delphoí**. Site of panhellenic sanctuary sacred to Apóllōn. Hosted the Pythian games.
Pythónikos	Historical figure. From Thḗbai. Father of Thrasydaíos. His name means "winner at Pythó."
Rhadámanthys	Mythological figure. From Krḗtē. Son of Eurṓpē and Zeus. A judge in Háïdēs.
Rheía	Deity. Daughter of Gaía and Ouranós. Married Krónos. Mother of Háïdēs, Dēmḗtēr, Héra, Hestía, Poseidón, and Zeus.

Glossary

Rhódos — The largest of the Dodecanese islands in the eastern Mediterranean Sea. Represented as the eponymous *nýmphē* whom Hélios married (O.7).

Salamís — Island in the Saronic Gulf. Héllēnes defeated the Persians at the Battle of Salamís in 480 BCE.

Salmoneús — Mythological figure. Son of Ainarétē and Aíolos. Grandfather of Pelías.

Sámos — According to tradition, the first winner in four-horse chariot race at Olympía. Son of Haliróthios.

Sarpēdón — Mythological figure. Son of Laodámeia and Zeus. King of Lykía. Fought in **Trojan War** on the side of the Tróes.

Selénē — Deity. The word means "moon." Daughter of Theía and Hyperíōn.

Semélē — Mythological figure. Daughter of Harmonía and Kádmos. Mother of Diónysos (father: Zeus). Lightning destroyed her when Zeus appeared to her in his full divine power and majesty.

Sériphos — One of the Cycladic islands.

Seven Against Thébai — Upon the death (or exile) of Oidípous a dispute arose between his sons Eteoklés and Polyneíkēs over the rule of Thébai. The brothers agreed to share power, Eteoklés ruling one year, Polyneíkēs the next. When Eteoklés refused to cede rule to his brother, Polyneíkēs went into exile to Árgos, where he married Argeía, daughter of Ádrastos. Ádrastos recruited six heroes to join Polyneíkēs in taking power of Thébai by force. Eteoklés prepared for this confrontation by recruiting six heroes to ally with him in defense of Thébai. The numbers are significant: sevengated Thébai had, as the epithet indicates, seven gates. The opposing forces met in battle with one attacker and one defender at each gate. Aiskhýlos' drama *Seven Against Thebes* depicts pairs of Argive aggressors and defenders of Thébai as follows: Tydeús-Melánippos, Kapaneús-Polyphóntēs, Etéoklos-Megareús, Hippomédōn-Hypérbios, Parthenopaíos-Áktōr, Amphiáraos-Lasthénēs, Polyneíkēs-Eteoklés. Other versions of the Seven Against Thébai story, including Píndaros' (P.8.39–56), depict **Ádrastos** as one of the Argive aggressors. All seven attackers died in battle, (except Ádrastos in versions of the story in which he appears). Especially notable deaths: Zeus struck Kapaneús with a lightning bolt; the earth swallowed Amphiáraos; Polyneíkēs and Eteoklés killed each other. The Kréōn of Sophoklés' *Antigone* condemns Polyneíkēs as a traitor and memorializes Eteoklés as a guardian of the homeland. When sons of the seven Argive aggressors reached adulthood—they are referred to as **Epígonoi**—Ádrastos led them on another military campaign against Thébai.

Sikelía (Sicily) — Mediterranean island located near the "toe" of Italy's "boot."

Sikyón — City in northern Pelopónnēsos near Asōpós River. Local athletic competitions were held there in honor of Apóllōn. Píndaros credits Ádrastos with the foundation of these games (N.9.9–10).

Sípylos — A city in Lydía.

Sísyphos — Mythological figure. Son of Ainarétē and Aíolos. King of Kórinthos. According to tradition, original founder of Kórinthos and games at Isthmós. See **Aíolos** for the patrilineal genealogy of major figures in the mythology of Kórinthos.

Skámandros — River near Troía.

Skýros — Southernmost island of the Sporades archipelago in the Aegean Sea.

Sōgénēs — Historical figure. From Aígina. Son of Thearíōn. Winner in boys' *péntathlon* at Neméa.

Sōkleídas — Historical figure. From Aígina. Member of the Bassídai family. Father of Praxidámas, great-grandfather of Alkimídas.

Glossary

Sólymoi	Name of people said to live near Lykía and Pamphylía. Bellerophóntēs destroyed them.
Sóstratos	Historical figure. Father of Hagēsías. Member of Iamídai family.
Spárta	Another name for Lakedaímōn. City located in south-central Pelopónnēsos. A Dorian community.
Spartoí	Mythological figures. The word means "the sown ones." Upon killing a dragon, Kádmos cast its teeth over the ground. From these sown teeth sprung a group of warriors who were celebrated as ancestors of some prominent families of Thébai.
stádion (plural: stádia)	A race course or the distance of that race course. Roughly a distance of 200 meters. Also the footrace of one *stádion* in length.
Strepsiádas (1)	Historical figure. From Thébai. Winner in *pankrátion* at Isthmós.
Strepsiádas (2)	Historical figure. From Thébai. Son of Diódotos. Uncle of Strepsiádas (1).
Stróphios	Mythological figure. King of Phōkís. Father of Pyládēs.
Stýmphalos	City in northeast Arkadía. Birthplace of Hermés (O.6.79). Píndaros represents Stýmphalos as mother of Arkadía (O.6.100). Héra was worshipped as Héra Parthenía, that is, as Héra of Unwedded Women, at Stýmphalos (Pausanias 8.22.2).
Styx	River of Háïdēs. Gods swore oaths by Styx.
Syrákousai (Syracuse)	A city of Sikelía.
Taínaros	A town near Cape Taínaron (modern Cape Matapan) in the southern Pelopónnēsos. In some mythological accounts, the site of the entrance to Háïdēs (1). Home of Eúphēmos.
Talaós	Mythological figure. Son of Bías. Father of Ádrastos. King of Árgos.
Tántalos	Mythological figure. Son of Ploutó and Zeus. King of Sípylos in Lydía. Father of Nióbē and Pélops. According to a common version of the story, the gods punished Tántalos by tantalizing him with food and drink that remain eternally out of reach, but Píndaros offers another account of his punishment: a great boulder suspended over Tántalos' head threatened eternally to crush him (O.1.55–60 and I.8.9–11).
Tártaros	The writers Hēsíodos and Hómēros locate this place in the deepest part of the *kósmos* (universe), below Háïdēs. Place where rebellious monsters and deities are locked away.
Täygétē	Mythological figure. Daughter of Plēiónē and Átlas. One of the Pleiádes. Central figure in foundation myth of Lakedaímōn/Spárta. After Zeus had sex with her, Täygétē hid herself under Mount Täygetos in Lakōniké. Täygétē was mother of the eponymous Lakedaímōn, who married the eponymous *nýmphē* Spárta, daughter of Eurótas.
Täygetos	Mountain range in Lakōniké, near Spárta.
Tegéa	City in Arkadía. Site of games in honor of Athēná.
Teiresías	Mythological figure. A descendent of Spartoí. From Thébai. A blind prophet.
Telamón	Mythological figure. Son of Endēís and Aiakós. Brother of Pēleús. King of Salamís. Father of Aías. Killed his half-brother Phókos. Attacked Troía with Hēraklés.
Tēlebóai	Mythological figures. A people who inhabited islands of the Ionian Sea off the coast of Akarnanía.
Télephos	Mythological figure. Son of Aúgē and Hēraklés. Adopted son of Teúthras, from whom he inherited his kingship over Mysía. He resisted the Héllēnes when their fleet arrived at Mysía en route to Troía.

Glossary

Telésarkhos	Historical figure. From Aígina. Father of Kléandros.
Telesiádas	Historical figure. From Thébai. Father of Mélissos.
Telesikrátēs	Historical figure. From Kyrénē. Winner in hoplite race at Pythó.
Ténedos	Island in northeastern Aegean Sea off the coast of modern Turkey.
Terpsías	Historical figure. From Kórinthos. Brother of Ptoiódōros.
Terpsikhórē	Deity. One of the nine Moúsai. The Moúsa of dance.
Teúkros	Mythological figure. Son of Hēsiónē and Telamón. Half-brother of Aías (1). When he returned to Salamís after the **Trojan War**, his fellow citizens exiled him as punishment for failing to ensure Aías' safe return from Troía (N.4.46). Teúkros founded a second Salamís on the island of Kýpros.
Teúthras	Mythological figure. King of Mysía. The plain of Teúthras (O.9.71) refers to Mysía.
Thalía	Deity. The name means "festivity" and is derived from the verb *thállein* (to flower, to flourish). One of the Khárites.
Theaíos	Historical figure. Son of Oulías. From Árgos. Victor in local games at Árgos called Hekatómbaia.
Theandrídai	Historical figures. Prominent family of Aígina.
Theariōn	Historical figure. Father of Sōgénēs. From Aígina.
Theárion	Historical figures. A group of dignitaries sent by Aígina to Delphoí.
Thébai (Thebes)	Principal city in Boiōtía. According to tradition, founded by Kádmos. Píndaros identifies it as his homeland. Hosted games in honor of Iólaos, son of Iphiklés and companion of Hēraklés (O.9.98–9).
Thébē	Mythological figure. *Nýmphē*. Daughter of Metópē and Asōpós. Sister of Aígina. Eponym of Thébai.
Theía	Deity. Mother of Ēós, Hélios, and Selénē (father: Hyperíōn).
Thémis	Deity. The word means "traditional custom." Daughter of Gaía and Ouranós. Mother of the Hórai (father: Zeus): Eunomía, Díkē, and Eirénē. She was the presiding deity at the oracle of Delphoí before the site became sacred to Apóllōn.
Themístios	Historical figure. From Aígina. Member of Psalykhiádai family. Maternal grandfather of Pythéas and Phylakídas.
Theógnētos	Historical figure. Uncle of Aristoménēs. Victor at Olympía.
Théra	Ancient name for Santorini, a Cycladic island in the southern Aegean. According to tradition, people of Théra founded Kyrénē in Libýē.
Therápnē	Town near Spárta located in hilly country along Eurótas River. Site sacred to the **Dióskouroi, Kástōr** and **Polydeúkēs**, was located here.
Thérōn	Historical figure. Ruler of Akrágas. Son of Ainēsídamos. Brother of Xenokrátēs. Uncle of Thrasýboulos. Member of Emmenídai family, which claimed descent from Kádmos, founder of Thébai. Victor in chariot race at Olympía 476 BCE. Thérōn became tyrant at Akrágas (*c.* 489–473 BCE), conquered Himéra (483 BCE), and, in alliance with Gélōn of Syrákousai (brother of Hiérōn), defeated a Carthaginian force under Hamilcar (480 BCE). Thérōn's daughter Damarétē was Gélōn's wife, and Thérōn's niece became Hiérōn's wife after Hiérōn succeeded Gélōn as tyrant of Syrákousai upon Gélōn's death (478 BCE). The people of Akrágas honored Thérōn as a hero after he died.
Thérsandros	Mythological figure. Son of Argeía, daughter of Ádrastos, and Polyneíkēs. Ádrastos' only son Aigialeús died when the Epígonoi attacked Thébai, leaving Thésandros as the only remaining descendent of Ádrastos (O.2.43–5). Thérōn and Emmenídai claim descent from him.
Thessalía	Region of Hellás north of Boiōtía.

Glossary

Thessaloí	Historical figures. People who live in Thessalía.
Thessalós	Historical figure. From Kórinthos. Member of Oligaithídai family. Father of Xenophón. Son of Ptoiódōros.
Thétis	Deity. Daughter of Dōrís and Nēreús. Married Pēleús. Mother of Akhilleús.
Thórax	Historical figure. From Thessalía. Member of Aleuádai family. Probably commissioned P.10.
Thrákē (Thrace)	Northeasternmost region of Hellás.
Thrasýboulos	Historical figure. From Akrágas. Son of Xenokrátēs.
Thrasydaíos	Historical figure. From Thébai. Victor in boys' footrace at Pythó 474 BCE.
Thrásyklos	Historical figure. From Árgos. Maternal relative of Theaíos. An athletic victor.
Thyónē	Mythological figure. Another name for **Semélē**.
Timásarkhos	Historical figure. From Aígina. Son of Timókritos. Winner of boys' wrestling at Neméa.
Timodēmídai	Historical figures. The word means "descendants of Timódēmos." Refers to a prominent family of Akharnaí.
Timódēmos	Historical figure. From Akharnaí. Winner in *pankrátion* at Neméa.
Timókritos	Historical figure. From Aígina. Father of Timásarkhos.
Timónoos	Historical figure. From Akharnaí. Father of Timódēmos. Member of the Timodēmídai family.
Timosthénēs	Historical figure. From Aígina. Son of Iphíōn. Older brother of Alkimédōn.
Tíryns	Mycenaean site in Argolid of Pelopónnēsos. Proítos is its mythological founder. Home of Hēraklés and his son Tlēpólemos.
Titánes (Titans)	Deities. Designation for six sons of Gaía and Ouranós: Ōkeanós, Koíos, Hyperíōn, Kreíos, Iapetós, and Krónos.
Titanídes (Titans)	Deities. Designation for six daughters of Gaía and Ouranós: Theía, Rheía, Thémis, Mnēmosýnē, Phoíbē, and Tēthýs.
Tityós	Mythological figure. Son of Elára and Zeus. A giant. Ártemis killed him.
Tlēpólemos	Mythological figure. From Tíryns. Son of Astydámeia and Hēraklés. Emigrated from Tíryns to settle Rhódos (O.7.20–3).
trident	Poseidón's weapon. A spear equipped with three sharpened prongs at the business end.
Tritōnís	A lake in Libýē. The word means "lake of Trítōn," seagod and son of Poseidón.
Tróes (Trojans)	Mythological figures. The people of Troía.
Troía (Troy)	Another name for Ílios. Ancient city located in modern Turkey, inland from the Dardanelles (known in antiquity as the Hellespont). Site of the **Trojan War**.
Trojan War	The Oath of Tyndáreōs (father of Helénē) obligated Helénē's many suitors to defend the marriage to which she finally agreed. After she married Menélaos, Páris, son of Hekábē and Príamos, abducted or seduced (depending upon version of the story) Helénē and brought her to his homeland of Troía. The Hellenic heroes bound by the Oath of Tyndáreōs assembled their forces and embarked upon a military expedition to Troía to recover Helénē and punish Troía. Menélaos' brother Agamémnōn served as commander of these forces. For the Akhaioí, other major Trojan War figures that appear in Píndaros' victory songs include Akhilleús, Aías, Odysseús, and Néstōr. The great hero of Troía is Héktōr. The Trojan War lasted ten years. The Akhaioí finally sacked Troía through the covert tactic of presenting a massive wooden horse as a pretend peace offering. The horse contained a large contingent of Hellenic warriors who descended at night and surprise-attacked the sleeping people of Troía.

Glossary

týkhē
The word means "fortune" or "chance." Píndaros personifies Týkhē as a daughter of Zeus (O.12.2).

Tyndarídēs
Plural:
Tyndarídai
Mythological figure(s). The word means "son of Tyndáreōs" and refers to **Kástōr**, to **Polydeúkēs**, or to both.

Typhós
Mythological figure. Son of Gaía and Tártaros. A monster who rebelled against Zeus' rule. Zeus buried him under Mount Aítna.

Tyró
Mythological figure. Daughter of Alkidíkē and Salmoneús. Mother of Pelías (father: Poseidón).

Tyrsanoí
Historical figures. Píndaros' Hellenic word for Etruscans. Hiérōn defeated an alliance of Carthaginian and Etruscan forces in a naval battle off the coast of Kýmē in 474 BCE.

Xánthos
River in Lykía, in the southwest of the Anatolian Peninsula. The city Pátara, site of an oracle of Apóllōn, was located near the mouth of this river.

Xenárkēs
Historical figure. From Aígina. Father of Aristoménēs. Victor in games at Pythó.

Xenokrátēs
Historical figure. From Akrágas. Son of Ainēsídamos. Member of Emmenídai family. Father of Thrasýboulos. Brother of Thérōn. Won in 490 BCE chariot race at Pythó.

Xenophón
Historical figure. From Kórinthos. Son of Thessalós. Member of Oligaithídai family. Winner in both *stádion* and *péntathlon* in 464 BCE at Olympía.

Zéphyros
Deity. The west wind.

Zétēs
Mythological figure. Son of Oreíthyia and Boréas. Brother of Kálaïs. One of the Argonaútai.

Zeus
Deity. Son of Rheía and Krónos. Divine king of gods and humans. Ultimate arbiter of *díkē* (justice). Husband of Héra. His sacred animal is the eagle. Brother of Dēmétēr, Háïdēs, Héra, Hestía, and Poseidón. Signature weapon: thunderbolt. Father of Aiakós, Alétheia, Apóllōn, Ártemis, Athēná, Héphaistos, Hēraklés, Hermés, Khárites, Moúsai, Polydeúkēs, and Týkhē. Had sexual encounters, often nonconsensual and violent, with Aígina, Alkménē, Danáē, Ganymédēs, Léda, Maía, Semélē (=Thyónē), Thébē, and Thétis, that resulted in the birth of gods and heroes, except in the case of Ganymédēs. Games held at both Olympía and Neméa honored him.

NOTES

Note on Text and Translation

1. Bruno Snell and Herwig Maehler, eds., *Pindari Carmina cum fragmentis. Pars I: Epinicia*. 8th ed. (Leipzig: Teubner, 1997).
2. Cecil Maurice Bowra, *Pindari Carmina cum Fragmentis,* 2nd ed. (Oxford: Oxford University Press, 1935).
3. William H. Race, ed. and trans., *Pindar. Olympian Odes. Pythian Odes* (Cambridge: Harvard University Press, 1997) and William H. Race, ed. and trans., *Pindar. Nemean Odes. Isthmian Odes. Fragments* (Cambridge: Harvard University Press, 1997).
4. See James Bradley Wells, trans., *Vergil: "Eclogues" and "Georgics"* (Madison: University of Wisconsin Press, 2022), xiii–xxix, for a more fully developed account of translation and poetic practices that I more briefly present here.
5. Lawrence Venuti, *The Translator's Invisibility: A History of Translation* (London and New York: Routledge, 2018).
6. Cf. Wells, *Vergil*, xx–xxvii.
7. Katherine R. De Boer, "Pindar's Peaceful Rapes," *Helios* 44, no. 1 (2017): 1.
8. De Boer, "Pindar's Peaceful Rapes," 1

Pronunciation Guide

1. Geoffrey Horrocks, *Greek: A History of the Language and Its Speakers* (London: Longman 1997), xix–xx.

Introduction

1. Introductions to Píndaros and his poetry include David C. Young, "Pindar," in *Ancient Writers: Greece and Rome*, ed. T. James Luce (New York: Charles Scriber's Songs, 1982), 157–77; Hayden Pelliccia, "Simonides, Pindar and Bacchylides," in *The Cambridge Companion to Greek Lyric*, ed. Felix Budelmann (Cambridge: Cambridge University Press, 2009), 240–62; and Christopher Brown, "Pindar," in *A Companion to Greek Lyric*, ed. Laura Swift (Hoboken, NJ: John Wiley & Sons, Inc., 2022), 333–45. For introductions to the lyric poetry of the Archaic period, see Leslie Kurke, "Archaic Greek Poetry," in *The Cambridge Companion to Archaic Greece*, ed. H. A. Shapiro (Cambridge: Cambridge University Press, 2007), 141–68; Felix Budelmann, ed., *The Cambridge Companion to Greek Lyric* (Cambridge: Cambridge University Press, 2009); James Bradley Wells, "Lyric: Melic, Iambic, and Elegiac," in *A Companion to Greek Literature*, ed. Martin Hose and David Schenker (Malden, MA: John Wiley & Sons, Inc., 2016), 155–74; and Laura Swift, ed., *A Companion to Greek Lyric* (Hoboken, NJ: John Wiley & Sons, Inc., 2022).
2. In the interest of economy, I do not cite sources in the introductions to each *epiníkion* or in the Glossary. In writing those introductions and in the process of translation itself, I have referred to the commentary by the Confederate officer and defender of slavery, Basil L. Gildersleeve, ed., *Pindar: The Olympian and Pythian Odes* (Amsterdam: Adolf M. Hakkert, 1965 [1890]), as well as: J. B. Bury, ed., *The Nemean Odes of Pindar* (London: MacMillan and Co., 1890); J. B. Bury, ed., *The Isthmian Odes of Pindar* (Amsterdam: Adolf M. Hakkert, 1965 [1892]); William J. Slater, *Lexicon to Pindar* (Berlin: Walter de Gruyter and Company, 1969); M. M, Willcock, ed., *Pindar. Victory Odes: Olympians 2, 7, 11; Nemean 4; Isthmians 3, 4, 7* (Cambridge: Cambridge University Press, 1995).

3. Cf. Gregory Nagy, *Pindar's Homer: The Lyric Possession of an Epic Past* (Baltimore: The Johns Hopkins University Press, 1990), 136–7.

4. Interested readers may learn more about ancient athletics by exploring these sources, upon which I have drawn in my overview of the topic: David C. Young, *The Olympic Myth of Greek Amateur Athletics* (Chicago: Ares Publishers, Inc., 1984), David Sansone, *Greek Athletics and the Genesis of Sport* (Berkeley: University of California Press, 1998), Stephen G. Miller, *Ancient Greek Athletics* (New Haven: Yale University Press, 2004), Zahra Newby, *Athletics in the Ancient World* (London: Bristol Classical Press, 2006), David Potter, *The Victor's Crown: A History of Ancient Sport from Homer to Byzantium* (Oxford: Oxford University Press, 2012), and Charles H. Stocking and Susan A. Stephens, *Ancient Greek Athletics: Primary Sources in Translation* (Oxford: Oxford University Press, 2021).

5. On the emergence of Panhellenism in the Archaic period (750–480 BCE), see Gregory Nagy, *The Best of the Achaians: Concepts of the Hero in Archaic Greek Poetry*, revised ed. (Baltimore: The Johns Hopkins University Press, 1999), 7–9.

6. Nigel Nicholson, *The Poetics of Victory in the Greek West: Epinician, Oral Tradition, and the Deinomenid Empire* (Oxford: Oxford University Press, 2016).

7. Anne Pippin Burnett, *Pindar's Songs for Young Athletes of Aigina* (Oxford: Oxford University Press, 2005).

8. On Píndaros' *epiníkia* for athletes from Kyrénē, see Simon Hornblower, *Thucydides and Pindar: Historical Narrative and the World of Epinikian Poetry* (Oxford: Oxford University Press, 2004), 243–7, and Richard Neer and Leslie Kurke, *Pindar, Song, and Space: Towards a Lyric Archaeology* (Baltimore: The Johns Hopkins University Press, 2019), 159–217.

9. Nagy, *Pindar's Homer*, 137, and Leslie Kurke, "The Economy of *Kudos*," in *Cultural Poetics in Archaic Greece: Cult, Performance, Politics*, ed. Carol Dougherty and Leslie Kurke (Oxford: Oxford University Press, 1993), 134.

10. Nagy, *Pindar's Homer*, 137.

11. Nagy, *Pindar's Homer*, 118–19.

12. Nagy, *Pindar's Homer*, 118. On language and imagery of rebirth in Píndaros' *epiníkia*, see also Kevin Crotty, *Song and Action: The Victory Odes of Pindar* (Baltimore: The Johns Hopkins University Press, 1982), 113–17, and Leslie Kurke, *The Traffic in Praise: Pindar and the Poetics of Social Economy* (Ithaca: Cornell University Press, 1991), 70–82.

13. Nagy, *Pindar's Homer*, 119–20.

14. Nagy, *Pindar's Homer*, 140–2.

15. Nagy, *Pindar's Homer*, 141.

16. R. R. R. Smith, "Pindar, Athletes, and the Early Greek Statue Habit," in *Pindar's Poetry, Patrons, and Festivals: From Archaic Greece to the Roman Empire*, ed. Simon Hornblower Simon and Catherin Morgan (Oxford: Oxford University Press, 2007), 111.

17. Nagy, *Pindar's Homer*, 137.

18. I adapt this account from Nagy, *Pindar's Homer*, 129–30, where interested readers will find detailed documentation of primary ancient sources and insightful analysis of them.

19. This discussion of the statue habit of the late-Archaic and early-Classical periods draws upon R. R. R. Smith, "Pindar, Athletes, and the Early Greek Statue Habit," 83–139. Nigel James Nicholson, *Aristocracy and Athletics in Archaic and Classical Greece* (Cambridge: Cambridge University Press, 2005) analyzes the aristocratic rhetoric of victory memorials with particular focus on strategies for representing or eliding the roles of chariot drives, mule wagon drivers, jockeys, and athletic trainers.

20. Kurke, *Traffic*, 260.

21. Nicholson, *Aristocracy and Athletics*, 11–15, includes vases and the dedication of tripods and bowls among the media for victory commemoration.

22. Smith, "Pindar, Athletes, and the Early Greek Statue Habit," 84.

23. The exhibition, "Chroma: Ancient Sculpture in Color," New York Metropolitan Museum of Art, July 5, 2022–March 26, 2023, assembled replicas of ancient sculpture that include their original polychromatic

features. See www.metmuseum.org/exhibitions/listings/2022/chroma, accessed February 15, 2023, and Vinzenz Brinkmann, Dreyfus Renée, and Ulrike Koch-Brinkmann, eds., *Gods in Color: Polychromy in the Ancient World*. San Francisco: Fine Arts Museums of San Francisco, 2017.

24. Smith, "Pindar, Athletes, and the Early Greek Statue Habit," 91–2.
25. Smith, "Pindar, Athletes, and the Early Greek Statue Habit," 87.
26. Smith, "Pindar, Athletes, and the Early Greek Statue Habit," 107–8.
27. Here I summarize evidence and analysis admirably presented in Smith, "Pindar, Athletes, and the Early Greek Statue Habit," 95–100 and 137–9.
28. Smith, "Pindar, Athletes, and the Early Greek Statue Habit," 97.
29. Donato Loscalzo, *La parola inestinguibile: studi sull'epinicio pindarico* (Rome: Edizioni dell'Ateneo, 2003), 86.
30. Kurke, *Traffic*, 5.
31. Kurke, *Traffic*, 260.
32. In this survey of sociological poetics, I lean heavily upon Kurke, *Traffic*.
33. *The Oxford English Dictionary Online*, www.oed.com, accessed February 15, 2023, s.v. *wealth* and *weal*.
34. Cf. Kurke, *Traffic*, 8–9 and 62–82.
35. Kurke, *Traffic*, 43.
36. Kurke, *Traffic*, 35–8.
37. Kurke, *Traffic*, 97–9.
38. Kurke, *Traffic*, 99.
39. Kurke, *Traffic*, 101.
40. Kurke, *Traffic*, 167.
41. Kurke, *Traffic*, 176. Kurke, *Traffic*, 195–224 further elaborates the envy and threat of tyranny that may result from the practice of *megaloprépeia* and how Píndaros' poetry navigates this thorny terrain.
42. Smith, "Pindar, Athletes, and the Early Greek Statue Habit," 102.
43. Smith, "Pindar, Athletes, and the Early Greek Statue Habit," 101.
44. Kurke, *Traffic*, 186–8.
45. Kurke, *Traffic*, 193.
46. Kurke, *Traffic*, 188–92.
47. Kurke, *Traffic*, 258.
48. Kurke, "The Economy of *Kudos*," 131–63.
49. William J. Slater, *Lexicon to Pindar* (Berlin: Walter de Gruyter and Company, 1969), s.v. κῦδος.
50. Émile Benveniste, *Indo-European Language and Society*, trans. Elizabeth Palmer (Coral Gables: University of Miami Press, 1973), 348.
51. Kurke, "The Economy of *Kudos*," 134.
52. Kurke, "The Economy of *Kudos*," 134–5.
53. Kurke, "The Economy of *Kudos*," 137–41.
54. Kurke, "The Economy of *Kudos*," 139–40. On the victory celebration, see also Nicholson, *Aristocracy and Athletics*, 34.
55. For further discussion of these passages as textual evidence for the reentry ritual, see Kurke, "Economy of *Kudos*," 140–1.
56. Young, *Olympic Myth*, 141.
57. Nagy, *Pindar's Homer*, 142.
58. Kurke, *Traffic*, 6.

59. Hans-Georg Gadamer, *Truth and Method* (New York: Seabury Press, 1975), 129, cited in Gregory Nagy, "Copies and Models in Horace *Odes* 4.1 and 4.2," *The Classical World* 87, no. 2 (1994): 416–17.

60. Here I draw from the thought of linguist Roman Jakobson who defines six factors of a speech event—addresser, message, addressee, context, code, and contact—that correspond to six functions of language in a speech event—emotive, poetic, conative, referential, metalingual, and phatic. See Roman Jakobson, "Closing Statement: Linguistics and Poetics," in *Style in Language*, ed. Thomas Sebeok (Cambridge: Technology Press of Massachusetts Institute of Technology, 1960), 350–77.

61. Dionýsios elsewhere characterizes Píndaros' language as *megaloprepés* (grand) (*De imit.* 6.2). On such ancient literary criticism and assessments of Píndaros' language, see Robert L. Fowler, *Pindar and the Sublime: Greek Myth, Reception and Lyric Experience* (London: Bloomsbury Academic, 2022), 3–4, and Hornblower, *Thucydides and Pindar*, 354–72.

62. The best comprehensive study of Píndaros' metaphors remains Deborah Steiner, *The Crown of Song: Metaphor in Pindar* (New York: Oxford University Press, 1986). Loscalzo, *La parola inestinguibile*, 125–50, insightfully explores Píndaros' artistic metaphors for building construction, treasuries, *stélai* (stone monuments), metalworking, the weaving of garlands or fabric, and embroidery.

63. For an introduction to theories of metaphor, see Steiner, *Crown of Song*, 1–17. For a trenchant analysis of metaphor in the context of a foundational study of language and cognitive science, see Roman Jakobson, "Two Aspects of Language and Two Types of Aphasic Disturbances," in *On Language*, ed. Linda R. Waugh and Monique Monville-Burston (Cambridge, MA: Harvard University Press, 1990), 115–33.

64. See Steiner, *Crown of Song*, 46, on water metaphors for poetry.

65. Cf. Steiner, *Crown of Song*, 52–65.

66. Steiner, *Crown of Song*, 28–39.

67. Slater, *Lexicon*, s. v. ἄφθιτος, —ον. Steiner, *Crown of Song*, 126–7, associates metaphors of nature's enduring abundance or fertility with immortality.

68. Nagy, *Best of the Achaians*, 176–7.

69. On the flora metaphor as a motif that unifies *Olympian 7*, see David C. Young, *Three Odes of Pindar: A Literary Study of Pythian 11, Pythian 3, and Olympian 7* (Leiden: E. J. Brill, 1968), 69–105. On *Olympian 7* as environmental literature, see Chris Eckerman, "Ancient Greek Literature and the Environment: A Case Study with Pindar's *Olympian 7*," in *A Global History of Literature and the Environment*, ed. John Parham and Louise Hutchings Westling (Cambridge: Cambridge University Press, 2017), 80–92.

70. Elroy Bundy, *Studia Pindarica* (Berkeley: University of California Press, 1986 [1962]), 5.

71. Bundy, *Studia Pindarica*, 6.

72. Drawing upon Bundy, *Studia Pindarica*, 8–11 and 36, a suggestive rather than exhaustive catalog of priamels in Píndaros' *epiníkia* includes: O.1.28–51, O.8.53–9, O.11.1–6, O.12.1–19, O.13.91–7, P.1.81–6, P.2.13–20, P.5.1–11, P.8.21–39, P.10.1–6, N.4.33–46, N.4.69–79, N.4.91–6, N.5.14–21, N.6.45–66, N.7.1–8, N.7.17–34, N.7.50–3, N.9.48–55 N.10.1–24, I.1.1–13, I.1.47–51, I.5.1–11, I.5.30–8, I.5.51–63, I.7.1–22. N.8.19–39 presents a particularly elaborated example of priamel, with summary priamel at N.8.19–22, illustrative exemplum at N.8.23–34, and a priamel at N.8.35–9 that recapitulates N.8.20–2.

73. On *poikilía* in Píndaros' *epiníkia* see James Bradley Wells, *Pindar's Verbal Art: An Ethnographic Study of Epinician Style* (Washington, DC: The Center for Hellenic Studies, 2009), 177–84. On the aesthetics of *poikilía*, see Pauline LeVen, "The Colours of Sound: Poikilia in Its Aesthetic Contexts," *Greek and Roman Musical Studies* 1 (2013): 229–42.

74. For a detailed description of each of these registers, see Wells, *Pindar's Verbal Art*, 67–73 on gnomic register, 73–7 on lyric register, 77–83 on the register of *angelía* (victory announcement), 83–8 on mythological narrative, and 89–128 on prayers.

75. On the ancient genre of discourse called *Kheírōnos Hypothékai* (Precepts of Kheírō), a form of wisdom poetry that blends gnomic statements, instructions, and mythological exempla and appears in a variety of traditional poetries, including *epiníkia*, see Richard P. Martin, *Mythologizing Performance* (Ithaca: Cornell University Press, 2020), 285–308.

76. Wells, *Pindar's Verbal Art*, 116–20, demonstrates how the implied second-person address entailed in the conative function of language is a feature of the register of prayers in Píndaros' *epiníkia*.

77. On the patterning among the five registers that occur in Píndaros' *epiníkia*, see Wells, *Pindar's Verbal Art*, 177–84 and 193–238.

78. William W. Cook and James Tatum, *African American Writers and Classical Tradition* (Chicago: University of Chicago Press, 2010), 217.

79. Victoria Moul, "*A Mirror for Noble Deeds*: Pindaric Form in Jonson's Odes and Masques," in *Receiving the Komos: Ancient and Modern Receptions of the Victory Ode*, ed. Peter Agócs, Chris Carey, and Richard Rawles (London: Institute of Classical Studies, University of London, 2012), 154–6.

80. Cf. Nagy, *Pindar's Homer*, 86 n20. Martin, *Mythologizing Performance*, 123–6, explores the cultural significance and mythopoetics of the *kithára* and the *lýra*.

81. Anastasia-Erasmia Peponi, "Lyric Atmospheres: Plato and Mimetic Evanescence," in *Music, Text, and Culture in Ancient Greece*, ed. Tom Phillips and Armand D'Angour (Oxford: Oxford University Press, 2018), 179. With the qualification that Roman Jakobson attends to the speech act, while Peponi considers the multimedia (song, dance, music) and correspondingly multisensory experience of choral performance, Peponi's beautiful reading (of Plátōn's characterization) of lyric poetry parallels Jakobson's definition of the poetic function of language: "The poetic function projects the principle of equivalence from the axis of selection into the axis of combination"; Jakobson, "Closing Statement," 358.

82. Loscalzo, *La parola inestinguibile*, 96–119, explores more fully the evidence for reperformance and the circulation of Píndaros' *epiníkia*. See Wells, *Pindar's Verbal Art*, 129–44, on the dialogical relationship between the original performance of *epiníkion* and reperformance.

83. For a succinct, detailed overview of the reception histories of Píndaros and his poetry, see John Hamilton, "Pindar (Pindarus)," in *The Reception of Classical Literature*, ed. Christine Walde in collaboration with Brigitte Egger, trans. and ed. Duncan Smart and Matthijs H. Wibier (Leiden: Brill, 2012), 306–11.

84. On Aristophánēs' reception of Píndaros, see John T. Hamilton, *Soliciting Darkness: Pindar, Obscurity, and the Classical Tradition* (Cambridge: Harvard University Press, 2003), 17–23.

85. In this discussion of Horace's poem, I draw from Richard F. Thomas, ed., *Horace, "Odes" Book IV and "Carmen Saeculare"* (Cambridge: Cambridge University Press, 2011), 103–21.

86. On Horace's mimesis as reenactment of the Pindaric model, see Gregory Nagy, "Copies and Models," 415–26. Penelope Wilson, "Pindar and his Reputation in Antiquity," *Proceedings of the Cambridge Philological Society*, no. 26 (1980): 97–114, examines Horace's *Odes* 4.2 and the writing of ancient commentators as evidence for receptions of Píndaros' poetry in antiquity.

87. Thomas, *Horace*, 112.

88. Thomas, *Horace*, 118.

89. Cf. Hamilton, "Pindar," 306, and John Hamilton, "The Gift of Song: German Receptions of Pindar," in *A Companion to Greek Lyric*, ed. Laura Swift (Hoboken, NJ: John Wiley & Sons, Inc., 2022), 438–41.

90. Moul, "*A Mirror for Noble Deeds*: Pindaric Form in Jonson's Odes and Masques," 141–56. See Hamilton, "The Gift of Song," 444–5, on formal imitation of Píndaros' *epiníkia* in seventeenth-century French and German poetry.

91. On the ode in English poetry and its alignments with ancient Hellenic and Roman models, see Paul H. Fry, *The Poet's Calling in the English Ode* (New Haven: Yale University Press, 1980).

92. Penelope Wilson "Pindar and English Eighteenth-Century Poetry," in *Receiving the Komos: Ancient and Modern Receptions of the Victory Ode*, ed. Peter Agócs, Chris Carey, and Richard Rawles (London: Institute of Classical Studies, University of London, 2012), 157–68. Cf. Fowler, *Pindar and the Sublime*, 9–10. For similar complaints about Pindarization in German poetry, see Hamilton, "The Gift of Song," 445–6.

93. Vassiliki Dimoula, "The Reception of Pindar's *Epinicians* and Nineteenth-Century 'Poetic Religion': Hölderlin and Kalvos," in *Receiving the Komos: Ancient and Modern Receptions of the Victory Ode*, ed. Peter Agócs, Chris Carey, and Richard Rawles (London: Institute of Classical Studies, University of London, 2012), 169–91. See Hamilton, "The Gift of Song," 447–9, for the reception of Píndaros in the *Sturm und Drang* movement of German Romanticism as a model for "emancipation from all conventions, an inspired transcendence of quotidian experience," and Hamilton, *Soliciting Darkness*, 237–65 on Goethe's engagement with Píndaros and 282–306 on Hölderlin's.

94. Stephen Rogers, *Classical Greece and the Poetry of Chenier, Shelley, and Leopardi* (Notre Dame: University of Notre Dame Press, 1974), 83–103.
95. Rogers, *Classical Greece and the Poetry of Chenier, Shelley, and Leopardi*, 143–9.
96. Robert de Brose, "Greek Lyric and Pindar in Brazil," in *A Companion to Greek Lyric*, ed. Laura Swift (Hoboken, NJ: John Wiley & Sons, Inc., 2022), 512–25.
97. Cook and Tatum, *African American Writers and Classical Tradition*, 207–60.
98. Reginald Gibbons, *Renditions* (Tribeca: Four Way Books, 2021), 75.
99. Gibbons, *Renditions*, 83.
100. Hans Urs von Balthasar, *The Glory of the Lord: A Theological Aesthetics. Volume IV: The Realm of Metaphysics in Antiquity*, trans. Brian McNeil, Andrew Louth, John Saward, Rowan Williams, and Oliver Davies, ed. John Riches. (San Francisco: Ignatius Press, 1989), 23; cf. 99 on *kháris* in Píndaros' poetry.
101. Von Balthasar, *The Glory of the Lord*, 92.
102. I paraphrastically translate the relevant original-language passages from the *Vita Ambrosiana* in Anders Björn Drachmann, ed., *Scholia Vetera in Pindari Carmina, Volumen 1: Scholia in Olympionicas* (Stuttgart: Teubner, 1997), 1.
103. Von Balthasar, *The Glory of the Lord*, 23.

BIBLIOGRAPHY

Balthasar, Hans Urs von. *The Glory of the Lord: A Theological Aesthetics. Volume IV: The Realm of Metaphysics in Antiquity*. Translated by Brian McNeil, Andrew Louth, John Saward, Rowan Williams, and Oliver Davies. Edited by John Riches. San Francisco: Ignatius Press, 1989.
Bauman, Richard. *Verbal Art as Performance*. Prospect Heights, Illinois: Waveland Press, 1977.
Benjamin, Walter. *Illuminations: Essays and Reflections*. Edited by Hannah Arendt, translated by Harry Zohn. New York: Schocken Books, 1968.
Benveniste, Émile. *Indo-European Language and Society*. Translated by Elizabeth Palmer. Coral Gables: University of Miami Press, 1973.
Bowra, Cecil Maurice. *Pindari Carmina cum Fragmentis*. 2nd ed. Oxford: Oxford University Press, 1935.
Brinkmann, Vinzenz, Dreyfus Renée, and Ulrike Koch-Brinkmann, eds. *Gods in Color: Polychromy in the Ancient World*. San Francisco: Fine Arts Museums of San Francisco, 2017.
de Brose, Robert. "Greek Lyric and Pindar in Brazil." In *A Companion to Greek Lyric*, edited by Laura Swift, 512–25. Hoboken, NJ: John Wiley & Sons, Inc., 2022.
Brown, Christopher. "Pindar." In *A Companion to Greek Lyric*, edited by Laura Swift, 333–45. Hoboken, NJ: John Wiley & Sons, Inc., 2022.
Budelmann, Felix, ed. *The Cambridge Companion to Greek Lyric*. Cambridge: Cambridge University Press, 2009.
Bundy, Elroy. *Studia Pindarica*. Berkeley: University of California Press, 1986 (1962).
Burnett, Anne Pippin. *Pindar's Songs for Young Athletes of Aigina*. Oxford: Oxford University Press, 2005.
Bury, J. B., ed. *The Nemean Odes of Pindar*. London: MacMillan and Co., 1890.
Bury, J. B., ed. *The Isthmian Odes of Pindar*. Amsterdam: Adolf M. Hakkert, 1965 (1892).
Cook, William W. and James Tatum. *African American Writers and Classical Tradition*. Chicago: University of Chicago Press, 2010.
Crotty, Kevin. *Song and Action: The Victory Odes of Pindar*. Baltimore: The Johns Hopkins University Press, 1982.
De Boer, Katherine R. "Pindar's Peaceful Rapes." *Helios* 44, no. 1 (2017): 1–27.
Dimoula, Vassiliki. "The Reception of Pindar's *Epinicians* and Nineteenth-Century 'Poetic Religion': Hölderlin and Kalvos." In *Receiving the Komos: Ancient and Modern Receptions of the Victory Ode*, edited by Peter Agócs, Chris Carey, and Richard Rawles, 169–91. London: Institute of Classical Studies, University of London, 2012.
Drachmann, Anders Björn, ed. *Scholia Vetera in Pindari Carmina, Volumen 1: Scholia in Olympionicas*. Stuttgart: Teubner, 1997.
Eckerman, Chris. "Ancient Greek Literature and the Environment: A Case Study with Pindar's *Olympian 7*." In *A Global History of Literature and the Environment*, edited by John Parham and Louise Hutchings Westling, 80–92. Cambridge: Cambridge University Press, 2017.
Fowler, Robert L. *Pindar and the Sublime: Greek Myth, Reception and Lyric Experience*. London: Bloomsbury Academic, 2022.
Fry, Paul H. *The Poet's Calling in the English Ode*. New Haven: Yale University Press, 1980.
Gibbons, Reginald. *Renditions*. Tribeca: Four Way Books, 2021.
Gildersleeve, Basil L., ed. *Pindar: The Olympian and Pythian Odes*. Amsterdam: Adolf M. Hakkert, 1965 (1890).
Hamilton, John T. *Soliciting Darkness: Pindar, Obscurity, and the Classical Tradition*. Cambridge: Harvard University Press, 2003.
Hamilton, John T. "Pindar (Pindarus)." In *The Reception of Classical Literature*, edited by Christine Walde in collaboration with Brigitte Egger, translated and edited by Duncan Smart and Matthijs H. Wibier, 306–11. Leiden: Brill, 2012.
Hamilton, John T. "The Gift of Song: German Receptions of Pindar." In *A Companion to Greek Lyric*, edited by Laura Swift, 437–52. Hoboken, NJ: John Wiley & Sons, Inc., 2022.

Bibliography

Hornblower, Simon. *Thucydides and Pindar: Historical Narrative and the World of Epinikian Poetry*. Oxford: Oxford University Press, 2004.
Hornblower, Simon and Catherin Morgan, eds. *Pindar's Poetry, Patrons, and Festivals: From Archaic Greece to the Roman Empire*. Oxford: Oxford University Press, 2007.
Jakobson, Roman. "Closing Statement: Linguistics and Poetics." In *Style in Language*, edited by Thomas Sebeok, 350–77. Cambridge: Technology Press of Massachusetts Institute of Technology, 1960.
Jakobson, Roman. "Two Aspects of Language and Two Types of Aphasic Disturbances." In *On Language*, edited by Linda R. Waugh and Monique Monville-Burston, 115–33. Cambridge, MA: Harvard University Press, 1990.
Kurke, Leslie. *The Traffic in Praise: Pindar and the Poetics of Social Economy*. Ithaca: Cornell University Press, 1991.
Kurke, Leslie. "The Economy of *Kudos*." In *Cultural Poetics in Archaic Greece: Cult, Performance, Politics*, edited by Carol Dougherty and Leslie Kurke, 131–63. Oxford: Oxford University Press, 1993.
Kurke, Leslie. "Archaic Greek Poetry." In *The Cambridge Companion to Archaic Greece*, edited by H. A. Shapiro, 141–68. Cambridge: Cambridge University Press, 2007.
LeVen, Pauline. "The Colours of Sound: Poikilia in Its Aesthetic Contexts." *Greek and Roman Musical Studies* 1 (2013): 229–42.
Loscalzo, Donato. *La parola inestinguibile: studi sull'epinicio pindarico*. Rome: Edizioni dell'Ateneo, 2003.
Martin, Richard P. *Mythologizing Performance*. Ithaca: Cornell University Press, 2020.
Miller, Stephen G. *Ancient Greek Athletics*. New Haven: Yale University Press, 2004.
Moul, Victoria. "*A Mirror for Noble Deeds*: Pindaric Form in Jonson's Odes and Masques." In *Receiving the Komos: Ancient and Modern Receptions of the Victory Ode*, edited by Peter Agócs, Chris Carey, and Richard Rawles, 141–56. London: Institute of Classical Studies, University of London, 2012.
Nagy, Gregory. *Pindar's Homer: The Lyric Possession of an Epic Past*. Baltimore: The Johns Hopkins University Press, 1990.
Nagy, Gregory. "Copies and Models in Horace Odes 4.1 and 4.2." *The Classical World* 87, no. 2 (1994): 415–26.
Nagy, Gregory. *The Best of the Achaians: Concepts of the Hero in Archaic Greek Poetry*. Revised ed. Baltimore: The Johns Hopkins University Press, 1999.
Neer, Richard and Leslie Kurke. *Pindar, Song, and Space: Towards a Lyric Archaeology*. Baltimore: The Johns Hopkins University Press, 2019.
Newby, Zahra. *Athletics in the Ancient World*. London: Bristol Classical Press, 2006.
Nicholson, Nigel James. *Aristocracy and Athletics in Archaic and Classical Greece*. Cambridge: Cambridge University Press, 2005.
Nicholson, Nigel James. *The Poetics of Victory in the Greek West: Epinician, Oral Tradition, and the Deinomenid Empire*. Oxford: Oxford University Press, 2016.
Pelliccia, Hayden. "Simonides, Pindar and Bacchylides." In *The Cambridge Companion to Greek Lyric*, edited by Felix Budelmann, 240–62. Cambridge: Cambridge University Press, 2009.
Peponi, Anastasia-Erasmia. "Lyric Atmospheres: Plato and Mimetic Evanescence." In *Music, Text, and Culture in Ancient Greece*, edited by Tom Phillips and Armand D'Angour, 163–82. Oxford: Oxford University Press, 2018.
Potter, David. *The Victor's Crown: A History of Ancient Sport from Homer to Byzantium*. Oxford: Oxford University Press, 2012.
Race, William H., ed. and trans. *Pindar. Olympian Odes. Pythian Odes*. Cambridge: Harvard University Press, 1997.
Race, William H., ed. and trans. *Pindar. Nemean Odes. Isthmian Odes. Fragments*. Cambridge: Harvard University Press, 1997.
Rogers, Stephen. *Classical Greece and the Poetry of Chenier, Shelley, and Leopardi*. Notre Dame: University of Notre Dame Press, 1974.
Sansone, David. *Greek Athletics and the Genesis of Sport*. Berkeley: University of California Press, 1998.
Slater, William J. *Lexicon to Pindar*. Berlin: Walter de Gruyter and Company, 1969.
Smith, R. R. R. "Pindar, Athletes, and the Early Greek Statue Habit." In *Pindar's Poetry, Patrons, and Festivals: From Archaic Greece to the Roman Empire*, edited by Simon Hornblower Simon and Catherin Morgan, 83–139. Oxford: Oxford University Press, 2007.
Snell, Bruno, and Herwig Maehler, eds. *Pindari Carmina cum fragmentis. Pars I: Epinicia*. 8th ed. Leipzig: Teubner, 1997.
Steiner, Deborah. *The Crown of Song: Metaphor in Pindar*. New York: Oxford University Press, 1986.

Bibliography

Stocking, Charles H. and Susan A. Stephens. *Ancient Greek Athletics: Primary Sources in Translation*. Oxford: Oxford University Press, 2021.

Swift, Laura, ed. *A Companion to Greek Lyric*. Hoboken, NJ: John Wiley & Sons, Inc., 2022.

Thomas, Richard F., ed. *Horace, "Odes" Book IV and "Carmen Saeculare."* Cambridge: Cambridge University Press, 2011.

Venuti, Lawrence. *The Translator's Invisibility: A History of Translation*. London and New York: Routledge, 2018.

Wells, James Bradley. *Pindar's Verbal Art: An Ethnographic Study of Epinician Style*. Washington, DC: Center for Hellenic Studies, 2009.

Wells, James Bradley. "Lyric: Melic, Iambic, and Elegiac." In *A Companion to Greek Literature*, edited by Martin Hose and David Schenker, 155–74. Malden, MA: John Wiley & Sons, Inc., 2016.

Wells, James Bradley, trans. *Vergil: "Eclogues" and "Georgics."* Madison: University of Wisconsin Press, 2022.

Willcock, M. M, ed. *Pindar. Victory Odes: Olympians 2, 7, 11; Nemean 4; Isthmians 3, 4, 7*. Cambridge: Cambridge University Press, 1995.

Wilson, Penelope. "Pindar and his Reputation in Antiquity." *Proceedings of the Cambridge Philological Society*, no. 26 (1980): 97–114.

Wilson, Penelope. "Pindar and English Eighteenth-Century Poetry." In *Receiving the Komos: Ancient and Modern Receptions of the Victory Ode*, edited by Peter Agócs, Chris Carey, and Richard Rawles, 157–68. London: Institute of Classical Studies, University of London, 2012.

Young, David C. *Three Odes of Pindar: A Literary Study of Pythian 11, Pythian 3, and Olympian 7*. Mnemosyne Supplement 9. Leiden: E. J. Brill, 1968.

Young, David C. "Pindar." In *Ancient Writers: Greece and Rome*, edited by T. James Luce, 157–77. New York: Charles Scriber's Sons, 1982.

Young, David C. *The Olympic Myth of Greek Amateur Athletics*. Chicago: Ares Publishers, Inc., 1984.

INDEX

agón (contest, gathering, ordeal) 2–4, 5, 7, 10, 17
angelía (victory announcement) 9, 10, 17, 77
    as register, *see under* register
aristocracy 5, 8, 10–12, 15
athletic games 3–5
    and ritual 5–8, 17–18

Bakkhylídēs 8

commemoration, *see* victory commemoration
Cowley, Abraham 29

games, *see* athletic games
Gay, Ross 29
Gibbons, Reginald 29–30
Gray, Thomas 29

Hēsíodos 1–2, 31, 98, 273, 277
Hölderlin, Friedrich 29
honey, *see méli* (honey)
Horace 27–9

Jonson, Ben 29

Kalvos, Andreas 29
Keats, John 29
kháris (grace, splendor, reciprocity) 15, 30–1, 87–8
khréos (duty) 11, 14, 15, 30
kléos (renown) 10–11, 13, 15, 23
Kórinna 20
kúdos (magical aura, talismanic power) 12, 15–18

Leopardi, Giacomo 29

megaloprépeia (grandeur) 18
megaloprépeia (munificence) 12–14, 17, 19
méli (honey) 30–1
metaphor 18–20, 32, 98, 134, 135, 174, 175, 203, 220, 234, 258, 277, 285

meter 25–6, 47
Milton, John 29

Neruda, Pablo 29
nóstos (return home) 10–11

oíkos (household) 10–11, 12, 15, 17

performance of epiníkion 8, 13, 15, 17, 18, 23–4, 25, 26–7
periodoníkēs 5, 65, 96, 245
Plátōn 30–1
poikilía (embroidery, orchestration) 21–2, 24, 25
priamel 20–1, 47, 94

Quintilian 27

reception of Píndaros 18, 27–31
register 1, 18, 21, 22–5
    angelía (victory announcement) 23–4, 25
    gnómai (proverbs) 22–3, 27, 29, 65
    lyric 23, 24, 25
    mythological narrative 24–5
    prayer 25
reintegration of athlete 16–18

Shelley, Percy Bysshe 29
Simōnídēs 2, 8
statue habit 8–9, 13, 14, 17
structure of epiníkion 21–2

Tolson, Melvin B. 29
tyranny 12

victory
    announcement, *see angelía* (victory announcement)
    commemoration 8–18
von Balthasar, Hans Urs 30, 31

xenía (ritualized guest-friendship, hospitality) 11–12, 15

www.ingramcontent.com/pod-product-compliance
Lightning Source LLC
Chambersburg PA
CBHW071800300426
44116CB00009B/1150